Reason™ 7 Power!:
The Comprehensive Guide

G.W. Childs IV

and Michael Prager

Cengage Learning PTR

CENGAGE
Learning®

Professional • Technical • Reference

Australia • Brazil • Japan • Korea • Mexico • Singapore • Spain • United Kingdom • United States

CENGAGE
Learning·
Professional • Technical • Reference

Reason™ 7 Power!: The Comprehensive Guide
G.W. Childs IV and Michael Prager

Publisher and General Manager, Cengage Learning PTR: Stacy L. Hiquet

Associate Director of Marketing: Sarah Panella

Manager of Editorial Services: Heather Talbot

Senior Marketing Manager: Mark Hughes

Acquisitions Editor: Orren Merton

Project Editor: Kate Shoup

Technical Reviewer: Kurt Kurasaki

Copy Editor: Kate Shoup

Interior Layout Tech: MPS Limited

Cover Designer: Mike Tanamachi

Indexer: Sharon Shock

Proofreader: Sue Boshers

Library of Congress Control Number: 2013948716

ISBN-13: 978-1-285-86657-4

ISBN-10: 1-285-86657-6

Cengage Learning PTR

20 Channel Center Street

Boston, MA 02210

USA

Cengage Learning is a leading provider of customized learning solutions with office locations around the globe, including Singapore, the United Kingdom, Australia, Mexico, Brazil, and Japan. Locate your local office at: **international.cengage.com/region**

Cengage Learning products are represented in Canada by Nelson Education, Ltd.

For your lifelong learning solutions, visit **cengageptr.com**

Visit our corporate website at **cengage.com**

Printed in the United States of America
2 3 4 5 6 7 15 14

To Pamela Moncrief: Thanks for keeping things fun while I was writing, editing, and stressing to finish this title.

Acknowledgments

A big thanks to God, for allowing me to write another book.

Thanks also to Cengage Learning for believing in me and for giving me the opportunity to write more.

Thanks to Orren Merton for keeping me grounded and focused on my titles and always being supportive.

Thanks to Kate Shoup for an excellent eye for detail and keeping things on track. It was great working with you.

A big thank you to Mike Prager for trusting me to carry on an amazing book that he grew and groomed over so many years. It's been a true honor to carry on something that you started and maintained so well.

Thanks to Leo Nathorst-Böös and the rest of the Propellerhead gang. I had some crazy problems during the last part of this book, and you guys really saved the day. And, thanks for making Reason, the coolest software on the planet!

Thanks to Bill and Suzanne Childs for continually supporting me when things are good and bad!

Thanks Pamela Moncrief for your companionship and keeping me in smiles.

Thanks to Allison, Tommy, Haley, and Lexi Parchman. Thanks to Alex, Jen, Will and Elizabeth Childs.

Thanks to Avoca Coffee (Garald LaRue and Jimmy Story) for giving me a nice place to work when home just isn't cutting it.

Thanks to all the guys at The Usual: Juan, Jose, Louis, Brad, Hampton, Josh, Jordan, Braeden, Evan, and Steve. It's nice to be able to get away from it all in the middle of the night.

About the Authors

Starting off as a small boy on a farm in a galaxy far, far away, **G.W. Childs** dreamed of sound and music. As he grew, he learned synthesis, sound design, song writing, and remixing. As a soldier in psychological operations, G.W. learned ways to creatively use sound; and as a touring musician performing with the likes of Soil & Eclipse, Deathline Int'l, and Razed in Black, he learned to bring music to the masses.

Still listening to his inner child, G.W. decided to work in video games as well and really stepped in to a galaxy far, far away, doing sound design on *Star Wars: Knights of the Old Republic II: The Sith Lords*; acting in *Star Wars: Battlefront*; and contributing to many other popular video game titles, TV shows, and so on.

But the call of synthesis never fully left his ears, so G.W. did a lot of sound design on the popular music application Reason 3, and Reason 4, and the amazing plug-in from Cakewalk, Rapture.

Excited to share knowledge from these wonderful adventures, G.W. has written books under the Cengage Learning banner, including *Creating Music and Sound for Video Games*, *Using Reason Onstage*, and *Making Music with Mobile Devices*. He has also written many highly acclaimed articles and video tutorials with MacProVideo and Ask.com.

Michael Prager has been involved with music technology for more than 15 years and has worked for such organizations as Guitar Center Management, Cakewalk, Steinberg, Disney Interactive, Spectrasonics, Q Up Arts, Sony Classical, audioMIDI.com, the Columbia College Hollywood, and *Keyboard Magazine*. Prager has worked on various Course Technology instructional DVDs and is the author of several books and CD-ROMs from Cengage Learning/Course Technology, including *Reason 4 Power!*, *Reason CSi Starter*, *Reason CSi Master*, and *Sampling and Soft Synth Power!*.

Contents

Chapter 6 Dr. Octo Rex: Close-Up   135

Chapter 7 The Malström: Close-Up   159

Chapter 8 Thor: Close-Up   173

Chapter 11 The Combinator: Close-Up

Chapter 12 Automation

Index

Introduction

From the moment Reason was first introduced, I knew that the entire game for electronic music had changed. It was the very first music software platform that behaved just like hardware. And, having been someone who had sunk quite a bit of my hard-earned money into music hardware, it was nice to finally see a new way of doing things without having to have so much room in my studio taken up. I mean, Reason even had all of the cords that I'd been paying so much money for over the years included free of charge!

Reason has grown a lot since then. More devices have been added, sure. A truly professional mixing board was added in as well. And, finally, audio. Since version 6, we have a complete studio that looks and sounds like hardware, but is all software. Its progression has been very similar to the way that it used to be when studios were all hardware. You'd buy a mixer, you'd buy a synth, a drum machine. And, over time, you'd add other items, like another drum machine, or you'd sell the one you had and get an even better one. As you got really adept, you'd get an even bigger mixing board. Propellerhead has been very generous with this studio!

Reason 6.5 came around very soon after Reason 6. With that update came a major breakthrough. Now, you could start buying new, individual effects, instruments, and various other forms of crazy hardware for your Reason studio. These rack extensions were not only ways for users to customize, but also for new developers, other than Propellerhead, to start adding new devices of their own. Well-respected companies like Korg, Cakewalk, and others began creating, and in some cases re-creating, classic devices that could be purchased for Reason as well. This was a huge jump going from Reason 5 to 6 to 6.5.

Reason 7 is here now, and this is the version that adds the polish. In fact, if there were ever a "pro" version, this would be it. Everything has been refined, including the way that you get around Reason and even the way you edit audio. Propellerhead has even added a way to send external MIDI to those hardware keyboards I talked about!

This book goes over these new refinements to Reason 7 as well as covering everything that Reason's always done. So, if you're new to Reason, you're in very good shape, as it's all right here in this book. You'll learn all about the classic devices stored within the giant virtual studio of Reason that you've probably heard about from so many other musicians. And, if you're an experienced Reason user, you'll be happy, too. All of the new features for Reason 7 are covered—everything from MIDI to amazing new features like the ability to create your own REX files.

Alright, now that you know what you're here for, let me grab the keys to the studio, and we'll start diving into Reason.

Getting Started

Introduction to Reason 7.0

Reason has been and always will be the quintessential software studio in the sense that all the gear you would ever need—and it does look like gear—is there at your fingertips. And, where other digital audio workstations (DAWs) have provided similar capabilities, none of them have gone as far as lovingly creating the mannerisms, look, and performance of the instruments that Reason emulates.

For example, Reason gives you cables to creatively route all your different virtual devices, as shown in Figure 1.1. You simply press the Tab button and turn the virtual "rack" around.

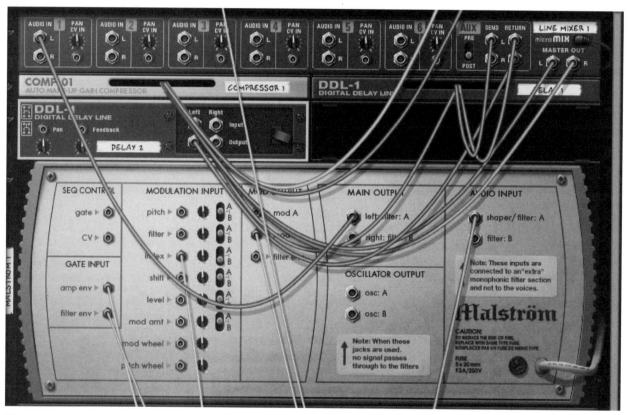

Figure 1.1
© Propellerhead Software AB.

Additionally, Reason gives you knobs, faders, buttons, and every other type of activator you would regularly see in any professional studio, as you can see in Figures 1.2 through 1.5.

Figure 1.2
© Propellerhead Software AB.

Figure 1.3
© Propellerhead Software AB.

Figure 1.4
© Propellerhead Software AB.

Figure 1.5
© Propellerhead Software AB.

The craziest thing about Reason, though—and this is mostly taken for granted these days—is that you can create an unlimited number of each device within Reason. The end result? You feel as though you're in a multimillion dollar studio, similar to the types used by iconic artists like the Beatles, Snoop Dogg, Van Morrison, and the Cars. But you're on your laptop or desktop computer!

In this first chapter, we go over what Reason is, what it isn't, how to create instruments and audio tracks, and more.

What Is Reason?

If you haven't figured it out by now, Reason is a piece of software that provides not only a studio, but also unlimited (unless you're using Reason Essentials) instruments and devices within a virtual rack that all work and act like the real hardware instruments.

As mentioned in the introduction, you also have cables that let you creatively route the way each device is connected to mixers, effects, and more. But if you're not into playing with cables, don't worry about it! Reason also has an invisible engineer that you never see or hear from that handles all the cabling for you. Bottom line: He's shy.

Furthermore, Reason also has a professional-grade sequencer/multitrack audio-recording platform that will enable you to create whatever is in your head and more.

And, if you have some outboard gear, such as MIDI keyboards, well, you've picked a great time to begin using Reason. In the past, Reason was set up to be more like an all-inclusive virtual studio. It was as if the developers did not think you'd want to use any gear other than the instruments provided with Reason. In Reason 7, that's changed. MIDI instruments (outboard drum machines, keyboards, keytar, etc.) can be set up very similarly to the virtual instruments that Reason is known for.

Let's begin by looking at four buttons you should become very intimate with if you plan on using Reason a lot. Because you did buy this book on Reason, I'll assume that's a yes, so let's move on. I hope you're excited!

Four Buttons for Four Windows

Reason has a few different screens that are highly important to its regular use. These screens are as follows:

▷ **The Mix screen (F5):** This screen holds the main Reason mixer that enables you to control the levels of not only your song, but also each individual instrument or track within your song (see Figure 1.6).

Figure 1.6
© Propellerhead Software AB.

▷ **The Rack (F6):** This screen emulates a hardware device rack that holds all your instruments, effects, and so on (see Figure 1.7).

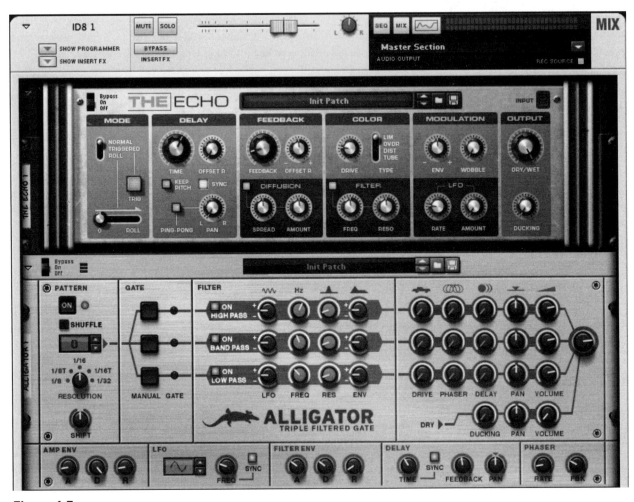

Figure 1.7
© Propellerhead Software AB.

▷ **The Sequencer (F7):** This screen is Reason's main recording/sequencing tool (see Figure 1.8). This is the place where you record your parts and audio and arrange them.

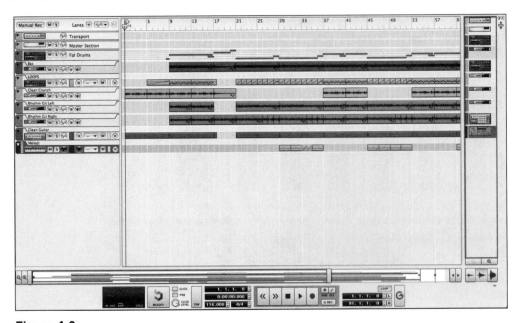

Figure 1.8
© Propellerhead Software AB.

▷ **The Tool window (F8):** This very handy window holds tools for editing MIDI (Musical Instrument Digital Interface) sequence parts, sample organization, and instrument creation (see Figure 1.9).

Figure 1.9
© Propellerhead Software AB.

Each function key indicated in the preceding list toggles open or close the window to which it's assigned. Also, you can press each button individually or simultaneously. For example, you can press F5 and F6 at the same time to open both the Mix screen and the Rack screen at the same time. If you press both buttons again, both the Mix screen and the Rack screen will disappear. I draw your attention to these particular buttons because they are the easiest form of navigation in Reason and will save you a lot of time if you use them!

NOTE: If your computer's function keys are tied up for other uses, you'll want to go into your System Preferences and disable their use by other system programs. For example, if you press F5 on a Windows machine, the Windows Media Player automatically appears. Apple computers also have their own default uses for function keys. Consult your operating system's Help menu or your owner's manual for more information. Failure to free up the function keys (F1–F11) may interfere with your use of Reason.

Now let's look at the Mix and Rack screens!

The Mix Screen (F5)

In earlier versions of Reason, you had to create a mixer to monitor and mix the multiple devices that you'd create. This is no longer the case. Beginning with version 6.0, Reason incorporated a very large, very powerful mixing board, called the Mix screen, that grows larger with each device you create.

When you open an empty Reason project, it won't look very significant. You'll see only the master channel strip on the right side of the screen (see Figure 1.10).

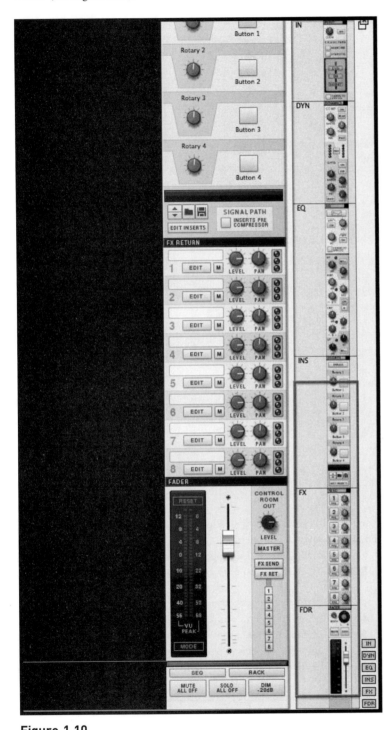

Figure 1.10
© Propellerhead Software AB.

As you begin to add more devices or audio tracks, more channel strips will appear with each individual track or device created (see Figure 1.11).

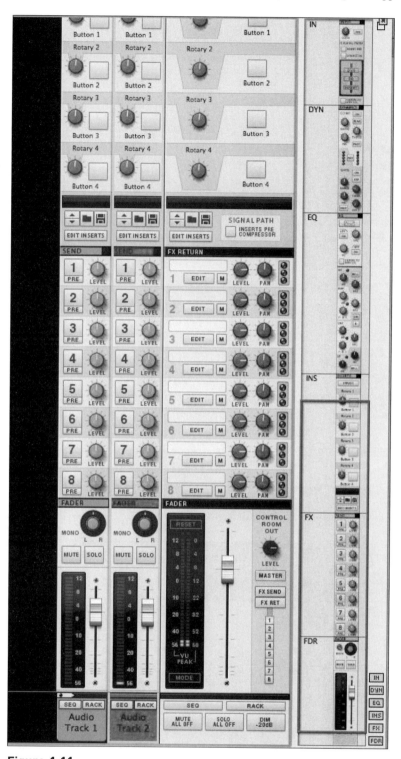

Figure 1.11
© Propellerhead Software AB.

As the Mix screen begins to grow in size, it can become very intimidating to behold because it has so many features. How much you use these features is completely up to you. In fact, Reason has small Show/Hide buttons that enable you to show more or fewer of the sections of the Mix screen (see Figure 1.12). These buttons are abbreviated with the names of each part of the Mix screen, and they are used to hide and reveal parts of the Mix screen that you do and do not need.

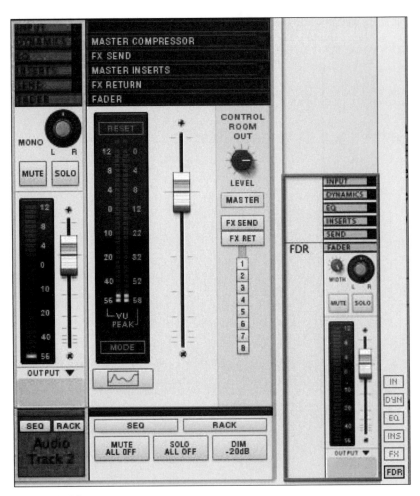

Figure 1.12
© Propellerhead Software AB.

I advise that you hide all but the Fader section at first to avoid being overwhelmed by all the different parts of the Mix screen (see Figure 1.13).

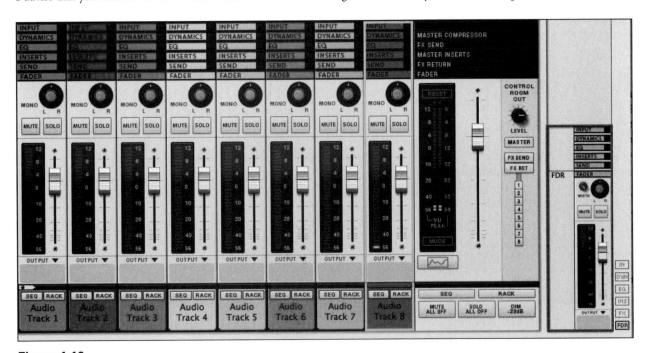

Figure 1.13
© Propellerhead Software AB.

Fader Section

The Fader section of the Mix screen enables you to control the volume of each audio track and device within your Reason song/project, as well as adjust how much of one track or instrument is within each speaker (see Figure 1.14).

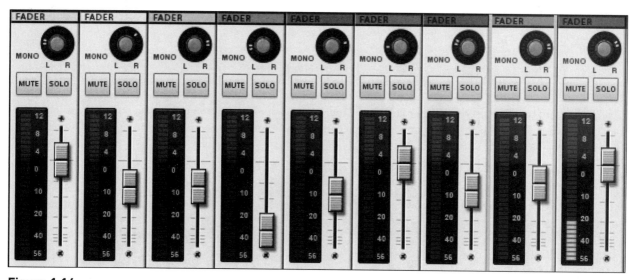

Figure 1.14
© Propellerhead Software AB.

For example, turning up the fader determines how loud an instrument/audio track is within a song (see Figure 1.15).

Figure 1.15
© Propellerhead Software AB.

Adjusting the Pan knob determines whether you hear more of an instrument/audio track in your left or right speaker (see Figure 1.16).

Figure 1.16
© Propellerhead Software AB.

There are also Mute and Solo buttons within the Fader section (see Figure 1.17). Mute does what it says it does: It instantly makes an audio track inaudible until you click the Mute button again. You'll always know when it's active for any particular track because it lights up orange.

Figure 1.17
© Propellerhead Software AB.

The Solo button will mute every track but the one you're soloing (see Figure 1.18). For example, if you click Solo on your bass track, you instantly hear only the bass track and nothing else in your project. You'll know when it is active because it lights up green. Just click the button again to stop this function.

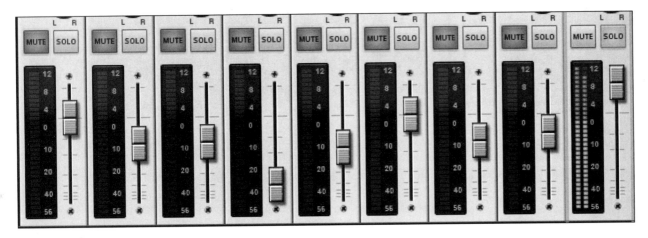

Figure 1.18
© Propellerhead Software AB.

The other sections of the Mix screen are definitely relevant but are not necessary in terms of finishing a song. They're described next.

Input Section

The Input section enables you to fine-tune the amount of signal coming into the audio track, as well as determine the order in which the signal will pass through different devices of the mixer (see Figure 1.19). For example, will it pass through the EQ section first or the Dynamics section?

Figure 1.19
© Propellerhead Software AB.

Dynamics Section

The Dynamics section of the Mix screen (see Figure 1.20) enables you to moderate how dynamic your audio track or instrument will be within your song. It's broken up into the following two sections:

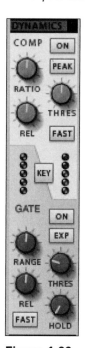

Figure 1.20
© Propellerhead Software AB.

▷ **Compressor:** A compressor smoothes out an audio signal (see Figure 1.21). For example, suppose you have recorded a singer, and she whispers through one section of the song and then starts screaming. The compressor will adjust the signal so that the whisper and the scream are both at the same perceived level of volume. Basically, you're not raising the volume one minute and then cupping your hands over your ears the next!

Figure 1.21
© Propellerhead Software AB.

▷ **Gate:** This tells the mixer to turn off all signals of a track when nothing is being played or between words (see Figure 1.22). For example, suppose you have recorded a very noisy guitar track. When the guitar is not playing, you hear a very loud hum that is not needed or wanted during the rest of the song. By adjusting the gate threshold, you can adjust at what volume the guitar will be cut off. If it plays above a certain level, it will be heard; if it's only a hum, the signal will be killed. This frees up a lot of space within your mix so that other instruments can shine!

Figure 1.22
© Propellerhead Software AB.

EQ Section

The EQ section enables you to adjust the frequency range of an individual track or instrument (see Figure 1.23). If you have a really thick guitar track, it can take up the frequency range of an entire song, keeping you from hearing the vocals, drums, and so on. You can use the EQ section to moderate this range.

Figure 1.23
© Propellerhead Software AB.

NOTE: You don't have to use the EQ section if you don't want to. Some people may prefer to bypass the Mix screen entirely and work only within the Reason Rack and Sequencer screens. Reason does have two separate EQ devices: the Master Class EQ (see Figure 1.24) and the smaller PEQ-2 Two-Band Parametric EQ.

Figure 1.24
© Propellerhead Software AB.

The EQ section is broken up into the following sections:

▷ **Filters:** As shown in Figure 1.25, this contains one low pass filter (LPF) and one high pass filter (HPF). Use the high pass filter to instantly kill low frequencies in one fell swoop. Use the low pass filter to kill all high frequencies in one fell swoop. Yes, it looks as though this is a mistake on my part, but that's how filters work. Low pass kills high frequencies, allowing only the "lows" to pass; high pass kills all low frequencies, allowing only the "highs" to pass.

Figure 1.25
© Propellerhead Software AB.

▷ **HF (High Frequency), HMF (High Mid Frequency), LMF (Low Mid Frequency), LF (Low Frequency):** Each subsection of the mixer, in this case, centers on certain areas within a frequency (see Figure 1.26). Use the HF, for example, to kill all the upper frequencies on a kick drum, while using the LF to boost the lower range of a kick drum to give it more bass.

Figure 1.26
© Propellerhead Software AB.

Inserts Section

The Inserts section enables you to control, from the Mix screen, effects that you've assigned specifically to individual tracks (see Figure 1.27).

Figure 1.27
© Propellerhead Software AB.

For example, suppose you create an RV7000 Reverb unit, a Line 6 unit, and a Master Class Compressor for your guitar track. After customizing all these effects devices, you decide that you'd like to have the ability to control specific knobs or buttons directly from the Mix screen as opposed to having to switch back and forth from the Rack screen to the Mix screen. Because the Inserts section is technically a Combinator, you can assign specific knobs or buttons from the effects directly to the Inserts section knobs and buttons. These assignments take place within the Rack screen's representation of the mixer (described in the section "The Reason Rack [F6]" later in this chapter). Before moving on, though, I'd like to point out the four buttons at the bottom of the Inserts section. The Browse patch button enables you to open the Reason browser and search for your own or premade FX settings created by Propellerhead Software.

To access premade insert FX, follow these steps:

1. Click the Browse Insert FX Patch button in the Inserts section of the Mix screen (see Figure 1.28).

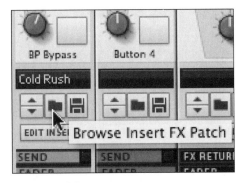

Figure 1.28
© Propellerhead Software AB.

2. Select Reason Factory Sound Bank on the left side of the browser (see Figure 1.29).

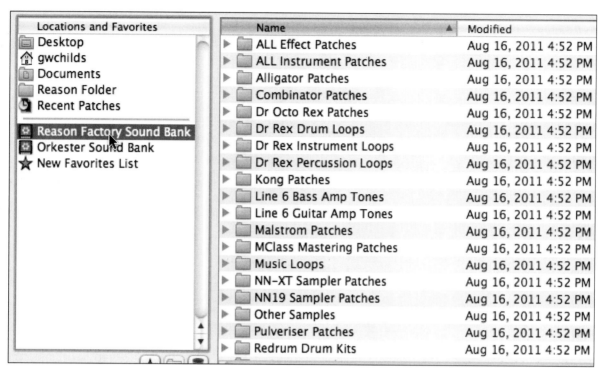

Figure 1.29
© Propellerhead Software AB.

3. Double-click All Effect Patches to enter this directory (see Figure 1.30).

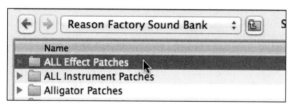

Figure 1.30
© Propellerhead Software AB.

4. Within the All Effect Patches directory, you'll notice folders that describe several specific production tasks (see Figure 1.31). Open the folder that would best suit your purposes and select one of the patches inside by double-clicking.

Master Section

There is also an Inserts section for the entire mix. It is known as the Master Inserts section (see Figure 1.32). It is located in the Master section of the Mix screen, on the far right side of the Mix screen. The Master section not only controls your overall mix output using the Master Fader (refer to "Fader Section," earlier in this chapter), but also controls the sound of the entire mix.

For example, using the Master Inserts section, you could assign a small chorus over the whole mix to give the mix a little extra thickness. Or you could simply use one of the premade patches from the Reason Factory Sound Bank to give your mix a whole new spin! The Master Section also has its own Dynamics section. Therein lies the Master Compressor, which you can use to tighten up your entire mix (see Figure 1.33).

And, finally there is the FX Send section, described in more detail in the next section.

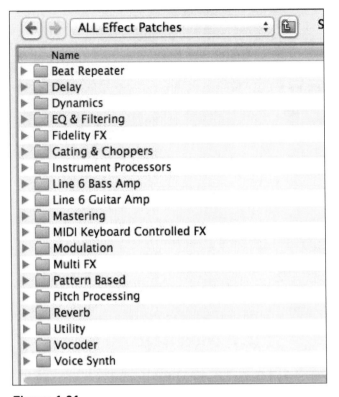

Figure 1.31
© Propellerhead Software AB.

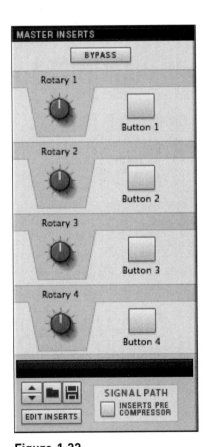

Figure 1.32
© Propellerhead Software AB.

Figure 1.33
© Propellerhead Software AB.

Send and Return Section

Sometimes you will want or need a few effects that can each be distributed to a variety of different tracks but stem from one source. The Send and Return section of the Reason Mix screen enables you to do just that (see Figure 1.34).

Figure 1.34
© Propellerhead Software AB.

As you can see, you get up to eight sends and returns within your project (see Figure 1.35). Once you've created a send effect, you can determine how much, if any, of the effect will be heard on the other tracks or channels by using the Send knobs.

Figure 1.35
© Propellerhead Software AB.

Here's how you do it:

1. Right-click on the Return section of the Mix screen and select Create Send FX (see Figure 1.36).

Figure 1.36
© Propellerhead Software AB.

2. In this example, in the Studio FX submenu, choose RV7000 (see Figure 1.37).

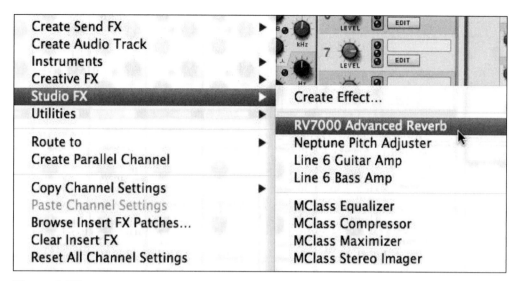

Figure 1.37
© Propellerhead Software AB.

3. On the tracks on which you want to also have the RV7000 reverb, click the numbered buttons (in this case, 1) and turn up the Send knob that corresponds with the Return (see Figure 1.38). For example, the RV7000 is in Return 1, so you can turn up the Send 1 knob on the track that you want to have reverb.

Figure 1.38
© Propellerhead Software AB.

The advantages of doing it this way are as follows:

▷ You can adjust one effect and affect several instruments at once as opposed to having to adjust each individual instrument when you decide you don't like something.

▷ You can create an atmosphere through effects that will draw your listener in further.

There are actually more uses for sends and returns, but I'll leave those for you to discover on your own.

Creating Audio Tracks/Adding Channels to the Mix Screen

Before going on, I'd like to show you that you can create additional channels in the Mix screen that will also show up as gear within your Reason Rack screen (covered next), as well as tracks within the Reason Sequencer (covered in the next chapter).

To begin, let's start by creating an audio track because, historically, it's the most common form of track to a mixer.

1. Open the Create menu.
2. Select Create Audio Track (see Figure 1.39), or press and hold Ctrl+T (Windows) or Command+T (Mac).

Instantly, an additional channel will appear in your Mix screen (see Figure 1.40).

If you press the F6 button on your keyboard, you'll notice a new track has appeared within the Rack screen, labeled as an audio track (see Figure 1.41).

On this audio track device, you can choose your recording input (from the Audio Input menu), mute, and solo, as explained earlier in this chapter, directly from the Mix screen.

Figure 1.39
© Propellerhead Software AB.

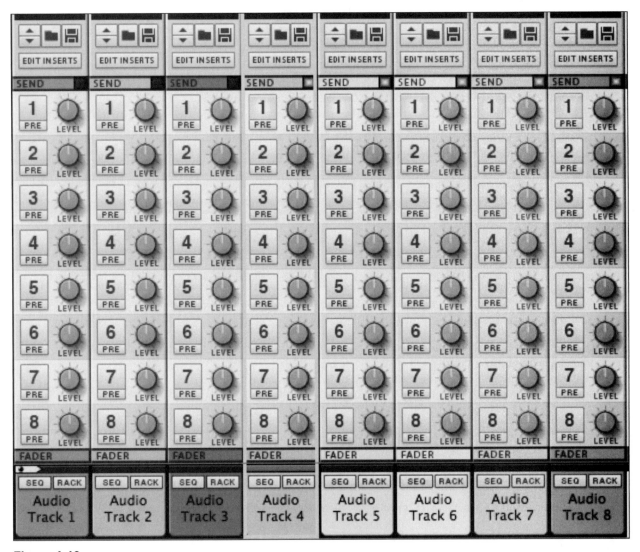

Figure 1.40
© Propellerhead Software AB.

Also, there are navigation buttons, such as Sequencer (labeled "Seq") and Mixer (labeled "Mix") buttons that take you to the labeled screens. There's even a button to take you to the Spectrum EQ! You can also choose the audio track output from the Audio Output drop-down menu, as well as control the volume and panning of your audio track, all from Audio Track device.

Now that we're here in the Rack screen, let's talk about it a bit.

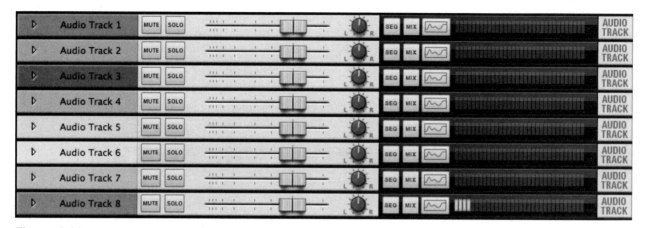

Figure 1.41
© Propellerhead Software AB.

The Reason Rack Screen (F6)

We've established now that Reason's Mix screen is your main area for mixing your song. This entails adjusting levels and EQs, adding FX, and so on. Now, let's talk about the screen that actually holds all the virtual devices that make up your virtual studio minus the mixer (see Figure 1.42).

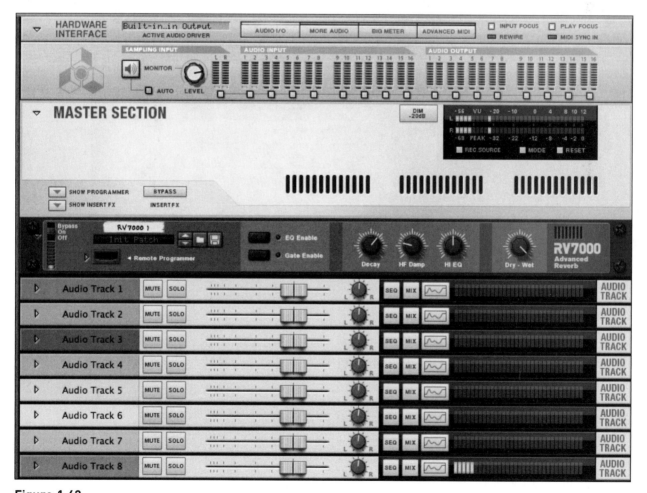

Figure 1.42
© Propellerhead Software AB.

Reason 7 Power!: The Comprehensive Guide

The Reason Rack screen—the most iconic portion of Reason, period—stores your virtual instruments, audio track devices, effects, line mixers, and more, but also takes it a step beyond this. These devices aren't just visually represented here; they actually work! From within the mixer, you can modify settings on the devices. And by pressing the Tab button, you can even adjust the signal flow to and from the devices to the mixer, and so on. Press the Tab button now!

See all the dangling wires in Figure 1.43? These aren't just for show! You can actually pull the wires and drag them to other inputs, outputs, or control voltage (CV) ports. If you aren't comfortable with this yet, don't worry; Reason doesn't require you to do anything with the wires. Remember, you have a virtual engineer that will take care of all that for you if you want.

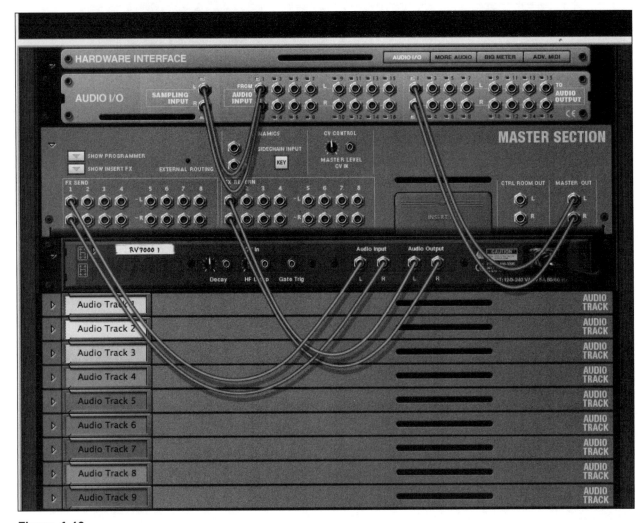

Figure 1.43
© Propellerhead Software AB.

Let's take a moment to go over the anatomy of the Reason Rack screen in its most simple form, meaning before there are several devices attached (see Figure 1.44). To begin, let's start with the hardware interface. You will always see this device in every Reason Rack screen, period. This is the virtual equivalent of the audio hardware you may physically have at your disposal, such as your audio interface or MIDI controller.

NOTE: Reason, like many DAWs, is compatible with ReWire, which is a protocol that allows two audio applications to work together. The ReWire protocol not only allows perfect synchronization between applications, but also enables you to send virtual audio cables between two applications to allow greater mixing potential. The audio inputs and outputs section of the hardware interface is your direct conduit to other applications. For more information on ReWire, see *Using ReWire: Skill Pack* by G.W. Childs (Course Technology PTR).

Audio Inputs and Outputs

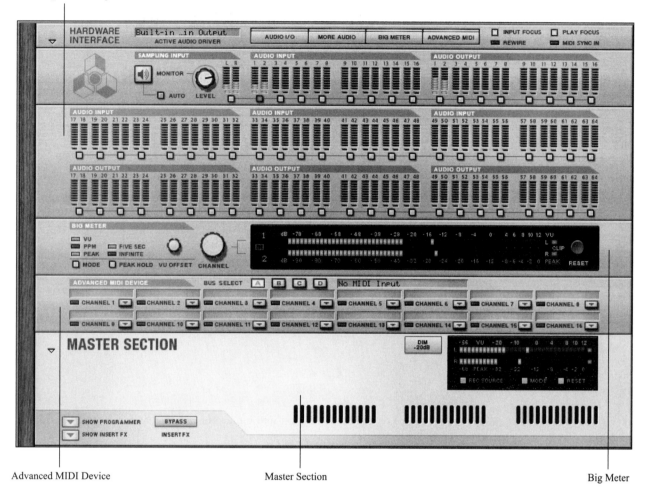

Advanced MIDI Device   Master Section   Big Meter

Figure 1.44
© Propellerhead Software AB.

The hardware interface consists of the following:

▷ **Audio Inputs and Outputs:** You use these audio inputs and outputs to enable the physical audio inputs and outputs on your audio interface. You also use them for rewiring to other audio applications. (See the preceding note on ReWire.)

▷ **Big Meter:** This device enables you to view the signal of either your main mix or another selected input or output. Additionally, it gives you options for how you'd like to view each signal.

▷ **Advanced MIDI Device:** This is essentially a virtual MIDI interface. You use this device to connect multiple MIDI devices into one Reason Rack or to enable another computer sending MIDI to control Reason.

▷ **The Master Section:** This interfaces with the Mix screen, covered earlier. Here, you connect your Master Section inserts within the Rack screen. This is also the place where your send and return FX are connected. Consider this the mixer's avatar within the Rack screen.

NOTE: When the Master Section is completely open, it looks and behaves very much like a Combinator (see Figure 1.45). Like the Combinator, it has assignable knobs and buttons that can be routed to specific functions. These functions are intended for the insert effects knobs, which are also present within the Mix screen.

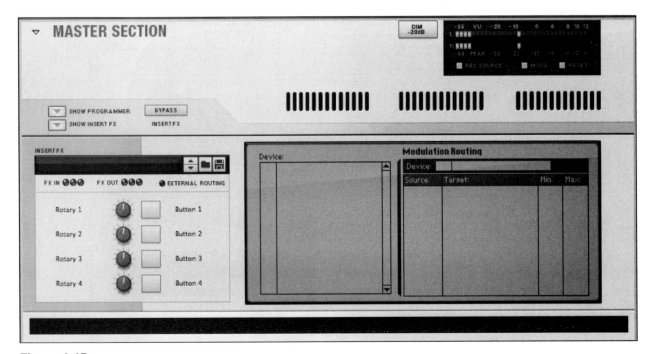

Figure 1.45
© Propellerhead Software AB.

Moving On

We've covered two of the major screens within Reason. In the next chapter, we'll get into the Reason screen that enables you to actually record and arrange your song: the Sequencer!

2

Recording

I N CHAPTER 1, "GETTING STARTED," you learned about two of the main screens in Reason: the Mix screen and the Rack screen. This was a major step forward! Now that you understand these two main screens, you're ready to move on to the main functions and to the rest of the main screens. But you can't finish up with the Rack screen before creating instruments first.

The Devices

If you were to ask Reason users, they'd say the greatest fun in Reason would have to be the devices or gear—or whatever you want to call them. But before you get to know each and every one of them individually (this book goes into great depth with each device in later chapters), let's talk about the three main types of devices and how to create them.

The three main types of devices are as follows:

▷ **Instruments:** These are the drum machines, synthesizers, and samplers—the devices you use to produce sound and make music.
▷ **Creative FX:** These effects tend to be a little more on the experimental and non-traditional side. For example, The Echo isn't just any old digital delay. It also incorporates subtle pitch-modulation functions and can be used to create spacious audio landscapes through feedback. If you're looking for something different, try Creative FX out. Trust me!
▷ **Studio FX:** These devices add that extra sparkle to both instruments and audio tracks. These effects include echo (delay), reverb (hallway-type effects), chorus (fattening effects), and more.
▷ **Utilities:** These devices require a little more understanding. They essentially perform very specific tasks that aren't necessarily normal music functions. For example, splitters, in the form of Spiders, enable you to do very interesting things with cables and signal flow. There are also step-sequencing-type devices, such as the Matrix and RPG-8 (which produces arpeggios). You even get extra mixers.

The reason I've broken down the device types into these four groups is simply that Propellerhead (the manufacturer of Reason) has done the same thing.

In an empty Rack screen (or in a current song of your own), try right-clicking (Windows) or Control-clicking (Mac) on the black area (see Figure 2.1).

At the bottom of the context menu that appears, you'll see four submenus: Instruments, Creative FX, Studio FX, and Utilities. If you open the Create menu, you'll see the same categories (see Figure 2.2).

Create a Reason Device

Now we can put all this together in a quick, ordered list of instructions and actually create an instrument:

1. Right-click in the black area of Reason or open the Create menu.
2. Choose Instruments. Then choose Redrum Drum Computer. (See Figure 2.3.)

The Redrum Drum Computer appears in the Rack screen (see Figure 2.4).

You also can choose Reason-specific instruments that you'd like to use. For now, select the Redrum device in the Rack and press Delete.

Create an Instrument

Sometimes you need instruments that are more well known than a Malström, Thor, or SubTractor. Sometimes you want something along the lines of a piano, guitar, bass guitar, or lead synth. When you run into this situation, it can be tedious to load up each device and then try going through all the presets of each device. This is where the Create Instrument command becomes very handy. It's also located in the Create menu.

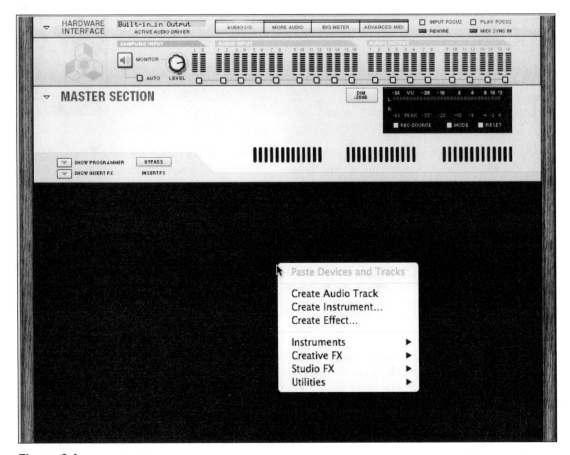

Figure 2.1
© Propellerhead Software AB.

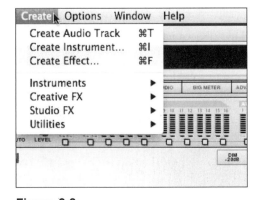

Figure 2.2
© Propellerhead Software AB.

Try it out now:

1. Open the Create menu and select Create Instrument (see Figure 2.5). Alternatively, can press Ctrl+I (Windows) or Command+I (Mac). The Patch Browser will appear. (See Figure 2.6.)
2. In the Patch Browser, choose Reason Factory Sound Bank if it isn't already selected (see Figure 2.7).
3. Type Piano in the Search For field, located in the upper-right corner of the Patch Browser (see Figure 2.8) and press Enter (Windows) or Return (Mac). Reason will display all the pianos in the middle of the Patch Browser (see Figure 2.9).
4. If your audio and controller are set up right, you'll be able to select and play any piano in the list. Select a piano (see Figure 2.10) and try playing your MIDI Controller (if it's available and set up).
5. If you find a piano you like, press Enter (Windows) or Return (Mac), and you'll see the device planted nicely in your rack.

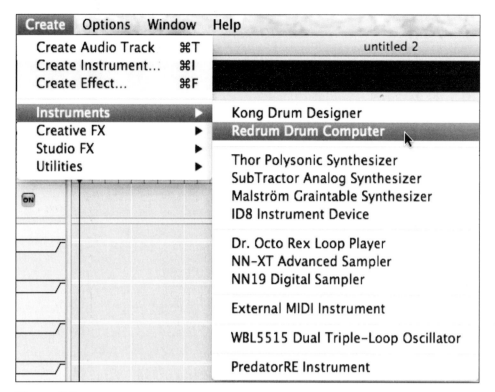

Figure 2.3
© Propellerhead Software AB.

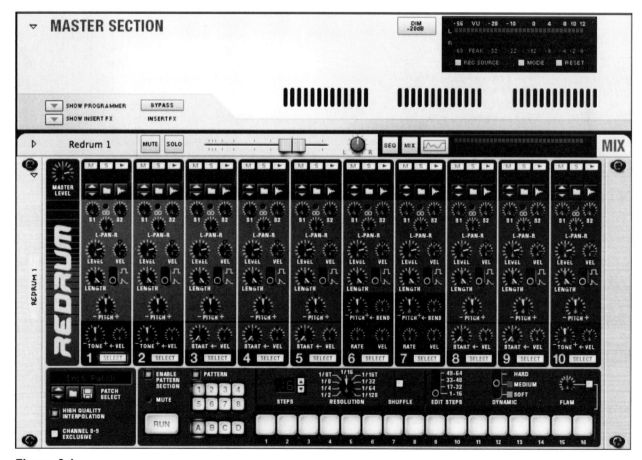

Figure 2.4
© Propellerhead Software AB.

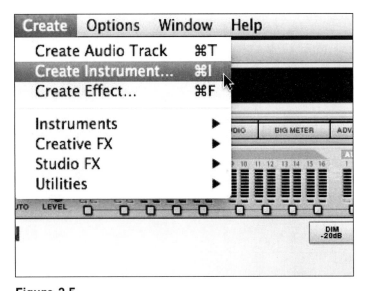

Figure 2.5
© Propellerhead Software AB.

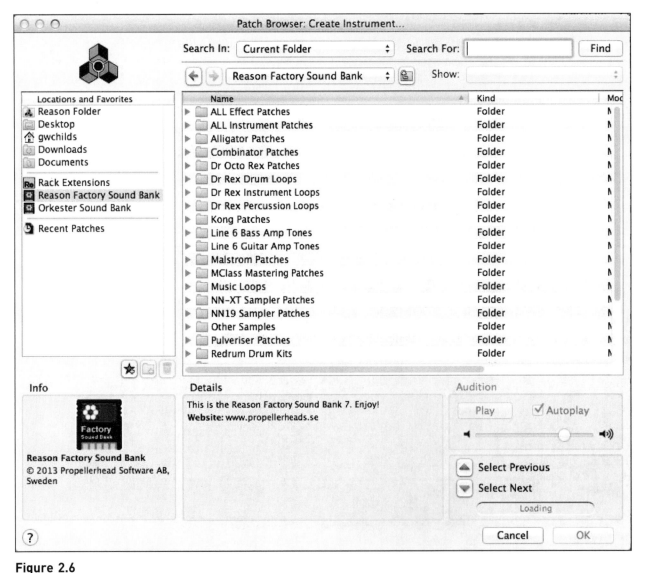

Figure 2.6
© Propellerhead Software AB.

Figure 2.7
© Propellerhead Software AB.

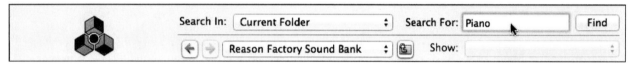

Figure 2.8
© Propellerhead Software AB.

Name ▲	Parent	Modified	Size
A Grand Piano.sxt	NN–XT Sa...er Patches	Aug 16, 2011 4:52 PM	1...B
B GrandPiano 1.0.sxt	NN–XT Sa...er Patches	Aug 16, 2011 4:52 PM	49 kB
CCRMA E Piano.zyp	Subtractor Patches	Aug 16, 2011 4:52 PM	1 kB
4-op Piano –GR.thor	Gordon Reid (GR)	Aug 16, 2011 4:52 PM	2 kB
4-op Piano ...I) –GR.thor	Gordon Reid (GR)	Aug 16, 2011 4:52 PM	2 kB
8 bit piano.thor	Poly Synths	Aug 16, 2011 4:52 PM	2 kB
8 bit piano.thor	Synth Poly	Aug 16, 2011 4:52 PM	2 kB
62 Detroit Upright.cmb	Acoustic Piano	Aug 16, 2011 4:52 PM	83 kB
62 Detroit Upright.cmb	Acoustic Piano	Aug 16, 2011 4:52 PM	83 kB
418 Piano.cmb	Acoustic Piano	Aug 16, 2011 4:52 PM	9 kB
418 Piano.cmb	Acoustic Piano	Aug 16, 2011 4:52 PM	9 kB
A Grand Piano.sxt	Piano	Aug 16, 2011 4:52 PM	1...B
A Grand Piano.sxt	Acoustic Piano	Aug 16, 2011 4:52 PM	1...B
Ac Bass & E...o Split.cmb	Splits	Aug 16, 2011 4:52 PM	10 kB
Ac Bass & E...o Split.cmb	Splits	Aug 16, 2011 4:52 PM	10 kB
Ac Bass+Ri...o Split.cmb	Splits	Aug 16, 2011 4:52 PM	12 kB
Ac Bass+Ri...o Split.cmb	Splits	Aug 16, 2011 4:52 PM	12 kB
Ambient Piano.cmb	Acoustic Piano	Aug 16, 2011 4:52 PM	83 kB
Ambient Piano.cmb	Acoustic Piano	Aug 16, 2011 4:52 PM	83 kB

Figure 2.9
© Propellerhead Software AB.

Name	▲	Parent	Modified	Size
8 bit piano.thor		Synth Poly	Aug 16, 2011 4:52 PM	2 kB
62 Detroit Upright.cmb		Acoustic Piano	Aug 16, 2011 4:52 PM	83 kB
62 Detroit Upright.cmb		Acoustic Piano	Aug 16, 2011 4:52 PM	83 kB
418 Piano.cmb		Acoustic Piano	Aug 16, 2011 4:52 PM	9 kB
418 Piano.cmb		Acoustic Piano	Aug 16, 2011 4:52 PM	9 kB
A Grand Piano.sxt		Piano	Aug 16, 2011 4:52 PM	1...B
A Grand Piano.sxt		Acoustic Piano	Aug 16, 2011 4:52 PM	1...B
Ac Bass & E...o Split.cmb		Splits	Aug 16, 2011 4:52 PM	10 kB
Ac Bass & E...o Split.cmb		Splits	Aug 16, 2011 4:52 PM	10 kB
Ac Bass+Ri...o Split.cmb		Splits	Aug 16, 2011 4:52 PM	12 kB
Ac Bass+Ri...o Split.cmb		Splits	Aug 16, 2011 4:52 PM	12 kB
Ambient Piano.cmb		Acoustic Piano	Aug 16, 2011 4:52 PM	83 kB
Ambient Piano.cmb		Acoustic Piano	Aug 16, 2011 4:52 PM	83 kB
Ambient PPG Piano .thor		Poly Synths	Aug 16, 2011 4:52 PM	2 kB
Ambient PPG Piano .thor		Synth Poly	Aug 16, 2011 4:52 PM	2 kB
B GrandPiano 1.0.sxt		Piano	Aug 16, 2011 4:52 PM	48 kB
B GrandPiano 1.0.sxt		Acoustic Piano	Aug 16, 2011 4:52 PM	49 kB
Bright EPiano.zyp		PolySynths	Aug 16, 2011 4:52 PM	1 kB
Bright EPiano.zyp		Electric Piano	Aug 16, 2011 4:52 PM	1 kB

Figure 2.10
© Propellerhead Software AB.

Creating an instrument is actually one of my favorite tricks in Reason. It speeds up the workflow in a big way because you can always find the instrument you're looking for easily.

If you like the piano you found, or any other device, click the New Favorites List button in the browser and drag that patch from the browser into the Favorites list (see Figure 2.11). Or, click the Add As Favorite button. This will enable you to find this patch in your Favorites list.

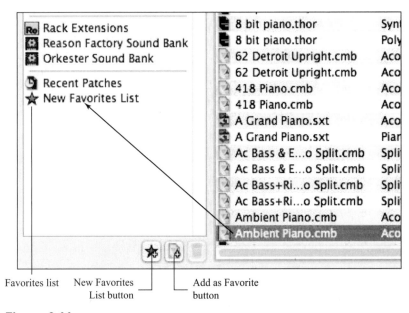

Favorites list   New Favorites   Add as Favorite
                 List button   button

Figure 2.11
© Propellerhead Software AB.

When you create the piano device, notice the additional device called Mix directly above the Redrum device (see Figure 2.12). Let's talk about the Mix Channel device as well as the Audio Track device.

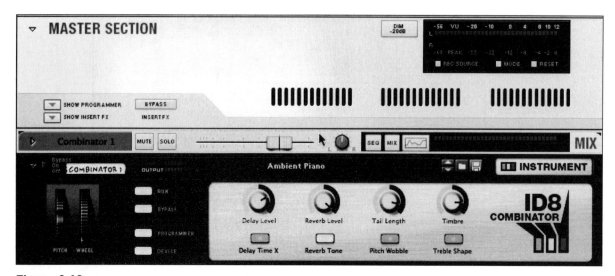

Figure 2.12
© Propellerhead Software AB.

The Mix Channel Device and Audio Track Device

The Mix Channel device is what connects the piano patch—or any other device you create—to the Mix screen. If you delete this device, you will no longer hear the drum machine.

Now let's take it a step further. Click the small arrow next to the Combinator 1 label (see Figure 2.13).

Figure 2.13
© Propellerhead Software AB.

This expands the Mix Channel device so that you can see more of what it has to offer. In Chapter 1, we talked about what the Mute and Solo buttons do in both the Mix screen and the Audio Track device. Also mentioned in Chapter 1 was the fact that the Audio Track and Mix Channel devices are almost identical, aside from the Input Selection. Very important: The Mix Channel device has inputs (L and R) on it for Reason instruments and devices, where the Audio Track device does not. Everything else is exactly the same. So, let's talk about the buttons that the Mix Channel and Audio Track devices have in common.

Click the Show Programmer button (see Figure 2.14). The Programmer lets you assign specific parameters of insert devices contained in your Mix Channel or Audio Track device. Contained *in*? Yep, you read that right! The Mix Channel and Audio Track devices are a form of the Combinator, which is fully explored in later chapters of this book. A Combinator is a Reason device that lets you combine many other devices, creating a much more specific and powerful device.

With regard to the Mix Channel and Audio Track devices, they merely let you contain effects devices in them to keep the Rack screen a little less cluttered and a little more organized. Plus, with the Programmer, you can assign specific functions of certain effects to the knobs or buttons of the Audio Track device, which will also be available also in the Mix screen. For example, I assign the Dry/Wet knob of the RV7000 to the first knob on my audio track so that I can adjust how much reverb my vocals have during a song. After assigning this in the Rack screen, I now have access to this same knob in the Mix screen.

Now, if you click the Show Insert FX button (see Figure 2.15), the Mix Channel or Audio Track device will display a black sub-rack area inside which you can stick effects.

With the effects condensed inside another device this way, you can keep a more tidy Rack screen, as well as know what devices are connected to what. (See the empty Rack screen in Figure 2.16 and filled Rack screen in Figure 2.17). This is far easier than having to root around behind the rack!

All right, before we move on to the sequencer, there's another type of track we need to discuss: MIDI tracks for outboard gear!

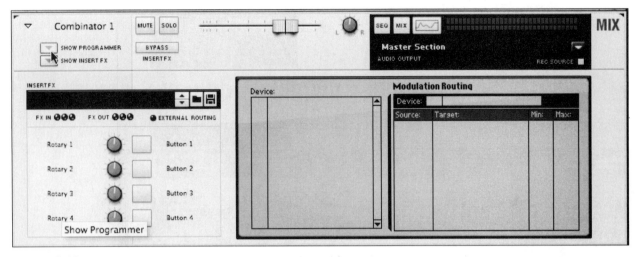

Figure 2.14
© Propellerhead Software AB.

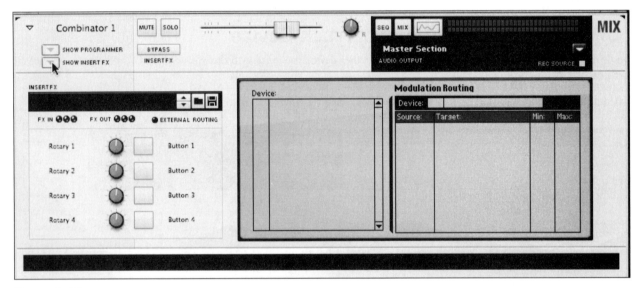

Figure 2.15
© Propellerhead Software AB.

Empty Rack screen

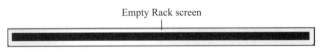

Figure 2.16
© Propellerhead Software AB.

Filled Rack screen

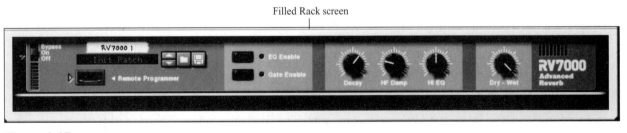

Figure 2.17
© Propellerhead Software AB.

Creating MIDI Tracks for External Devices

Okay, bear with me here. This is where things can get a little confusing. But, don't worry! If you read this section carefully, you should be just fine!

The confusion comes from MIDI, and the way it works with all software applications when outboard hardware, like keyboards, are concerned. You see, MIDI does not transmit audio. When you hook a MIDI cable up to an external keyboard that actually has onboard sounds, sending a cable from MIDI OUT on your computer's audio/MIDI interface to the MIDI IN on your keyboard (or drum machine) does not ensure audio will be heard. The MIDI cable, shown in Figure 2.18, simply gives your computer control over the keyboard. A separate audio cable has to be run from the keyboard back into your computer's audio interface. If all this seems confusing, don't worry. I'm going to walk you through it.

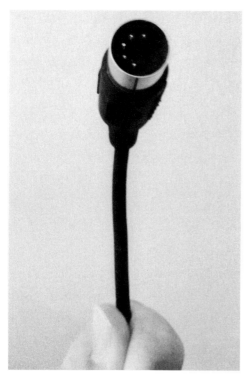

Figure 2.18
© G.W. Childs IV.

Before we begin, there are a couple of things you'll need/want in order to complete this exercise. If you don't have them, don't worry; just move on to the "What Is a Sequencer?" section later in this chapter. When you do finally have everything, just come back to this section later.

Here's what you'll need:

▷ **A free audio input that works with Reason, on your computer:** If you have an audio interface, even better. If you're lacking an interface, the built-in line in on a Mac computer will work. PC built-in line ins can be a little tricky to set up. If you have any trouble, consult your computer's owner's manual. Regardless of what type of computer you have, an audio interface will serve you best for audio latency, sound quality, and so on.

▷ **A MIDI interface:** Another reason to get an audio interface (if you don't have one) is that they tend to have MIDI inputs as well. Even if your audio interface does not have a MIDI input, you can purchase MIDI interfaces relatively cheaply. Also, some USB controllers have MIDI interfaces as well, where external MIDI devices can be hooked up and controlled by your computer.

▷ **A MIDI-compatible device:** When I say MIDI-compatible device, I'm referring to keyboard synthesizers that generate sounds on their own. I'm not referring to typical USB controllers that just have keyboards and knobs. I'm also referring to drum machines that have built-in sounds, pattern sequencer, and voice parameters that can be controlled separately. If you're unsure of your external devices, refer to their respective manuals. An example, My Roland XP-50, is shown in Figure 2.19. Another, a Boss DR-550 drum machine, is shown in Figure 2.20. Please verify that the device does have a MIDI IN port on it. (You may need to consult the device's manual for additional setup that can only be done in the device.)

Figure 2.19
© Moog Music.

Figure 2.20
© Akai Music Company.

Once you've assembled these requirements, continue on with the following steps. You're going to love this!

NOTE: As I mentioned, you may have a USB controller that has built-in MIDI ports as well. If this is the case, you can use the MIDI OUT port. Just hook this port to the MIDI IN port of your external device.

---

1. Verify that the MIDI OUT port of your MIDI interface is connected to the MIDI IN port of your external MIDI device. (See Figure 2.21.)

Figure 2.21
© Moog Music.

2. Connect an audio cable from your external MIDI device's audio output to an audio input on your computer or your computer's audio interface (see Figure 2.22). If you have multiple audio inputs, make sure you remember the audio port's designated number. For example, if you hook the audio cable to input 3, remember this number!

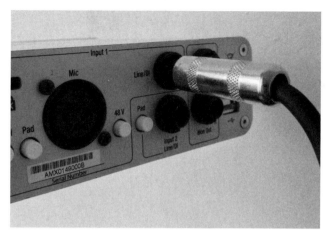

Figure 2.22
© G.W. Childs.

3. Now for the fun part! In Reason, open the Create menu, choose Instruments, and select External MIDI Instrument (see Figure 2.23). This device is known as the EMI, and it is a virtual MIDI interface that specifically controls external hardware. On this device, you'll notice that you can send MIDI program changes, which means that you can program your hardware device to switch to different sounds. You can also choose particular control parameters that exist in your hardware device that can be controlled with the EMI's encoder knob (with the CC toggle on) and numerical scroll. And, you can choose which MIDI channel you want to control on your external device. (The MIDI channel should be paid attention to, as some devices work only on certain channels, and other devices can have a different sound on each of the 16 channels. If you find your device is not working at the end of this section, you may try changing this number.)

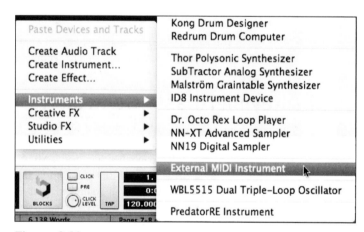

Figure 2.23
© Propellerhead Software AB.

4. Now you need to set up audio coming from your MIDI device. Press Ctrl+T (Windows) or Command+T (Mac) to create an audio track. Then expand the device so that you can select the proper audio input on your audio interface. (Hopefully, you remembered the input number!) Finally, open the Audio Input and select the audio port to which your device is connected. (See Figure 2.24.)

5. Press F7 on your computer keyboard to open the Sequencer screen. Then click the EMI track. A small keyboard icon appears under the small device shown in the track list. This causes Reason to focus on this device for MIDI control. This is a function that you'll use with external and internal devices. If you want to control a Reason synth, click the icon in the track list, so that the keyboard icon appears. Click on the EMI icon in the track list to direct control to your external hardware. (See Figure 2.25.)

6. While in the Sequencer screen, click the Enable Monitoring for Track button on the audio track (see Figure 2.26). This monitors incoming audio so that you can audition what the external hardware is emitting.

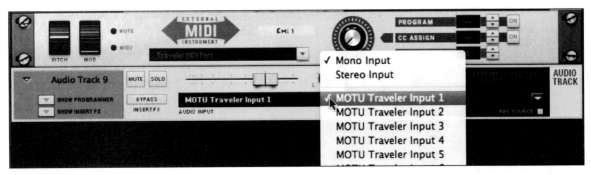

Figure 2.24
© Propellerhead Software AB.

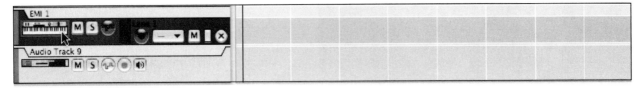

Figure 2.25
© Propellerhead Software AB.

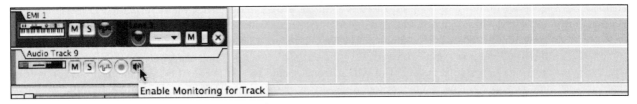

Figure 2.26
© Propellerhead Software AB.

7. Press a key on the your MIDI controller or use the onscreen piano keys, which you can access by pressing F4 key on your computer keyboard. If you press a key and you hear sound, you've done it! If not, go back and make sure you're sending audio to the right audio input, verify that the MIDI device is functional, etc.

What If You're Using an External MIDI Keyboard as a Controller?

One other scenario is one in which someone has an external MIDI device that they are using as a master MIDI controller for Reason. If this is your situation, you have it extremely easy! Your MIDI OUT port will be going into Reason already and set up via the Control Surfaces as a MIDI <Other> Device tab in the Reason Preferences dialog box. To use the sounds in your external MIDI controller, just send a MIDI cable from the MIDI OUT on your computer's MIDI interface to the MIDI IN on your device. Then select the proper MIDI port on the EMI, as instructed on step 3 in the preceding section. As you go forward with your song creation, when you want to use your controller's built-in sounds, select EMI in the sequencer. Note, however, that you'll need to set this up every time you start a new song unless you code it into a template.

If You Can't Get It to Work...

If your external MIDI device is not behaving, try pressing a key on the external device or a button that normally causes a sound to emit. If sound is coming into Reason, there is a MIDI setup problem. Either you're using the wrong MIDI port or MIDI is disabled in the device. You may need to consult the device's manual. There's usually a section in the manual on using the device with a computer.

Next, let's take a look at actually recording MIDI with the sequencer!

What Is a Sequencer?

In my opinion, terms like *sequencing* and *sequencer* tend to intimidate and confuse those interested in computer-based music. There was a point when computer-based music and MIDI were predominantly used by people like myself, who were comfortable with such terms, silly as they were.

So, what is a sequencer? It's a recorder!

The sequencer allows you to create audio tracks and MIDI tracks, record on each individual track, and have them play together at the same time. It's very similar to the multitrack recording devices used during the 1970s, 1980s, and 1990s. The main difference is that the sequencer enables you to arrange the parts you record in a visual manner. In fact, the sequencer is actually fully visual. Here's a small feature list of what you can do with a sequencer:

▷ See each note you've played.
▷ Erase individual and multiple notes. (This applies more to virtual instruments than audio.)
▷ Copy sections of recordings in your project and paste them into multiple locations.
▷ Have the computer tighten up MIDI parts (virtual instrument parts) you recorded using a feature known as *quantization*.

Now that you have a better idea of what a sequencer does, let's actually use Reason's Sequencer screen to record some regular audio!

Recording an Audio Track

This exercise for recording an audio track assumes that you are still working in an empty Reason project. If not, please create one. Also, make sure you've set up your audio device properly in your Reason preferences. If you are unsure how to do this, consult your manual. If you are carrying over from the previous exercise, delete the piano and Mix device by selecting them and pressing Delete.

To record the track, follow these steps:

1. Press Ctrl+T (Windows) or Command+T (Mac). Your project should look like the one shown in Figure 2.27.

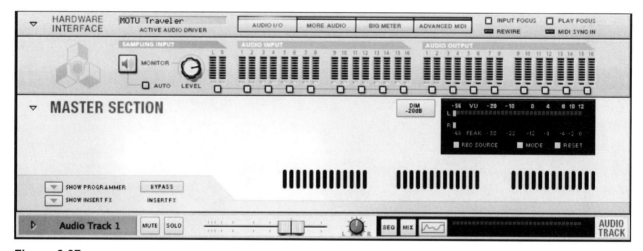

Figure 2.27
© Propellerhead Software AB.

2. Click the small arrow near Audio Track 1 (or 2 or 3 if you already have more audio tracks in your project). See Figure 2.28.

Figure 2.28
© Propellerhead Software AB.

3. Select your Audio Input (see Figure 2.29).
4. Press F7 to open the Reason Sequencer (if it's not already open). See Figure 2.30.
5. Click in the timeline where you'd like the recording to start (see Figure 2.31). This moves the song position pointer to the appropriate starting location.
6. Click Record (see Figure 2.32).

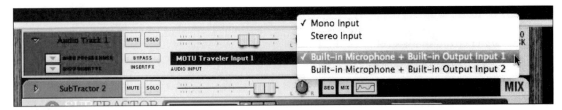

Figure 2.29
© Propellerhead Software AB.

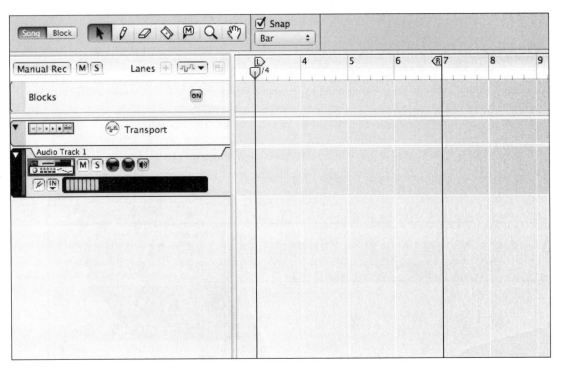

Figure 2.30
© Propellerhead Software AB.

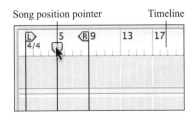

Figure 2.31
© Propellerhead Software AB.

Figure 2.32
© Propellerhead Software AB.

Now you can sing, play, strum, whistle, clap, or chortle (what's a chortle?) to your heart's content! When you finish your recording, you'll see your recorded part in the Sequencer screen. Click to move the song position pointer to the beginning of the recording to hear it again. If you don't like your work, you can always choose Undo Record Track from the Edit menu (see Figure 2.33).

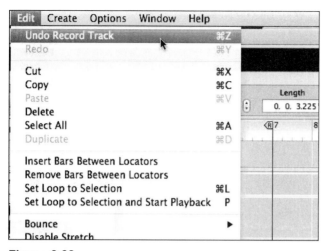

Figure 2.33
© Propellerhead Software AB.

Keep in mind that this is recording at its most basic level. There are way more tricks and methods to record audio parts in Reason. Another great way of doing this is through loop recording. Let's check out this process next!

Loop Recording

When I'm engineering a recording session, one method of recording I've come to rely on quite a bit is loop recording. What's so great about it is that you can set up a portion of the song that you want to focus on and record, say, a verse in the song. Next, you can set up Reason to record in this section of the song, over and over again. When you get to the end of the section you want to record, Reason restarts this section seamlessly. You can keep recording the parts with multiple takes and then later go back and choose the parts you like the most.

Let's try this out now! Keep the track that you created in the previous exercise; just delete the recorded part. Next, do the following:

1. In the Sequencer screen (F7), Ctrl-click (Windows) or Option-click (Mac) in the timeline where you'd like your loop to start. In this case, choose measure 1. This will move the left loop locator to this location (see Figure 2.34).

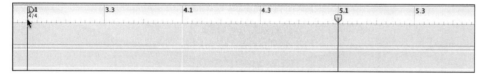

Figure 2.34
© Propellerhead Software AB.

TIP: Using loop locators is a simple way to tell Reason which area you would like to repeat during either recording or playback. You can use loop recording in audio to perfect a certain part, to easily build harmonies, and so on. You can also use loop recordings with virtual instruments such as drums to easily build amazing drum loops and complex instrument parts.

---

2. Alt-click (Windows) or Command-click (Mac) measure 3. This moves the right loop locator to measure 3 (see Figure 2.35). The right loop locator marks the end of the loop, whereas the left loop locator shows the beginning. If you cannot see measure 3, feel free to use the Magnifying Glass tool to zoom in, found in the tool bar (not shown).
3. Press L on your computer keyboard to trigger Loop mode. You can also click the Loop button in the transport bar (see Figure 2.36).
4. Now that your loop is established in the Sequencer screen, click on measure 1 to position the song position pointer (the line that moves over each part of your song as the song plays) at the beginning of the loop. You can also press 1 on your computer's numeric keypad. To position the song position pointer at the left loop indicator, Option-click the left arrow button (Mac) or Alt-click the right arrow button (Windows). See Figure 2.37.

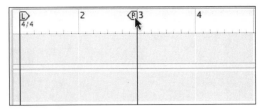

Figure 2.35
© Propellerhead Software AB.

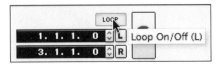

Figure 2.36
© Propellerhead Software AB.

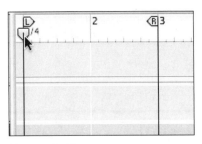

Figure 2.37
© Propellerhead Software AB.

5. Click the Record button to start recording the same audio part over and over again (see Figure 2.38). Record for as long as you want. Don't worry about what the sequencer is doing; just have fun. Once you've recorded yourself singing, drumming, whatever you do, click the Stop button (in the transport bar) or press the spacebar. Do not delete the audio part…until I tell you to.

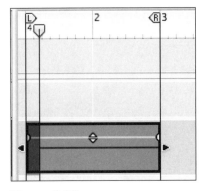

Figure 2.38
© Propellerhead Software AB.

It's nice to be able to record uninhibited like that, isn't it? Just imagine how it's going to be when you start incorporating drums, synths, and so on!

In the next section, I show you how to see all the different takes you recorded during your looped section. Moving on!

Working with Multiple Takes from Loop Recording

After doing all that recording, you may be wondering what happened to all the other audio you recorded while the sequencer was looping. The audio actually wasn't deleted each time the song position pointer came around; instead, it was stuffed inside the small audio clips that were left after you clicked Stop.

In this exercise, I show you how to see the recorded audio parts and select the parts you want to use. Follow these steps:

1. Double-click the recorded clips from the previous exercise. Alternatively, press Ctrl+E (Windows) or Command+E (Mac). This will take you into Edit mode (see Figure 2.39). If there are no comp layers on the audio track, then you will go in to the Slice Editor (covered in Chapter 6, "Dr. Octo Rex: Close-Up"). If this happens to be the case, click the Open in Comp Edit button.

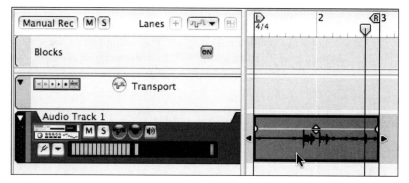

Figure 2.39
© Propellerhead Software AB.

2. You are now seeing all your previous takes, but one of them is grayed out (or dimmed) and another is in color (see Figure 2.40). What's happening here is that Reason is assuming the last take—the colored one—is your preferred take. To tell Reason that you think differently, double-click on a dimmed take to select it as your preferred take. If you want, press the spacebar and double-click through different takes till you hear one you like.

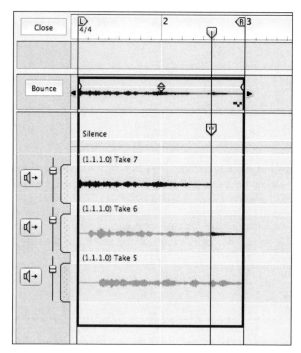

Figure 2.40
© Propellerhead Software AB.

3. You may discover that there are two takes you like a lot, but not necessarily the whole part of each take. For example, you may discover that you like how you sang the first part of a verse, but you don't care for how you ended it. But there is another version of you singing this same part that has a brilliant ending but a bad beginning. To put them both together, press R to open the Razor tool (see Figure 2.41).

Figure 2.41
© Propellerhead Software AB.

4. With the Razor tool selected, click after the beginning of the verse recording that you like. Then press Q to switch to the Pointer tool and click on the ending part that you like. The beginning part of the first recording and the ending part of the second recording will appear in color (see Figure 2.42). If you play your looped section now, you'll hear the audio accordingly. Neat, eh?

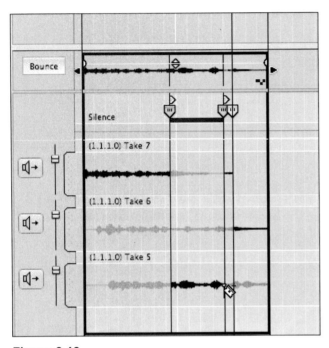

Figure 2.42
© Propellerhead Software AB.

This act of using the Razor tool is what's known as *comping*. You combine two or more takes and use a bunch of individual pieces to make one perfect recording. It's been done in pro studios for years. In fact, during the 1970s and 1980s, recording engineers actually used razor blades to cut pieces of audio tape and then pieced them together, much like what you're doing here!

Now that you're knee deep in Reason's audio capabilities, you could run into a situation that commonly occurs in which you have access to an almost unlimited number of audio tracks. Even if this isn't the case, it soon will be. So let's start talking about a way to keep things organized and sounding good at the same time. Let's talk about submixing.

Output Buses and Submixing

As your song ramps up in production, something always happens: More and more tracks appear. After all, you're going to want to double vocals, add some harmonies, and record multiple drum takes, guitar takes, and on, and on, and on, right? As these additional tracks start to appear, it can get harder and harder to manage everything going on. One way that professional engineers handle tons of audio tracks is through the use of submixing.

When you submix, you direct the output of certain Mix Channel and Audio Track devices to a very special type of mixer channel. In Reason's case, this type of channel is known as an Output Bus. The beauty of routing audio to an output bus is simple: You can create a special, smaller mix in your overall mix. Once your submix is done, you only have to deal with one fader—the one that controls the output bus.

Let me give you an example. Suppose you have, over the course of your production of a song, wound up with 13 vocal tracks. Your current vocal mix sounds wonderful, but you've decided that you'd like to be able to fade out all of the vocals at once. This can be tedious when you have 13 different faders to deal with! So, what you'd do is create an output bus and assign all of your vocal track outputs to this particular bus. Once you've done this, all you need to do is lower the fader of the ouput bus, and voilà! All your vocal tracks are lowered at once!

Let's try setting this up right now. In the last exercise, you recorded some audio files. Let's create a submix through an Output Bus.

1. Select an audio track in the Mix screen of your most recent Reason project. Make sure this project has more than a couple of audio tracks, preferably several similar tracks. For example, select one of your several drum tracks. If you don't have a Reason project like this available, feel free to create four audio tracks and then just follow along. (See Figure 2.43.)

Figure 2.43
© Propellerhead Software AB.

2. Shift-click every other track that pertains to this type of group of audio tracks. For example, select all the drum tracks while pressing the Shift button. If you just created four empty audio tracks, go ahead and select all of these tracks while pressing the Shift button in the Reason Mix screen. (See Figure 2.44.)

3. Here's where the magic takes place. Once you've selected all your tracks (they'll all have a light blue field around each track/channel), press Ctrl+G (Windows) or Command+G (Mac). Alternatively, open the Edit menu, choose Route To, and select New Output Bus (see Figure 2.45). This will cause an output bus to appear and for all of the previously selected tracks to be output to this bus.

4. Now try lowering the fader of the output bus with the song running. Notice how all these channels that are routed to this bus lower in volume when this fader level is decreased. (See Figure 2.46.) What's even better is that effects can also be assigned to this one bus. All insert effects created for this bus will affect all of the tracks being input into this bus. This is a wonderful way to save valuable processing power and build a very powerful submix in one shot. Not bad!

Submixing with output buses is a wonderful way to keep your mixes organized, processor-efficient, and sounding good. As you move forward, keep this technique in mind. This can save you a lot of headaches, especially if you are collaborating with someone else. By labeling your tracks and output buses, it's easy to know what's going on and ultimately, refine that master mix.

Keep in mind that output buses work on audio tracks as well as instrument tracks—in fact, on any track that appears in the Mix screen that isn't already being routed to another bus. That being said, let's start taking a look at something else Reason does very well: instruments and MIDI.

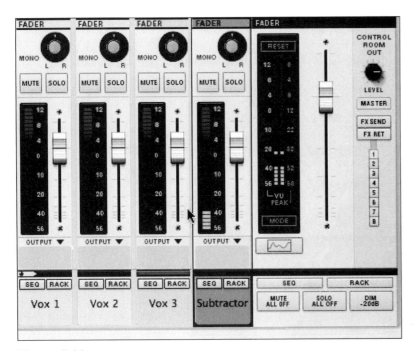

Figure 2.44
© Propellerhead Software AB.

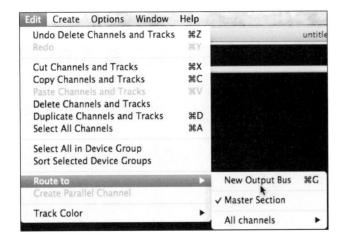

Figure 2.45
© Propellerhead Software AB.

Recording with Reason Instruments

Before we get started, you should understand that recording Reason instruments is different from recording audio from live instruments. For Reason instruments, such as Thor or SubTractor, the actual audio is not recorded; instead, the performance is captured as a MIDI sequence of events. Another way of looking at this is that the sequencer records how you play the Reason instrument. For example, the sequencer records not only the note, but how hard you hit the key and how long you hold the key down.

For example, say I record a synthesizer part in Reason using SubTractor. When Reason is recording what I'm playing, it's not actually recording the sound of the SubTractor; it's recording what my hands are doing as I play. When I play back the recording, it's playing back what my hands did, and then it cues the SubTractor in the same fashion. If I decide I don't like one of the notes I played, I can go into the track and individually delete a note, and then it's fixed. This type of recording is known as *sequencing*.

Recording a MIDI sequence is different from recording actual audio. For example, if I were to play a bad note while recording an actual guitar with a microphone, depending on where the note was placed in the recording, I may or may not be able to edit it out.

Figure 2.46
© Propellerhead Software AB.

In this exercise, I'd like for you to create another blank Reason project. That way, you don't have some nasty looping audio playing over and over again while you try to record the synth part! Once you've got everything set up, follow these steps:

1. Create an instrument using the Create Instrument key command (or open the Create menu and choose Create Instrument). In the Reason Factory Sound Bank, type Piano in the Search For field, select a piano from the list (see Figure 2.47), and press Enter (Windows) or Return (Mac).
2. Set up your loop points the same way you did in steps 1 and 2 in the section "Loop Recording" earlier in this chapter. Your left loop locator should be on measure 1 and your right loop locator on measure 4 (see Figure 2.48). Don't forget to put Reason in Loop Record mode by pressing L.
3. Enable the click track by pressing the C button on your keyboard. This enables the metronome. You can also select the Click button on the transport bar (see Figure 2.49).

> **TIP:** The metronome audibly indicates how fast (tempo) your current Reason project is playing. It's important, especially when using instruments, to record with the metronome so that you know whether you're in or out of time. This is especially important when you get into quantizing. More on this later!

4. Start recording the sequence (see Figure 2.50). When you get to the R loop locator, don't stop! Keep recording. When you feel as though you have enough material, press the spacebar to stop recording.
5. Play back your track, letting it loop a couple of times. Notice anything you like? Don't like? Regardless, double-click on your recorded clip in the Sequencer screen (see Figure 2.51).
6. Now you should be in Edit mode (see Figure 2.52). It will look different than it did when you edited audio. You'll see segments that represent all the notes that you played. Try selecting a note segment with your cursor.
7. With a note selected, try moving it around while the loop plays (see Figure 2.53). Notice how easily you can change things around after you've recorded.
8. Now, with a note or two selected (you can select several by clicking and dragging around many notes), press the Delete button. You just deleted notes that you recorded (see Figure 2.54)!

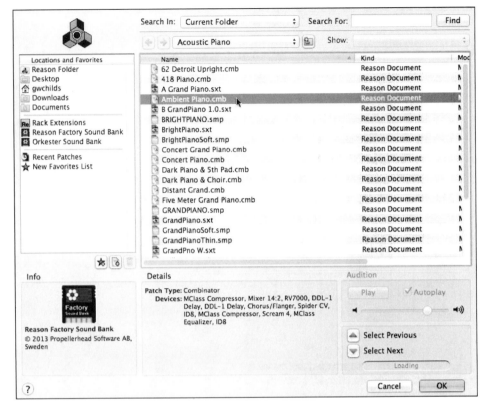

Figure 2.47
© Propellerhead Software AB.

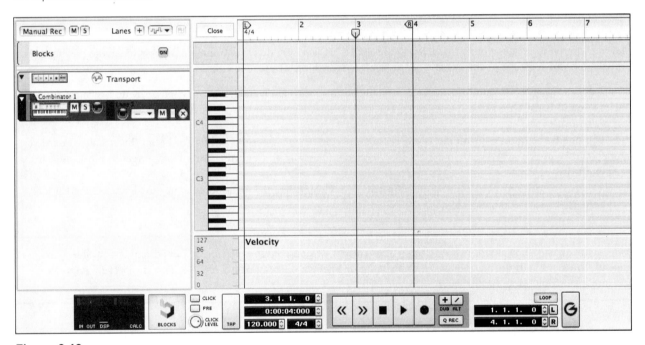

Figure 2.48
© Propellerhead Software AB.

Figure 2.49
© Propellerhead Software AB.

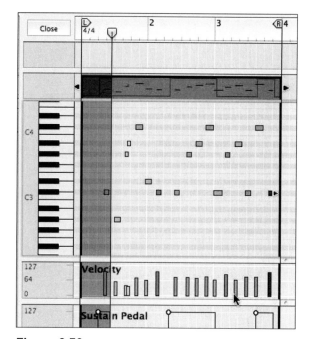

Figure 2.50
© Propellerhead Software AB.

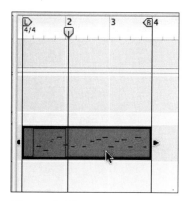

Figure 2.51
© Propellerhead Software AB.

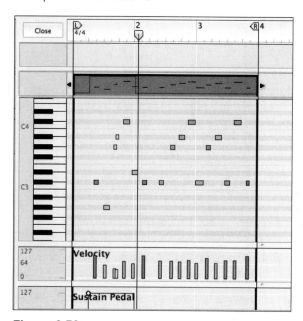

Figure 2.52
© Propellerhead Software AB.

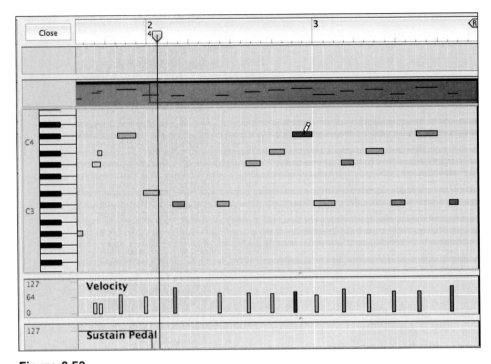

Figure 2.53

© Propellerhead Software AB.

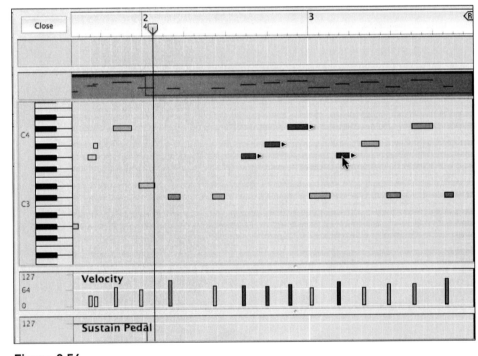

Figure 2.54

© Propellerhead Software AB.

Moving On

Congratulations, you just did your first MIDI edit! Be aware that this is only the tip of the iceberg with MIDI, and there will be more. Make sure you save what you recorded here; you'll be using it in the next chapter.

In the next chapter, we expand on cnstrument recording. Also, we get into some really cool effects that Reason includes, specifically Reason 7! See you in the next chapter!

Recording and Effects

3

IN CHAPTER 2, "RECORDING," YOU GOT YOUR FIRST TASTE OF RECORDING NOT ONLY AUDIO TRACKS, but also MIDI tracks. In this chapter, we're going to expand on recording...and recording with effects. But before we do anything, let's get into something that's really important for recording and editing virtual instruments: quantization!

Quantization

I hope you saved your recorded material from Chapter 2. Remember that I had you play some stuff for four measures? What I'd like for you to do now is listen to what you played along with the click track. Does it sound like it's in perfect time with the click track or does it sound sluggish? Could it be better? Worse? Regardless, I'd like to show you a trick that can save you a lot of editing time.

Remember when I had you move around and then delete notes in Chapter 2? This exercise was obviously helpful, but what if you could speed up your workflow even more and have Reason do some of the work for you?

Well, it can! The Quantize function is simple in the sense that you tell Reason what kind of notes you were playing (1/16, 1/8, 1/32, and so on), and based on what you tell it, it tries to take all those played notes and align them in the timing of the notes that you suggest.

> **TIP:** If you're new to music and don't know the difference between the timing of a 1/16 note and an 1/8 note, let me fill you in on a secret: It's almost always 1/16! It's true—if you listen to most pop songs, you'll notice that there are never more than 16 notes played between each kick and snare beat. In fact, Reason is always set to quantize at 1/16 notes by default. So, odds are, quantizing anything you play will most likely set it up in perfect timing.

Here's an example of using Quantize: Suppose you play some drums off a MIDI keyboard. While you're playing, everything sounds great. But when you click the Stop button and play back your recording, you notice that the timing, while close, is erratic. Maybe your hi-hat is a little lazy or your snare is a little fast. Also, you want this to sound good...and quickly! In this case, you'd do the following:

1. Drag to select around the played drums. Notice how the notes played appear to be slightly off the grid lines (see Figure 3.1).

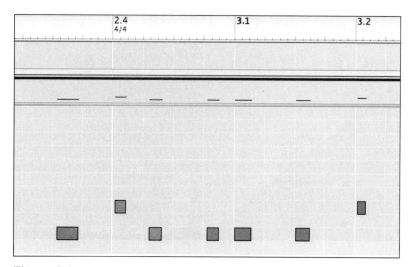

Figure 3.1
© Propellerhead Software AB.

2. Select the drum notes in need of help.

3. Open the Edit menu and select Quantize. Alternatively, press Command+K (Mac) or Ctrl+K (Windows). Now, the notes played are perfectly lined up with the grid lines (see Figure 3.2).

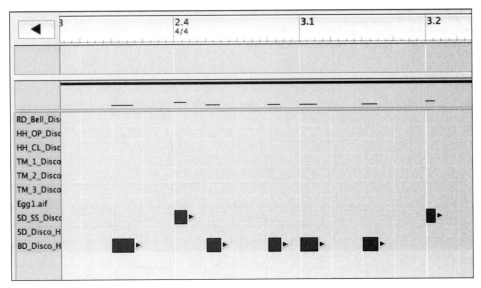

Figure 3.2
© Propellerhead Software AB.

Try applying quantization to what you played in the last section of Chapter 2:

1. Double click on the MIDI clip to enter Edit mode, and then hold down your mouse button and drag a selection box around the notes you played (see Figure 3.3). If you'd like to do this in the regular Arrangement mode of the Sequencer screen, simply select the clip(s) you'd like to quantize (see Figure 3.4) and move on to the next step.

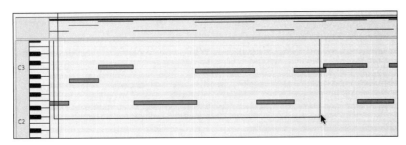

Figure 3.3
© Propellerhead Software AB.

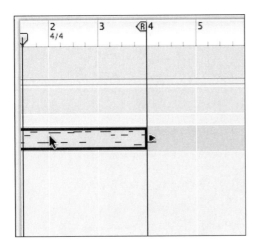

Figure 3.4
© Propellerhead Software AB.

2. Open the Edit menu and select Quantize (see Figure 3.5). Alternatively, press Command+K (Mac) or Ctrl+K (Windows).

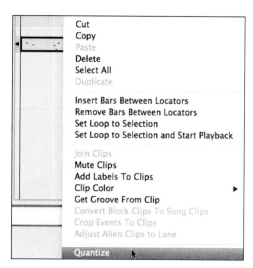

Figure 3.5
© Propellerhead Software AB.

3. Play back your part and listen to the difference. If you decide that you like the recording better without quantization, you can always choose Undo Record Track from the Edit menu.

If you'd like to try different quantization settings, press the F8 button to open the Tool Window (see Figure 3.6). To switch to the Sequencer Tools screen, click the Wrench/Screwdriver button at the top.

Figure 3.6
© Propellerhead Software AB.

You can also reduce quantization in the Tool Window. This capability can be handy when you want to retain some of the humanity of what you played but still need it to be a little "tighter."

> **TIP:** Having to remember to activate the Quantize function on each part you record can get annoying. To solve this problem, you can enable Auto-Quantize (Q Rec) on the transport bar (see Figure 3.7). This will automatically quantize everything you record!

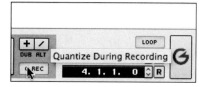

Figure 3.7
© Propellerhead Software AB.

Quantization is just one of the many handy functions that Reason has to make your production experience fun, exciting, and simple!

Because we're talking about functions that simplify the writing, recording, and production process, I'd like to show you another function of Reason that really speeds up song structure and makes song writing fun. Make sure that you hold on to what you did in the preceding exercise; you'll be using it in the next!

Blocks

Great songs always have a few things in common, regardless of genre. Let's break them down:

▷ There is always an opening to the song.
▷ There is always an in-between part of the song that tells the story.
▷ There is always a crescendo, or climax, of some sort.
▷ There is some sort of musical solo or breakdown.
▷ Each song has an end! Everything comes to an end, right?

These song parts actually have names:

▷ Intro (song opening)
▷ Verse (storytelling portion of the song)
▷ Chorus (climax)
▷ Bridge (musical solo/breakdown)
▷ Outro (song end)

A while back, Propellerhead realized that people were spending a lot of time on simple loops that they had recorded in Loop mode (see Chapter 2) but weren't actually completing songs! In fact, this is quite common with computer music: You get so much virtual gear that you don't know what to do with all of it!

To combat this growing problem of song stagnation, Propellerhead created a system known as *blocks*. Blocks allow you to compose separate parts in a loop-recording style of sorts. Then, once you have all your parts recorded and ready to go, you can piece them together to form a full song. The idea is like baby blocks that have big letters on them. You take one big letter block and stick it with a few other letter blocks to form a full word.

Let's look at how this system works!

In this exercise, I show you how to convert the last part you played and recorded into a block. Then I show you how to create another block and chain the two blocks together. Let's get started!

> **NOTE:** If it looks like something in the Reason 7 sequencer is missing, it's probably the Edit Mode button. If you need to enter Edit mode, simply double-click on a clip or press Ctrl+E (Windows) or Command+E (Mac). Exiting Edit mode is also easy; either click the Close button, as illustrated in step 1 below, or just press Ctrl+E (Windows) or Command+E (Mac) again.

1. Click the close button in the upper-left corner of the Sequencer screen. The button should be white, not blue. You should now be in Arrangement mode (see Figure 3.8).

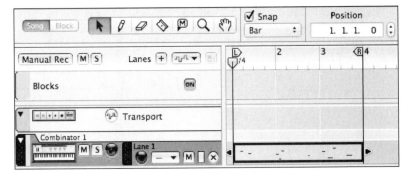

Figure 3.8
© Propellerhead Software AB.

2. Select the recorded clips in your Sequencer screen from the preceding exercise. Then press Command+C (Mac) or Ctrl+C (Windows). Alternatively, open the Edit menu (see Figure 3.9) and choose Copy.

Figure 3.9
© Propellerhead Software AB.

3. Click the Block button, next to the sequencer toolbar. (See Figure 3.10.)

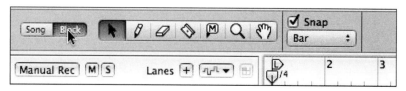

Figure 3.10
© Propellerhead Software AB.

4. Welcome to Block mode. You'll notice in the upper-left corner that the screen already says "Block 1." When you enter Block mode, Block 1 is ready and waiting for your use. Press Command+V (Mac) or Ctrl+V (Windows) to paste your work into Block 1. Alternatively, choose Paste from the Edit menu (see Figure 3.11).

5. Congratulations! You've just created your first block. You'll notice that there are loop locators inside the block as well. Place the left and right loop locators at the beginning and end of your recorded part (see Figure 3.12). This will mark where, when the block loops, your part will play.

6. Drag the E icon, for "end of block," to the end of your recorded part (see Figure 3.13). The farther out this marker is placed from the end of your part, the longer the gap after the end of your part when you use this block later in Arrangement mode.

7. Open the Blocks menu (see Figure 3.14). and choose Block 2.

8. In Block 2, record a new part via Loop mode or by just clicking Record (see Figure 3.15). The loop locators still work the same way, so don't let the fact that you're in Block mode intimidate you. If you forgot how to loop record, refer to Chapter 2.

9. When your recording is finished, place the loop locators at the beginning and end of your recorded part and place the end marker at the very end of the part (see Figure 3.16).

10. Click the Song button to switch back to Arrangement mode (see Figure 3.17).

11. Enable the Pencil tool (see Figure 3.18).

12. Now we're going to have a little fun. With the Pencil tool, draw in the Blocks lane of your Sequencer. Draw a block for at least nine measures (see Figure 3.19). You may need to use the Zoom All function from the Window menu (see Figure 3.20).

13. Draw another block next to your first block (see Figure 3.21).

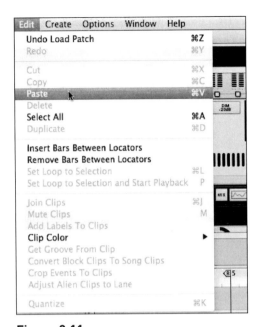

Figure 3.11

© Propellerhead Software AB.

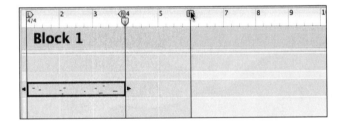

Figure 3.12

© Propellerhead Software AB.

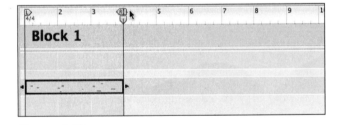

Figure 3.13

© Propellerhead Software AB.

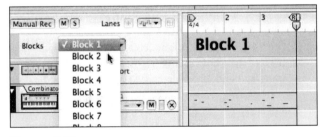

Figure 3.14

© Propellerhead Software AB.

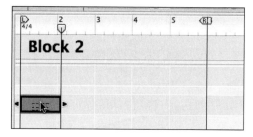

Figure 3.15
© Propellerhead Software AB.

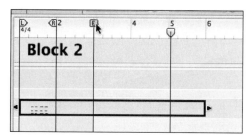

Figure 3.16
© Propellerhead Software AB.

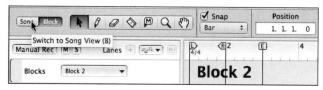

Figure 3.17
© Propellerhead Software AB.

Figure 3.18
© Propellerhead Software AB.

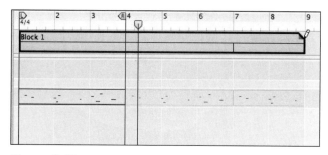

Figure 3.19
© Propellerhead Software AB.

14. Switch back to the Selection tool (arrow). Select the second block region, click on the Block 1 label to access the drop-down menu, and choose Block 2 (see Figure 3.22).

15. You'll notice that you now have two chained blocks in the Sequencer (see Figure 3.23). If you move the song position pointer to the beginning of the song and click the Play button, you'll hear both blocks play back to back.

Notice that your original recorded clip from the previous exercise is still in the Sequencer screen. Clips sitting on the timeline in Song mode will shadow clips in blocks, and so for both blocks to play, you will need to select and delete this clip. You don't need it anymore because you have it contained in a block!

Figure 3.20
© Propellerhead Software AB.

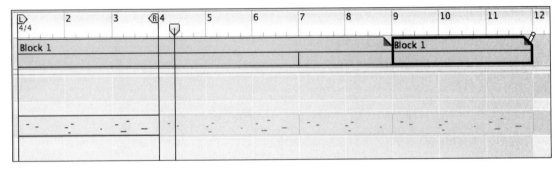

Figure 3.21
© Propellerhead Software AB.

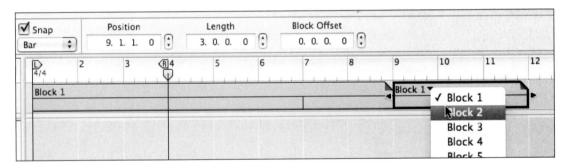

Figure 3.22
© Propellerhead Software AB.

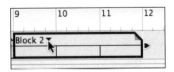

Figure 3.23
© Propellerhead Software AB.

I hope that, through this simple exercise, you can see the implied power of blocks. With blocks, you can draw in pieces of music instead having to copy, paste, and so on. Making a change in a block will apply globally to regions drawn in Song mode. It's important to note that multiple instrument tracks are contained in each block, so you'll definitely want to use it as an arrangement tool.

Okay, now that you've had some time with blocks and recording, let's have a little fun with effects.

Effects

While instruments and audio are definitely the building blocks of any song, if you don't have effects, they are really, really boring. Let's take a guitar, for example. If you just play a guitar by itself, it's this twangy, almost bell-like thing. Don't get me wrong; an acoustic on its own can be quite beautiful. But if it's an electric guitar by itself, you could almost play a rubber band and get a more interesting sound. It's not until an amplifier is hooked up that it begins to sound even remotely interesting.

However, even amps are rather limited. They generally only give you distortion, and that's it. That's why you pick up reverb pedals that make the guitar sound as if it's in a long, cavernous hallway. That's why you pick up echo pedals that make the guitar sound as if it's got a distant cousin in the background or that you're simply amazing at finger-picking, and so on.

These examples of effects are just the tip of the iceberg—especially when it comes to Reason.

Reason's effects include the following:

▷ **Amp modeling:** Line 6 Guitar and Bass Amp
▷ **Distortion:** Scream 4, D-11 Foldback Distortion
▷ **Reverb/delay/echo:** RV7000, DDL-1 Delay, RV-7 Reverb
▷ **Chorus/flange, phaser:** CF-101 Chorus/Flanger, PH-90 Phaser, UN-16 Unison
▷ **Filters:** ECF-42 Filter
▷ **Corrective effects (such as equalizers, compressors, and limiters):** MClass EQ, Compressor, Comp-01, PEQ-2 Compressor, MClass Stereo Imager, Maximizer
▷ **Pitch correction:** Neptune, BV512 Vocoder

These effects are all amazing. They take Reason from being a quaint bundle of instruments to being a powerhouse virtual studio without rival.

Three effects that I really like are as follows:

▷ **Echo:** A delay unit designed to make feedback loops fun and exciting
▷ **Alligator:** A filter gate that can be MIDI controlled like an instrument
▷ **Pulveriser:** A filtered compressor that can make anything sound hard and dirty (literally, there is a Dirt knob)

I like them so much because they do far more than what they are described as doing. For example, The Echo can double as a chorus type effect, and can give your music rhythmic stutters.

These descriptions may not raise your eyebrows much, but don't be too quick to judge. As we begin exploring them, you may have your musical life changed.

First, how do you set up an effects device? In the last couple of exercises, you were using a Piano device to create sounds. Let's try adding an effects device to this unit so you can hear and play simultaneously. Follow these steps:

1. On the Piano device you've been using for the last several exercises, position the cursor over a non-control area such as the rack ear and right-click to access the context menu. From the menu, choose Creative FX, and select The Echo (see Figure 3.24).

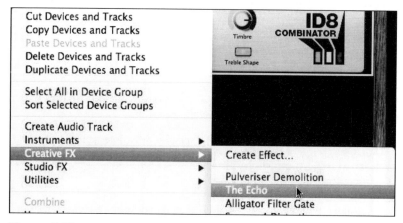

Figure 3.24
© Propellerhead Software AB.

2. The Echo effect pops into the Reason Rack. Press the Tab key to turn the Rack around (see Figure 3.25).

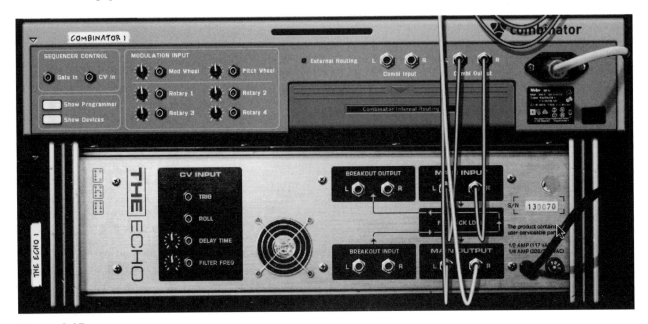

Figure 3.25
© Propellerhead Software AB.

You'll notice that the cabling is already taken care of. The Piano device is going into The Echo, and The Echo is routed to the Mix Channel device. But wait a minute! Remember when I said that you can store effects inside the Mix Channel device? Well, you can, and this will be very important to you if you really want most of your control coming from the mixer, as many producers do. The reason you would create The Echo inside the Mix Channel device is so that you can map knobs on the Mix Channel device to the Insert device—in this case, The Echo.

3. Delete The Echo by selecting the unit and then pressing the Delete key. Alternatively, right-click on the rack ear of The Echo and choose Delete Devices and Tracks from the menu that appears (see Figure 3.26).

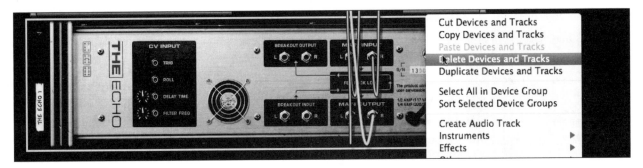

Figure 3.26
© Propellerhead Software AB.

4. Position the cursor on a region that is not a control on the Mix Channel device, right-click to access the context menu, choose Creative FX, and select The Echo (see Figure 3.27).

5. Notice that The Echo now resides inside the Mix Channel device (see Figure 3.28). Also notice that the cabling goes into the Insert FX inputs as opposed to the input sockets. Instead, the Piano device goes there directly. Press Tab.

Okay, now that you've seen a couple of the ways to route effects into your Reason Rack, let's spend a little time getting to know The Echo since we've got it running.

The Echo

Many musical acts of the past and present have used delay as more of an instrument in itself as opposed to just a basic effect. For example, U2's the Edge has created the illusion that he plays extremely fast and complicated guitar parts, when in reality he times his strums

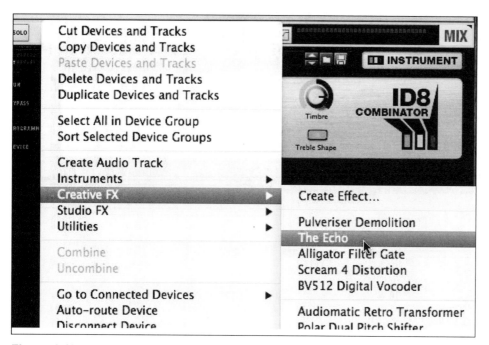

Figure 3.27
© Propellerhead Software AB.

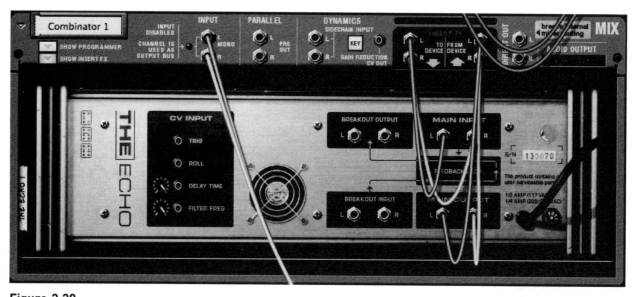

Figure 3.28
© Propellerhead Software AB.

between echo repetitions. The Edge is an extremely talented guitarist, and I'm not bashing his play style; he's amazing. That's just a trick of his that he has used throughout his career.

Also, many electronic acts (myself included) will use echo or delay to make extremely intricate bass and drum loops. Delay/echo makes it easy because it doubles, triples, and in some cases, quadruples what is being played. Figure 3.29 shows Reason's tool for this, The Echo.

Now try this exercise:

1. Play your original sequence from the earlier exercise. Place the Sequencer in Loop mode, with your loop points at a place where you can seamlessly loop your work for a while (see Figure 3.30).
2. Adjust the Dry/Wet knob and the Time knob while your part plays (see Figure 3.31). Notice how this completely changes the feel of the original piano part.

Figure 3.29
© Propellerhead Software AB.

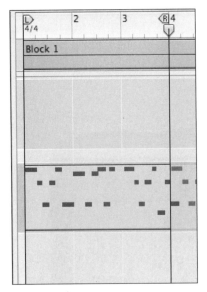

Figure 3.30
© Propellerhead Software AB.

Figure 3.31
© Propellerhead Software AB.

3. Pretty cool, eh? Let's make things even more interesting! Turn the Feedback knob gradually until you get it quite far, around 5 o'clock (see Figure 3.32). Notice how the piano now gets very, very psychedelic. It almost becomes a wall of sound. This is very reminiscent of old reggae, dub, ska, and so on, but can be used for any kind of music you want. When you want that wall, just raise the feedback.

4. If you want to really trick out the feedback loop, start toying with the Filter, LFO (low-frequency oscillator), Modulation, Color, and Diffusion sections (see Figure 3.33).

Figure 3.32
© Propellerhead Software AB.

Figure 3.33
© Propellerhead Software AB.

TIP: You can also use The Echo as a triggered device by changing its mode. The modes are as follows (see Figure 3.34):

▶ **Normal:** What you used in the preceding exercise.

▶ **Triggered:** The Delay effect is bypassed until you click the Trig button. You can trigger this rhythmically in very cool ways. Try tapping!

▶ **Roll:** The Delay effect and feedback are bypassed but can be gradually increased by using the Roll crossfader. This mode is great for triggering feedback loops and so on.

Figure 3.34
© Propellerhead Software AB.

5. All right, now you can put The Echo in Bypass mode, as shown in Figure 3.35.

Figure 3.35
© Propellerhead Software AB.

Alligator

Gating is a tool that has been used in electronica of all sorts, but the methodology has been kept relatively hidden. This is mainly because the means for creating the gating effect haven't been exactly easy to set up.

The Alligator changes this. As soon as you plug it in, you will instantly hear the gating effect, but with added dimension. You see, the Alligator, doesn't just gate; it gates between filters—thus, the Alligator Filter Gate menu command shown in Figure 3.36, which you use to launch the Alligator. (Right-click on the Mix Channel device, choose Creative FX, and choose Alligator Filter Gate.)

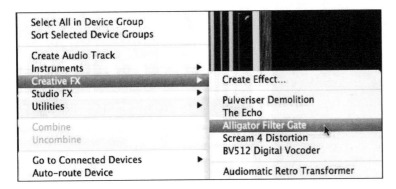

Figure 3.36
© Propellerhead Software AB.

The Alligator features a rhythm generator that activates the gates. The lamps in the Gate section blink on and off according to the pattern settings and also indicate how the signal is being rhythmically directed through the Filter section (see Figure 3.37). You can override the pattern by clicking the Manual buttons to hold a gate open. (More on this later.)

Figure 3.37
© Propellerhead Software AB.

You'll notice that each filter—the high pass, band pass, and low pass—can be modified in big, crazy ways with Delay, Drive, LFO, Phaser, and more (see Figure 3.38). That means each triggered filter can sound very, very different from another.

Figure 3.38
© Propellerhead Software AB.

The Pattern section gives you synced, premade patterns for bouncing between different filters (see Figure 3.39). Try running your piano sequence while the pattern (always enabled by default) is playing. Use the resolution to change the timing and the number arrows to choose the pattern.

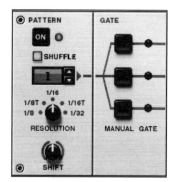

Figure 3.39
© Propellerhead Software AB.

You can even set up the Alligator as a playable effect. Right-click on the Alligator and select Create Track for Alligator. You'll now be able to trigger filters from MIDI keys F#1, G#1, and A#1. Neat, eh? For now, put the Alligator in Bypass mode.

Pulveriser

Compression is the friend of the knowledgeable producer for two reasons:

▷ It takes the dynamics out of very dynamic parts (vocals, guitar, drums, and so on) and makes them sit pretty in a mix.
▷ It can make things much bigger, meaner, and phatter.

The latter is what the Pulveriser (see Figure 3.40) excels at. To open the Pulveriser, right-click the Mix Channel device, choose Creative FX, and select Pulveriser Demolition.

Figure 3.40
© Propellerhead Software AB.

But the Pulveriser is far more than just a compressor! It's basically a compressor and distortion unit with a filter with an LFO. (If you don't get what any of that means, you'll know by the end of this book.)

Okay, so let's try it out:

1. Create a Dr. Octo Rex. To do so, position the cursor on an empty area of the Rack screen and right-click to open a context menu. Then choose Instruments and select Dr. Octo Rex Loop Player (see Figure 3.41). Leave it loaded with its default patch, which is Acoustic Drums | College 130-1.drex (see Figure 3.42).
2. Click the Run button on the Dr. Octo Rex to hear the drum loop. When you have an idea what these drums sounds like, click the Run button again. Then right-click on the Dr. Octo Rex, choose Creative FX, and select Pulveriser Demolition to create another Pulveriser (see Figure 3.43). Make sure to right-click on an empty part of Dr. Octo Rex. Right-clicking on a knob will open a different menu.
3. Click the Run button on the Dr. Octo Rex and listen to the difference made just by adding a Pulveriser. Nasty, eh?

Figure 3.41
© Propellerhead Software AB.

Figure 3.42
© Propellerhead Software AB.

Figure 3.43
© Propellerhead Software AB.

4. Turn the Squash knob to 11 o'clock and the Dirt knob to 3 o'clock (see Figure 3.44). Then click the Run button on the Dr. Octo Rex again. There's a major difference with a subtle setting like this. Try experimenting with the Squash now. Notice how much more aggressive the drums get as you raise it.

Figure 3.44
© Propellerhead Software AB.

5. Let's make it even more interesting! Try moving the Tremor to Volume knob to 3 o'clock (see Figure 3.45).
6. Increase the Tremor Rate to 4 o'clock (see Figure 3.46). Hear the ringing? Try adjusting the Tremor Waveform with the arrow buttons. Using these effects, you can create all sorts of crazy textures!

Figure 3.45
© Propellerhead Software AB.

Figure 3.46
© Propellerhead Software AB.

Not Enough? Try the Prop Shop!

Once upon a time, you were limited to the instruments and effects that Propellerhead included with Reason. This is no longer the case. Reason can now be expanded and customized with additional instruments, known as rack extensions, that can be purchased from the Propellerhead shop. That's right: You can customize your Reason rack with additional pieces of gear.

Purchasing rack extensions is easy. Head to http://shop.propellerheads.se. Instantly you'll be transported to the Rack Extensions online store (see Figure 3.47), which contains synthesizers, effects, utilities, and more.

Figure 3.47
© Propellerhead Software AB.

It's important to note that while there are some additional devices created by Propellerhead, the creators of Reason, most Rack Extensions are from outside companies. And these third-party developers are not slouches by any stretch. In fact, they include major developers like Korg, Rob Papen, FXpansion, even Cakewalk!

Oh, and check this out: You can demo anything in the Prop Shop for up to 30 days. This little nugget of information should have you scurrying to the website right now! In fact, let me suggest some rack extensions for you to check out:

▷ **Korg MonoPoly:** This is a killer subtractive synth that has that vintage sound that will spruce up any track you bring it into. It also features a killer arpeggiator. (See Figure 3.48.)

▷ **Rob Papen Predator RE:** This is another amazing synth that features three oscillators, tons of effects, and an arpeggiator that will almost write the song for you. (See Figure 3.49.) Rob Papen is a renowned sound designer with a roster of users who span several years of the Billboard charts. Keep an eye on anything from this developer.

▷ **Audiomatic Retro Transformer:** Audiomatic is an incredible device from Propellerhead itself. It can be used to add vintage-style coloration to your audio. Seriously, run your mix through it and choose the Tape setting. Suddenly, your song will sound like it was recorded on an old reel to reel. Have a taste for vinyl? Well, there's a setting for that, too. This rack extension is free for Reason 7 users. (See Figure 3.50.)

Figure 3.48
© Propellerhead Software AB.

Figure 3.49
© Propellerhead Software AB.

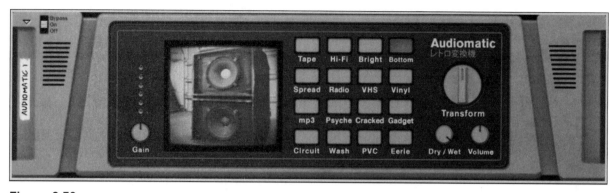

Figure 3.50
© Propellerhead Software AB.

▷ **BitSpeek LPC Vocoder from Sonic Charge:** Have a taste for Speak & Spells? If so, you'll love this device. With BitSpeek, shown in Figure 3.51, you can process your voice through the very same algorithm used to make the Speak & Spell voice. In other words, you can instantly sound like an old 8-bit computer. But there's more: It's also possible to use your MIDI keyboard to control the pitch of the recorded audio once it's running through BitSpeek. It's like having a Speak & Spell with auto-tune!

Figure 3.51
© Propellerhead Software AB.

▷ **Buffre Beat Repeater from Peff:** Do you DJ? Do you dabble in electronica? Do you like sick, glitched-out breaks that change things up a bit? If you answered "Yes" to any of these questions, then you should definitely check out Buffre (see Figure 3.52). Aside from having one of the coolest-looking front and back panels of any of the third-party rack extensions, Buffre delivers precision stutters that can be triggered from your MIDI controller. If you get higher up in the octaves while stuttering, looping audio can even become melodic.

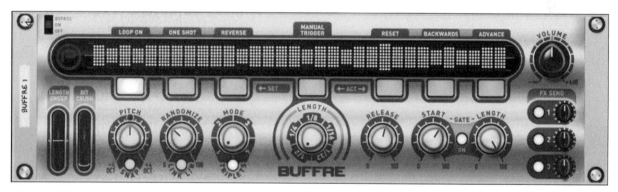

Figure 3.52
© Propellerhead Software AB.

Prices on each of the rack extensions vary from developer to developer. And of course, the price listed may not always be the price you're willing to pay. But keep in mind that developers are always having sales. And, if something looks appealing, try it! See if it's even worth your hard-earned cash.

Moving On

As you can see, Reason is packed with some powerful pieces of gear...and it can be expanded with even more powerful pieces of gear!

Okay, now we can start spending some time with some of the individual instruments in Reason. Let's move on!

4

The Reason Sequencer: Close-Up

T HE REASON SEQUENCER IS BASICALLY THE BRAIN OF THE ENTIRE PROGRAM (see Figure 4.1). It is the compositional tool that enables you to record your performances, edit them, and then play them back with accuracy and precision. This chapter examines the individual parts of the Reason Sequencer screen and discusses how to use the Sequencer to its limits.

Track List   Song/Edit/Block view   Tool Window

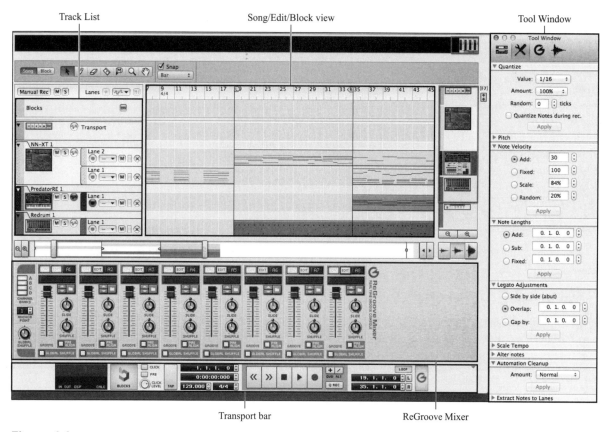

Transport bar   ReGroove Mixer

Figure 4.1
© Propellerhead Software AB.

A sequencer is responsible for performing three tasks:

▷ Recording MIDI/audio data
▷ Editing MIDI/audio data
▷ Playing back MIDI/audio data

Importing and Exporting MIDI Files: The Reason sequencer can import and export MIDI files. This is a great feature for users who like to surf the Web and download MIDI files of their favorite songs. Additionally, you can export your songs in Reason as MIDI files for other users to download into their favorite MIDI sequencers.

To import a MIDI file, simply choose Import MIDI File from the File menu and then locate the MIDI file with your Windows or Mac file browser to import it. After you import the MIDI file, just keep these rules in mind:

▶ Imported sequencer tracks are automatically routed to an instance of the ID8 per MIDI track. Additionally, each instance of the ID8 will have a patch loaded that hopefully resembles the original sound if that data is contained within the MIDI file. Otherwise, the instance of the ID8 will load a Grand Piano patch as the default patch.

▶ All the controller data saved within a MIDI file, such as modulation wheel adjustments and pitch bend changes, is imported along with the rest of the data. In some cases, however, this controller data might not work as intended with Reason devices. You might have to remove the controller information, which is covered toward the end of this chapter.

To export a MIDI file, first set your end (E) marker to the right-most position of your song. Then choose Export MIDI File from the File menu, and Reason does the rest. Just remember the following:

▶ The tempo of the Reason song is stored in the MIDI file.
▶ All the exported sequencer tracks are set to MIDI Channel 1 by default. This is true because Reason is not a MIDI channel–dependent program, like Cubase and Logic.
▶ All the exported sequencer tracks retain their given names from Reason.

The rest of this chapter explores every inch of the Reason Sequencer screen, including the following topics:

▷ The basic layout
▷ The Track List
▷ The Sequencer screen toolbar
▷ The Tool Window
▷ The Transport panel
▷ How to sequence a live performance
▷ How to sequence written data
▷ How to record a live performance
▷ How to edit a live performance
▷ The ReGroove Mixer

The Basic Layout and Tools

Before you begin your exploration of the Reason Sequencer screen, it's important to have a general understanding of the basic layout of its common and unique views and functions.

The Song View and Edit Mode

When you first look at the Sequencer screen, the Song view is probably the first point of interest you will notice. This is the place where all the MIDI and audio data for your Reason song is stored, arranged, and displayed.

> **NOTE:** All the data displayed in the Reason Sequencer screen is also referred to as *clips*. Clips are groups of data that can be easily moved around, selected, deleted, cut into smaller clips, and more.

Typically, a sequencer displays its MIDI/audio data in a linear fashion, meaning that the information is read from left to right. A song begins on the far left and progresses to the right as the song plays. The timeline of these events in the Reason Sequencer screen is governed by the ruler, which is located at the top of the Song view and runs parallel to it. Looking at Figure 4.2, you can see that the ruler displays *bars*, or measure counts for every other bar. When you read through the next part of this section and use the Zoom tools, you'll find that the ruler can display much smaller and finer increments.

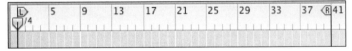

Figure 4.2
© Propellerhead Software AB.

Several kinds of data are displayed in the Song view:

▷ Note/audio information
▷ Controller information
▷ Automation information
▷ Pattern change information

NOTE: If you're familiar with other DAWs, you're probably used to seeing track lanes that feature a lot of data, which can be viewed through various drop-down menus and so on. Reason works similarly, but through a feature called "lanes," which are multiple tracks of data contained within a single sequencer track. Looking at Figure 4.3, you can see a track that includes two lanes of data. The first lane is the note data and the second lane is automation data for the Filter Frequency parameter of the Reason synth where this track is routed, which is the SubTractor. Also note that the second lane has an On/Off switch, which disables the automation data from playing back. This is also the same for pattern lanes, which you'll read about shortly. Additionally, every lane has a Delete Lane button marked ×, which deletes just the lane and not the entire sequencer track.

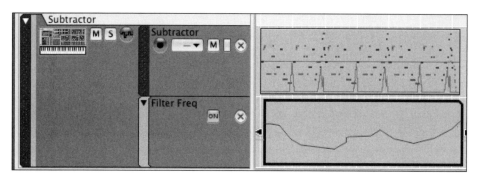

Figure 4.3
© Propellerhead Software AB.

The Sequencer screen also has an alternate viewing mode, called Edit mode. In this view, all the data in a song can be edited and new data can be created (see Figure 4.4). As you read further in this chapter, you will find that there are many creative possibilities and different faces to the Edit mode.

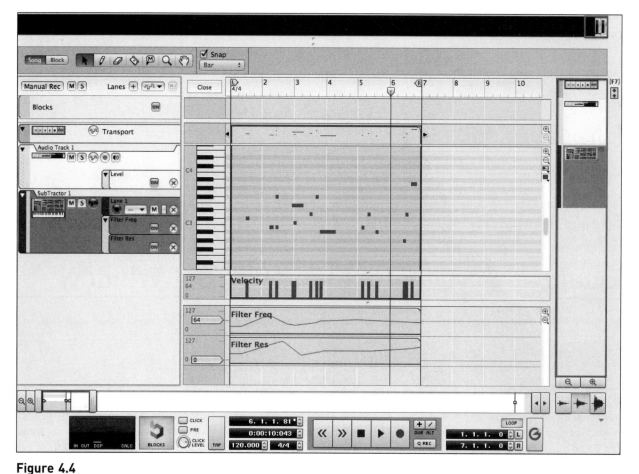

Figure 4.4
© Propellerhead Software AB.

The Zoom Tools

The Reason Sequencer screen includes Zoom tools that can help you get a close-up look at any data in a particular track. They also give you a better view of an overall song.

▷ The first pair of Zoom tools is located in the lower-left corner of the Sequencer screen. These tools enable you to zoom in and out horizontally on any event(s) in the Sequencer screen (see Figure 4.5).

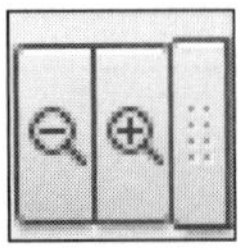

Figure 4.5
© Propellerhead Software AB.

▷ The second pair of Zoom tools is located in the lower-right corner of the Navigator. These tools enable you to zoom in and out vertically on every sequencer track while in Song or Block view (see Figure 4.6).

Figure 4.6
© Propellerhead Software AB.

▷ Two additional pairs of Zoom tools become visible when you enter Edit mode. They are located in the upper-right corner of the Sequencer screen. You use the topmost pair to zoom in or out on the Clip Overview and use the lower pair to zoom in or out on the data being edited (see Figure 4.7).

Figure 4.7
© Propellerhead Software AB.

Sizing Up the Sequencer

The size of the Sequencer screen can be easily adjusted in two ways:

▷ Click on the Maximize button, located in the upper-right corner of the Sequencer screen. Note that after you maximize the Sequencer screen, the Maximize button becomes a Restore button, which you use to return the window to its default position. You can also use the F7 key to maximize the Sequencer screen.

▷ Click and drag on the divider between the Sequencer screen and the Reason Rack screen.

The Sequencer Screen Toolbar and Tool Window

Both the toolbar and the Tool Window are used to perform numerous tasks in the Sequencer screen. This section discusses each of these (see Figure 4.8).

Let's first discuss the Sequencer screen toolbar, starting at the far-left corner.

Accessing Edit Mode

Like all DAWs, Reason features a main view that acts as your arrangement window. In Reason's case, this is the Song view that we've been working in. There's also another view known as Edit view. You can reach this mode a few different ways. One is to use the Options menu, shown in Figure 4.9. The quickest way is to press Ctrl+E (Windows) or Command+E (Mac). You can also double-click on a clip to enter Edit mode, but double-clicking on an audio clip with no comp layers opens the Inline Editor for timing adjustments.

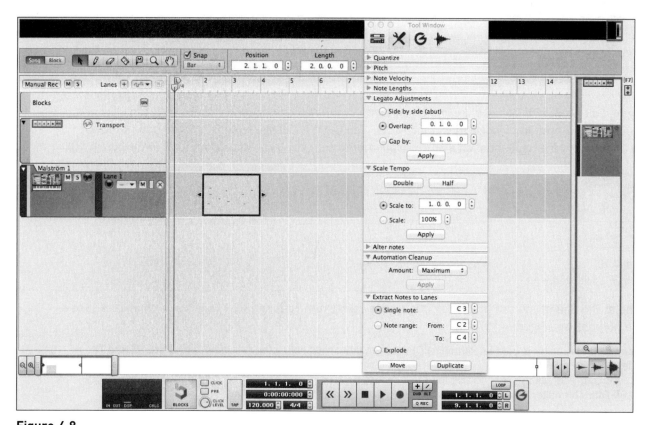

Figure 4.8
© Propellerhead Software AB.

Figure 4.9
© Propellerhead Software AB.

TIP: Looking at Figure 4.9, you can also see another option, Switch to Block View, which switches the Reason Sequencer screen to Block view. In case you missed this feature, refer to Chapter 3, "Recording and Effects."

Changing Edit Modes: When you are in the Edit mode of the Reason Sequencer screen, you can view and edit your performances and sequences in a few ways. You use the Change Note Edit Mode pop-up menu, which is located to the upper-right area of the Sequencer screen, just below the Zoom tools (see Figure 4.10).

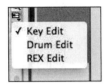

Figure 4.10
© Propellerhead Software AB.

Looking at the figure, you can see three options (Key Edit, Drum Edit, and REX Edit), each of which serves a unique purpose (see Figure 4.11).

- ▶ **Key Edit:** This editor is used to edit the MIDI data related to the SubTractor, Malström, Thor, NN-19, and NN-XT devices.
- ▶ **Drum Edit:** This editor is used to edit the MIDI data of Redrum.
- ▶ **REX Edit:** This editor is used to edit the MIDI data of the Dr. Octo Rex Loop Player.

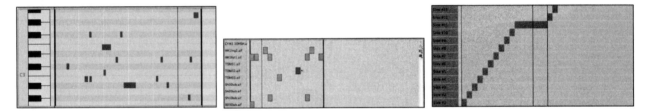

Figure 4.11
© Propellerhead Software AB.

Just below the Change Note Edit Mode menu is the Note Lane Performance Parameter Automation menu (see Figure 4.12). This menu enables you to show and hide different controller parameters such as the Mod Wheel and Aftertouch and all the parameters that can be automated. You'll learn more about this later in the chapter. For now, just be aware that these menus are available and you'll be calling on them from time to time.

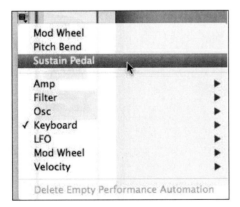

Figure 4.12
© Propellerhead Software AB.

The Toolbar

To the right of the Song/Block buttons is the toolbar, containing the Sequencer screen editing tools (see Figure 4.13). These seven buttons are used to view, write, or edit data in both the Song and Block views, as well as in Edit mode.

Figure 4.13
© Propellerhead Software AB.

> **Selector tool:** Also known as the *pointer*, this tool enables you to select an individual event or group. You also can use it to select a group of events and groups by clicking and dragging a marquee box around them.
> **Pencil tool:** This tool enables you to draw MIDI events and groups. Additionally, you can use it to draw in controller and velocity information on an event-by-event basis. You can also hold down the Ctrl (Windows) or Option (Mac) key, and the Pencil becomes a crosshair tool that you can use to click and drag straight lines or smooth diagonal lines.
> **Eraser tool:** This tool enables you to delete single events and groups. Additionally, you can delete a group of events by clicking and dragging a marquee box around them and then releasing the mouse button.
> **Razor tool:** This tool enables you to cut sequencer data by splitting clips.
> **Mute tool:** This tool enables you to mute selected clips of events in a song.
> **Magnify tool:** This tool enables you to get a close-up look at a group or event.
> **Hand tool:** This tool enables you to scroll through a Reason song. Select it and then click and drag to the left or right while in the Song or Edit view. The song position pointer shifts along with you.

Keyboard Shortcuts: Each tool button has a keyboard shortcut assigned to it. This makes it easy to switch tools quickly without using the mouse. Here's a list of the buttons and their shortcut keys:

▶ **Selector:** Q
▶ **Pencil:** W
▶ **Eraser:** E
▶ **Razor:** R
▶ **Mute:** T
▶ **Magnify:** Y
▶ **Hand:** U

Snap Controls

To the right of the editing tools are the Snap (short for "Snap to Grid") controls (see Figure 4.14). These perform two tasks:

> They assign a minimum note length value to the Pencil tool.
> They assign a minimum note length value for shifting MIDI events.

Figure 4.14
© Propellerhead Software AB.

Snap supports a wide variety of note values, ranging from bar (whole notes) to 1/64 notes. After selecting a note value, you can then use the Pencil, Line, or Selector tool to draw, edit, or shift clips in the Song view or events in the Edit view.

It's important to understand how Snap works, so let's try a couple of exercises. Get yourself ready by starting a new Reason song, creating an instance of SubTractor, and creating a clip by using the Pencil tool to click and drag between the left and right locator points. When you're finished, it should look something like Figure 4.15.

1. Use the Selector tool to double-click on the clip. This opens the Key Lane Editor for the SubTractor. The velocity lane should also be viewable by default.
2. Select a note value of 1/8 from the Snap menu.
3. Make sure the Snap button, located to the right of the Snap Value menu, is active.

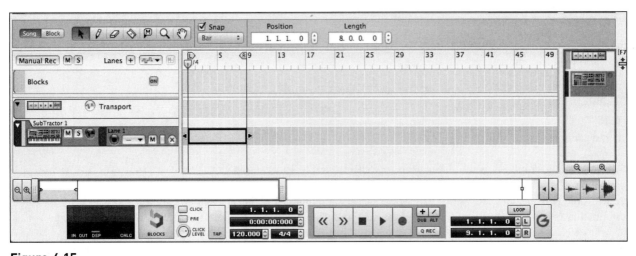

Figure 4.15
© Propellerhead Software AB.

4. Select the Pencil tool and click to create a few events in the key lane. Notice that each note is a 1/8 note in length (see Figure 4.16).

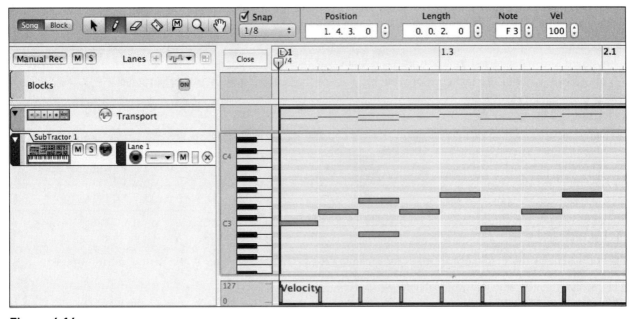

Figure 4.16
© Propellerhead Software AB.

5. Click the Close button to switch to Song view.

In the next exercise, you'll use the Selector tool in Song view. For the sake of simplicity, keep using the song you started in the preceding example and make sure that the Snap to Grid button is still active before you begin this exercise.

1. Switch to Song view and choose 1/2 from the Snap menu. This assigns a half note value.
2. Click the Selector tool. Now click and drag the SubTractor clip to the left or right, and you will notice it moving in half-note increments.
3. Choose a smaller note value from the Snap menu, such as 1/8.
4. Try moving the clip again, and you will see that it moves in much smaller increments than before.

> **NOTE:** Located just to the right of the Snap menu is the Snap to Grid button (keyboard shortcut S). This button turns the Snap function on and off. You have just seen how the Snap works when activated. Try turning off the Snap to Grid button and using the Selector tool to move around a few clips. You will notice that the moving clips are not governed by the Snap note value. Rather, you can move clips around freely, which is typically referred to as *free time*. This enables you to make very fine adjustments to a performance.

Additional Toolbar Features

In addition to all the tools discussed in the preceding sections, the Sequencer screen toolbar provides other tools and features. Just to the right of the Snap tools, there may appear to be a lot of empty, unused space. I say "may appear to be" because some of these additional tools and features do not appear unless a clip has been selected (see Figure 4.17).

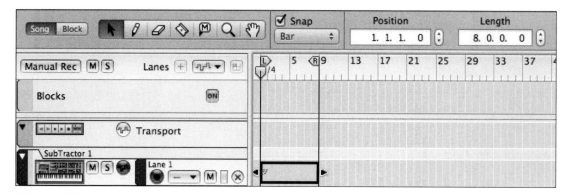

Figure 4.17
© Propellerhead Software AB.

The Track Parameter Automation button and menu operate in the same fashion as the Performance Parameter Automation menu that you looked at earlier in this chapter (review Figure 4.12). The purpose of this button and menu is to create an automation lane on the selected sequencer track. Looking at Figure 4.18, you can see that most of the automated parameters are listed, such as the parameters on the SubTractor.

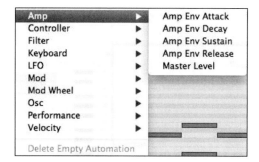

Figure 4.18
© Propellerhead Software AB.

The Manual Record button performs a simple yet useful task. Whenever you select a track in the Reason Sequencer screen, the track is automatically set to Record Enabled. Although this feature is great when you're first creating your Reason song, it can get a bit cumbersome when you are in the mixing stage because you don't want to risk accidentally recording over your audio tracks. Activate the Manual Record button and select any track in your Reason song, and you'll see that the track is not Record Enabled.

Moving along to the right, the Create Pattern Lane button enables you to create a lane for changing patterns with either the Matrix or Redrum, which are both pattern-based Reason devices. You also can use it to create a lane for changing loops with Dr. Octo Rex. Note that this button is grayed out until an instance of one of the aforementioned Reason devices has been created.

Now, select the Pencil tool and a couple of new drop-down menus appear just to the right of the Pattern Lane button.

▷ **Time Signature:** This drop-down menu is used to automate time signature changes for your Reason song. To use it, simply hold down the Alt (Windows) or Option (Mac) key on your keyboard and click on the Time Signature display in the Transport panel. A new time signature lane is created on the transport sequencer track. At this point, select your new time signature from the menu and use the Pencil tool to draw in the new time signature along the transport sequencer track.

▷ **Pattern/Loop:** This is used to automate pattern changes for either the Matrix or Redrum. It also can be used for automating loop changes with Dr. Octo Rex. To use it, hold down the Alt (Windows) or Option (Mac) key on your keyboard and click on the Pattern section of either the Matrix or Redrum, or the Loop Slot section of Dr. Octo Rex. A pattern select lane is created on the sequencer track of the aforementioned Reason devices. At this point, select your new pattern from the menu and use the Pencil tool to draw the new pattern in the lane.

▷ **Block:** This is used to assign any selected clip of song data in a song to a block, which is part of the Block view. This is a feature that enables you to create a dynamic arrangement of your song by assigning groups of MIDI data to blocks that can then be rearranged quickly. This feature is covered in the previous chapter.

Lastly, some additional settings are displayed in the Inspector when dealing with MIDI clips in Edit mode. Open any Reason song that contains MIDI tracks, switch to Edit mode, and select a MIDI note. At this point, you see the newly displayed options at the top of the screen in an area called the Inspector (see Figure 4.19). They are as follows:

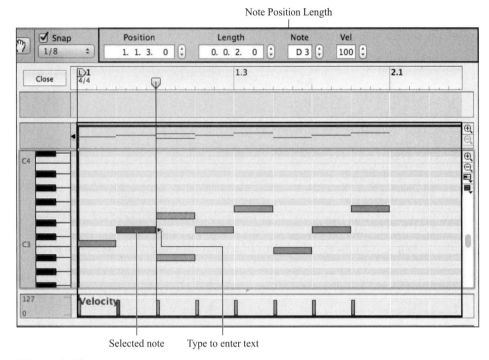

Figure 4.19
© Propellerhead Software AB.

▷ **Position:** This option displays the MIDI note's position in bars, beats, 1/16 notes, and ticks.
▷ **Length:** This option displays the MIDI note's length in bars, beats, 1/16 notes, and ticks.
▷ **Note:** This option displays the note's pitch in numeric form. Note that this option is not actually labeled "Pitch" (or anything, for that matter).
▷ **Vel:** This option displays the note's velocity.

Note that you also can view the Position and Length options in Song view when a clip is selected in the Sequencer screen.

The Tool Window

Reason 7's Tool Window is probably one of the best workflow features I've ever used in a sequencing program (see Figure 4.20). It can help create new instances of any Reason device, edit your MIDI performances, edit samples, and edit/alter your grooves via ReGroove, which you'll learn about later in this chapter. It can even be used to transpose the pitch of audio and MIDI clips! In other words, it's Reason's creative hub.

The Tool Window is divided into four sections: the Device palette, the Sequencer tools, the Groove settings, and the Song Samples section. This discussion focuses only on the Sequencer tools and Song Samples section; you'll learn about the Groove settings later in this chapter.

Sequencer Tools

To start, let's meet the family of Sequencer tools (refer to Figure 4.20).

Quantize

Quantization helps to correct timing problems. The easiest way to explain this concept is to think of quantizing as an invisible magnet that pulls and pushes MIDI events to a determined note value, which is assigned via the Quantize Notes section of the Sequencer tools (refer to Figure 4.20). It's an indispensable tool for rhythmically challenged (or non-robotic) people who need rhythms that are tight and punchy.

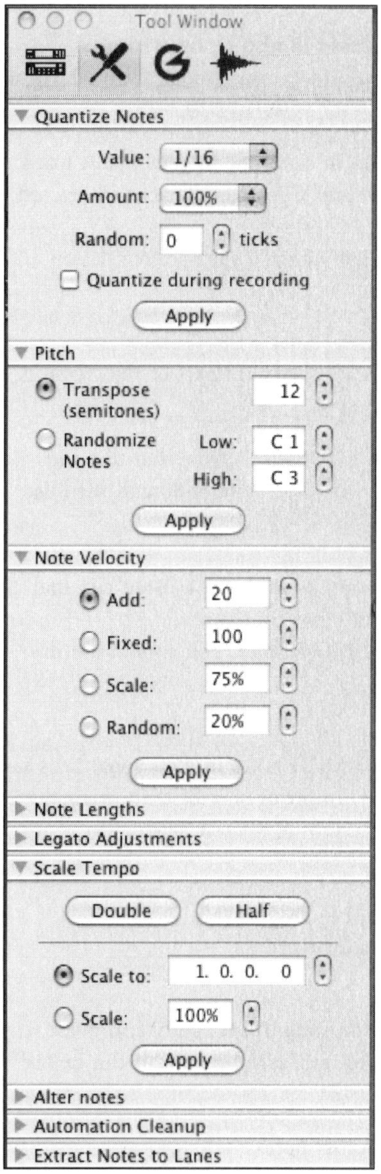

Figure 4.20
© Propellerhead Software AB.

To use this tool, you must select a clip from any sequencer track that has MIDI note data or a group of MIDI notes in Edit mode. After you do this, the Apply button in the Quantize tool becomes active. Assuming that you've done this, let's look at the individual parameters:

▷ **Value:** This menu determines the note value to use for quantization. Like the Snap menu, it has a range of bar to 1/64 and all points in between. However, unlike the Snap menu, it has an additional Shuffle option, which is used in combination with the ReGroove mixer. More on this later.

▷ **Amount:** This menu determines the amount of quantization to apply to a clip or to a group of selected MIDI notes. It has a range of 5% to 100%.

▷ **Random:** This option applies a randomized feeling to your MIDI notes in tick increments. It has a range of 0–120 ticks. The purpose of this function is to introduce a looser feeling to your music to prevent it from feeling too tight and rigid. Think of real drummers; as much as they might try, it's difficult to hit every note right in time without some sort of variation. This introduces a randomization into their playing, which is what gives the performance its charm. The Random function can help make this possible.

▷ **Quantize During Recording:** When selected, this performs real-time quantization after the MIDI event has been recorded. The amount of applied quantization is determined by the selected note value and quantization strength.

PITCH

The Pitch tool enables you to alter the pitch of an audio or MIDI performance in your song. This process can also be referred to as *transposition* because it can be used to introduce key changes to your song. As shown in Figure 4.20, you have two options from which to choose when using this tool:

▷ **Transpose:** This option enables you to transpose the pitch of your audio or selected MIDI notes in semitone increments. It has a range of +/−127 for MIDI clips. For audio, the combined transpose values in the Tool Window and Clip Inspector cannot exceed +/−12.50 semitones.

▷ **Randomize:** This option enables you to randomize the pitches of your selected MIDI notes based within a specifically selected note range. Simply assign a Low and High setting and then click the Apply button.

NOTE VELOCITY

The Note Velocity tool is used to assign varying velocities to the MIDI performances in your song. It's an important part of the creative process because it can help introduce dynamics to your music, making it much more interesting to listen to.

▷ **Add:** This setting allows you to add a specific amount of velocity to a selected clip or group of MIDI notes. Note that this adds velocity to what has already been recorded, which simply means that if you have a MIDI note with a velocity of 80 and then use this tool to add 20, the resulting value is 100.

▷ **Fixed:** This setting enables you to apply a fixed velocity value to your selected MIDI notes.

▷ **Scale:** This setting enables you to apply a scaled feeling to your selected MIDI notes. A good example of this is a drum clip that has a lot of dynamics. Using the Scale setting is a great way to make those variations in velocity more pronounced.

▷ **Random:** This setting enables you to introduce randomization to the velocities of your selected MIDI notes. You should use this feature sparingly because it might create some velocities that are unpleasant to listen to.

NOTE LENGTHS

The Note Lengths tool is used to add, subtract, or fix the length of the selected clip or group of selected MIDI notes in your song. Let's say you would like to take a track of sustained chords played through the NN-XT and make the notes play longer or shorter than originally recorded. Note Lengths is the right tool for the job.

▷ **Add:** This option adds length to your selected MIDI notes by bars, beats, 1/16 notes, or ticks.

▷ **Sub:** This option subtracts length from your selected MIDI notes by bars, beats, 1/16 notes, or ticks.

▷ **Fixed:** This option applies a fixed length to your selected MIDI notes by bars, beats, 1/16 notes, or ticks.

LEGATO ADJUSTMENTS

The Legato Adjustments tool is used to adjust the amount of legato for the selected notes in your Reason song. It's a handy and quick way to make a series of notes flow evenly without gaps between the notes. It's also a tool that can be used to overlap notes, and it can be used to introduce a gap between notes. The options are as follows:

▷ **Side-by-side:** This option extends the length of a selected note to the beginning of the next selected note.

▷ **Overlap:** This option overlaps the lengths of selected notes by bars, beats, 1/16 notes, or ticks.

▷ **Gap by:** This option creates a gap between selected notes by bars, beats, 1/16 notes, or ticks.

SCALE TEMPO

The Scale Tempo tool is used to alter the perceived tempo of an audio or MIDI performance. With the Scale Tempo tool, you can make a bass line or lead sound as if it's playing back at half or double the tempo at which it was originally recorded. Additionally, Scale Tempo alters any automation, controller, or pattern data to make sure everything sounds correct as it plays back. The options are as follows:

▷ **Double/Half:** These buttons double or cut in half the original tempo of the selected MIDI notes or audio data, speeding up or slowing down the tempo, respectively. You can also use the Scale setting to create the same effect by assigning a value of 200% to double the tempo or 50% to cut the tempo in half.

▷ **Scale:** This option allows you to alter the tempo of your selected MIDI notes or audio by less common values than the Double and Half buttons. Simply set your desired value and click the Apply button.

ALTER NOTES

The Alter Notes tool is a bit of an *avant-garde* feature because it alters the pitch, length, and velocity of your selected MIDI notes in a random fashion. However, this tool is not confined to a specific note or velocity range as you saw with the Note and Velocity tools. All you need to do is assign a percentage value and then click on the Apply button to see what Reason will randomly cook up for you. Just remember, there's always an opportunity to undo what you've done by selecting Undo Alter Notes from the Edit menu.

AUTOMATION CLEANUP

The Automation Cleanup tool is used to optimize or clean your automation data in a Reason song. You may notice that as you begin to write in automation data, it tends to get a little messy due to all the automation points created along the timeline of the sequencer track. To use this tool, simply select a clip with automation written onto it, determine the amount of cleanup needed (options range from Minimum to Maximum), and click the Apply button. You'll take a better look at this feature in Chapter 12, "Automation," which discusses automation at length.

EXTRACT NOTES TO LANES

The Extract Notes to Lanes tool is used to move or duplicate a specific note or range of notes to a separate clip on a new note lane within a sequencer track. This is a useful tool to have when you are working with a device, such as a Redrum sequencer track. You can split the separate notes onto their own tracks for further editing. The tool includes the following parameters:

▷ **Single Note:** This parameter enables you to select a single note to extract.

▷ **Note Range:** This parameter enables you to select a range of notes to extract.

▷ **Explode:** This parameter places every note of a sequence onto its own note lane.

Song Samples Section

The Song Samples section is used to list all of the audio samples loaded in a Reason song. This includes samples used within a device such as the NN-XT and recorded audio performances. This section can also be used to record, edit, duplicate, delete, and export a sample.

The Song Samples section includes the following options:

▷ **Play:** This will play any selected sample. Also note the Autoplay feature and the volume slider.

▷ **Start Sampling:** This will record new audio samples to be used in your song.

▷ **Duplicate:** This will create a duplicate file of any selected sample.

▷ **Delete:** This will delete any selected sample.

▷ **Export:** This will export any selected sample to an AIFF or WAV file.

The Transport Panel

Although some might consider the Transport panel a separate entity from the Reason Sequencer screen, I disagree, because the Sequencer screen is dependent on the Transport panel to function properly. With that in mind, the next part of the tour is dedicated to the features and functionality of the Transport panel (see Figure 4.21).

Figure 4.21
© Propellerhead Software AB.

In the center of the Transport panel are the Stop and Play controls of the Reason Sequencer screen. They look similar to the buttons on a tape machine or DVD player. There is really no mystery as to what each button does, but there are a few variations that make these buttons more adaptable to the Reason environment.

▷ Clicking the Stop button stops the sequencer wherever it is playing within a sequence. If you click the Stop button a second time, the song position pointer returns to the left locater. Clicking the Stop button a third time causes the song position pointer to return to the beginning of the sequence. This is called the *return-to-zero* function.

▷ Clicking the Play button causes the Reason sequencer to begin playing. There are no additional features on this button.

▷ Clicking the Rewind button shuttles the song position pointer backward to any point in a Reason song. The button can be used while the song is playing or when the sequencer is stopped. When it is clicked once, the song position pointer jumps back one bar. When you click and hold the button, the song position pointer scrolls back even faster.

▷ Clicking the Fast Forward button shuttles the song position pointer forward to any point in a Reason song. As with the Rewind button, it can be used while the song is playing or when the Reason sequencer has stopped. When you click the button once, the song position pointer jumps forward one bar. When you click and hold the button, the song position pointer scrolls forward even faster.

▷ Clicking the Record button triggers Reason's sequencer to record audio or MIDI data. If the Record button is clicked while the sequence is stopped, playback begins and recording commences on any record-enabled tracks or lanes. If the sequence is already playing, you can click the Record button to input MIDI or audio data on the fly. This is also referred to as *punching in*.

Know Your Key Commands: The key to becoming a seasoned Reason user is to learn the keyboard shortcuts linked to the graphical user interface controls in the program. Because I just went over the basic transport controls, here is a quick list of their corresponding key commands:

▶ **Stop button:** The 0 (zero) key on your numeric keypad, press the spacebar, or Shift+Enter (Windows) or Shift+Return (Mac). Pressing 0 twice or Shift+Enter or Shift+Return twice returns to zero.
▶ **Play button:** The Enter key on your numeric keypad or the spacebar
▶ **Rewind button:** The 7 key on your numeric keypad
▶ **Fast Forward button:** The 8 key on your numeric keypad
▶ **Record button:** The * (asterisk) key on your numeric keypad

---

NOTE: Located just to the left of the Transport controls is the Song Position readout. This is a numeric readout indicating where you currently are located in your sequence in bars, beats, 1/16 notes, or ticks. Click Play, and notice that the indicator constantly calls out position readings. Just below this is another Song Position readout that is in hours, minutes, seconds, and milliseconds. If you want to jump to a specific point in your song, you can double-click in either Song Position readout, type a value, and then press Enter (Windows) or Return (Mac).

Alt or Dub?

Located just to the right of the Transport controls are a couple of buttons that determine how Reason records a new audio or MIDI performance. These buttons are as follows:

▷ **Dub:** Select this button, and Reason creates a new note lane in your selected MIDI track without muting the previous note lane. Or, in the case of audio, a new audio track is created with the same settings as the previous audio track, also without muting the previous audio track. This allows you to record additional material into your sequence while listening to what you have already recorded for that same part.
▷ **Alt:** Select this button and Reason creates a new note lane in your selected MIDI track while muting the previous note lane. Or, in the case of audio, a new audio track is created with the same settings as the previous audio track (and the previous audio track is muted). This allows you to record a new take without having to listen to what was previously recorded.

Quantize During Recording

Located just to the lower right of the main Transport controls is the Quantize During Recording function (labeled Q Rec). When activated, this button performs real-time quantization after the MIDI event has been recorded. The amount of applied quantization is determined by the note value and quantization strength selected in the Quantize Notes section of the Sequencer tools in the Tool Window.

Tempo and Time

Located below the Song Position readouts are the Tempo and Time Signature readouts, in which you can make adjustments to the song tempo and time signature.

▷ Tempo refers to the speed of the song played by the sequencer. Tempo is measured in beats per minute (BPM) and can be adjusted anywhere from 1 to 999.999. This gives you many possibilities when writing and recording songs within Reason. Note: You can adjust the tempo by using the + and – keys on your numeric keypad.
▷ Time signature specifies the beats per bar (such as 1, 2, 3, 4, and so on) and what counts as a beat (that is, 1/2 note, 1/4 note, 1/8 note, and so on).

TIP: Just to the left of the Tempo and Time Signature readouts is the Tap button. You use this button to set the tempo of your song by clicking in succession. This tool is handy if you want to determine the tempo of a favorite track of yours and write something similar in tempo. While listening to the song, use the Tap button and click along with the beat. Reason then sets the tempo of the song.

Locators: The Key to Looping

To the right of the main Transport controls are the locator points and looping controls. If you recall from Chapter 2, "Recording," you learned a little bit about Reason's locator points. Although there are many ways to describe them, the easiest way is to think of them as a pair of bookends. Just like on a shelf of books, locator points act as the virtual bookends of a sequence. You have a left locator, which is used as a starting position, and a right locator, which is used as an ending position. These locator points can be used together to create a loop for a specific number of measures. Here's how:

1. Set your left locator to measure 1 by using the arrow keys next to the numeric values or by double-clicking on the numeric value and typing the desired value.
2. Using the same method, set your right locator to measure 9.
3. Just above the locators in the Transport panel is the Loop button. Click on it to activate the loop feature. This can also be done by pressing the / (forward slash) key or the L key on your keyboard.
4. Click Play and watch as the position indicator moves to the right. As soon as it reaches the right locator point, it jumps back to the left locator point.

After a looping point is created, you can listen to a specific part of your song over and over to edit the MIDI or audio data.

> **NOTE:** The key to any electronic or dance music is the incorporation of loops and repetition. As you'll learn in future chapters, a few virtual sound modules in Reason help to easily create these loops for you.

> **TIP:** If you press the Alt button while the Loop function is turned on, Reason still creates a new note lane on your selected sequencer track, but it mutes only the note data between the left and right locators and not the entire note lane.

The Click Control and Blocks

To the left of the Tempo and Time Signature fields of the Transport panel is the Click control. When activated, this function provides a metronome sound that is accented on the first beat of every measure. Just clicking on the Click button turns it on; you adjust the volume of the click by using the Click Level knob below. Note that the click sound itself is quite loud, so exercise caution when adjusting the volume.

Additionally, there is a Pre button, which, by default, gives you one measure of clicks before recording. This is more commonly known as a *precount*. The number of precount bars can be adjusted in the Options menu. You can choose to have up to four precount bars.

Just to the left of the Click controls is the Blocks button. This button is simply used to turn the Blocks function on and off. Try clicking on it, and you'll notice that the Block button next to the Song button is hidden and the Blocks sequencer track is hidden.

The In/Out, DSP, and Calc Indicators

To the far left of the Transport panel are the In/Out, DSP, and Calc indicators. The In/Out (I/O) indicators represent Reason's audio input and output signals. Note that when the inputs or outputs are overloaded, Reason indicates this by displaying the word "Clip" in bright red just above either the input or output. It is important to keep an eye on the audio I/Os because you really don't want to clip in the digital domain. Trust me—it sounds terrible! Figure 4.22 shows a graphical example of digital clipping.

The DSP meter is a real-time indicator of how much of the computer's CPU is being used in a given Reason song. As you begin to accumulate more and more virtual synths, real-time effects, and equalizers in a song, this meter tells you how much more CPU you have left until your audio "drops out." The Calc indicator is used to display Reason's progress when stretching or transposing audio. We'll dig into this later in the chapter.

Creating and Managing Tracks

Now that you've covered the basics of the Transport panel, you're ready to move to the left side of Reason's Sequencer screen, called the Track List. This is the place where all the tracks in a song are created and maintained. If you are not new to the concept of sequencing and recording, this section should look similar to other programs you have used. If you are new to this whole game, you'll be happy to know that understanding this portion of the Sequencer screen is a snap.

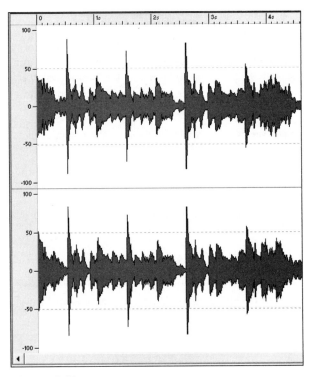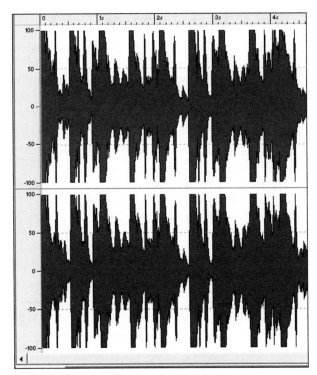

Figure 4.22
© Propellerhead Software AB.

Creating and Deleting Sequencer Tracks in Reason

There are a few ways to create a sequencer track in Reason:

▷ A sequencer track is automatically created whenever a Reason device is created. This includes audio and synth tracks.

▷ You can right-click (Windows) or Ctrl-click (Mac) on any Reason device without a sequencer track and select Create Track for [*name of device*]. A good example of this is reMix, which doesn't automatically get a sequencer track when an instance is created. Conversely, you can select any Reason device with a sequencer track, right-click on it, and select Delete Track.

After creating a sequencer track, you can name it anything you want by double-clicking on the name of the sequencer track and typing (up to 36 characters).

If you want to delete a sequencer track from Reason, you also have a few choices:

▷ Highlight the sequencer track and press the Delete or Backspace key on your keyboard. Note that this deletes the sequencer track and the Reason device to which it's routed. And in case you forget, a window pops up to remind you.

▷ Highlight the sequencer track and choose Cut Track and Device from the Edit menu or press Ctrl+X (Windows) or Command+X (Mac). Again, this removes both the sequencer track and the Reason device to which it's routed.

▷ Right-click on the Reason device and select Delete Track. This just removes the sequencer track and not the Reason device.

The Track Parameters

After you create a sequencer track, it's time to look at its parameters (see Figure 4.23).

▷ **Track name:** This is the where the name of the sequencer track is displayed.

▷ **Track icon:** This icon represents the Reason device to which the sequencer track is routed. This icon also displays incoming MIDI messages by making use of a green LED.

▷ **Mute/Solo:** Marked simply with an M and an S, the Mute and Solo buttons are used to mute or solo individual tracks from within the Track List. Also note the M and S buttons at the top of the Track List. These are the All Mute Off and All Solo Off buttons, which unmute/solo any sequencer tracks below that are muted or soloed.

▷ **Record Enable Parameter Automation:** This button is used to place the sequencer track in a Record Ready mode to record automation data. Note that it is automatically activated when a sequencer track is created.

▷ **Record Enable:** This button is used to put the sequencer track into Record Ready mode to record your performance. Note that like the previous parameter, it is also automatically activated when you create a sequencer track.

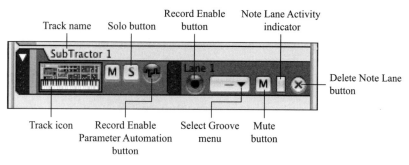

Figure 4.23
© Propellerhead Software AB.

▷ **Select Groove:** This menu is used to assign a sequencer track to a ReGroove channel. You'll learn more about this later in this chapter.
▷ **Note Lane Activity:** This LED represents data as it plays back a sequence. You don't see it in action while you record—just when a sequence is playing back.
▷ **Delete Note Lane:** This button is used to delete a lane of data from a sequencer track.

Moving Tracks

After you begin to accumulate a few tracks, you might want to organize the tracks by moving them up and down in the Track List. For example, you might prefer to have the Redrum and Dr. Octo Rex tracks at the top of the Track List, followed by the bass track, and then the chord and lead tracks. This is very easy to do. Here's how:

1. Click in the far-left section on the sequencer track that you want to move.
2. Click and drag with your mouse until you reach the desired position.
3. Release the mouse button. The track will drop into place.

> **TIP:** Looking at the top-left corner of every sequencer track, you can see an arrow pointing down, which means that the sequencer track is being displayed in its "expanded" mode. Click on this arrow to minimize, or collapse, the track. This is a great way to save space in your Track List, especially when you have 20 or 30 tracks of sequences playing back.

Sequencing a Live MIDI Performance

Now that you have taken your first detailed look at the Sequencer screen, it's time to press forward and record your first live sequencer track. In this section, you'll do the following:

▷ Create an instance of Redrum
▷ Record a drum pattern live
▷ Edit that pattern with quantization and dynamics

> **TIP:** Before you start this exercise, make sure your MIDI keyboard is turned on and connected to your computer. Additionally, make sure Reason has selected the keyboard as the Master Keyboard. You can do this by selecting it from the Control Surfaces tab of the Preferences dialog box. (Of course, if you don't have a MIDI controller handy, you can press F4 and play with your mouse or your computer keyboard!)

To record a drum pattern with Redrum:

1. Start a new Reason song.
2. Create an instance of Redrum by opening the Create menu, choosing Instruments, and selecting Redrum. A Redrum sequencer track is created and is armed to receive MIDI from your keyboard.
3. Take a second to turn off the Enable Pattern Section setting in the Redrum interface. This enables you to trigger and record live MIDI data from Redrum without using its pattern sequencer.

4. Because Redrum is already armed to receive MIDI data, you can press the C1 key on your MIDI keyboard. This key should trigger the kick drum sample. Also note that C#1 is typically the snare drum sample in any Redrum kit. The 10 channels on Redrum are mapped to keys C1 through A1 on your MIDI keyboard. Take a moment now to familiarize yourself with which key triggers which sound in your Redrum kit before you start recording.

5. In the Transport panel, make sure that the Loop section is activated. Set the right locator to bar 5. This provides you with four empty measures to record a four-bar loop. Also make sure that both the Click and Pre settings are turned on so that you have a full measure count in and a metronome to play against. Finally, make sure that you set the tempo to one you're comfortable playing. If this is your first time, I suggest 90 BPM.

6. Click the Stop button twice to send the position indicator back to measure 1. Now click on the Record button to start recording. The position indicator should begin moving to the right and start recording MIDI data.

7. When the sequencer starts recording data, play the kick drum sample on beats one and three until the position indicator reaches measure 5, at which time it will jump back to measure 1 and begin recording more MIDI data.

8. When the position indicator jumps back to measure 1 and begins recording again, play the snare sample on beats two and four until it reaches measure 5, at which point it will jump back to measure 1 again.

9. When the position indicator jumps back to measure 1 and begins recording again, play the hi-hat sample (typically found on the G#1 key) on beats one, two, three, and four until it reaches measure 5, at which point it will jump back to measure 1 again.

10. Click Stop in the Transport panel or press the spacebar on your computer keyboard to stop the recording. Notice that there is now MIDI data displayed in the Song view of the Sequencer screen (see Figure 4.24).

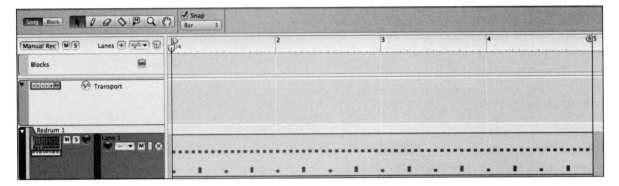

Figure 4.24
© Propellerhead Software AB.

Editing Your Performance

At this point, you have recorded the performance. If this was your first time recording a live MIDI performance using a sequencer, the timing might not have been as tight as you wanted. In this section, you learn how to fix any timing problems and move events around by using the Editing tools. Before you begin, switch to Edit mode by double-clicking on a MIDI clip. Because you are working with Redrum, the Redrum Lane Editor is displayed by default (see Figure 4.25). Use the Zoom tools to close in on the Redrum group that you are going to work on.

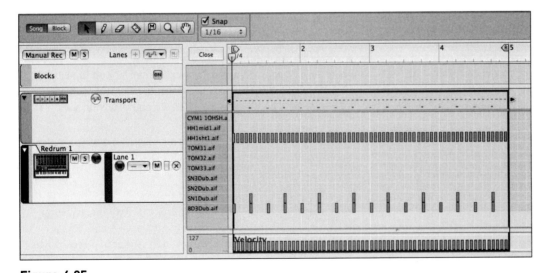

Figure 4.25
© Propellerhead Software AB.

Quantize: Timing Corrections

The first thing you are going to do is correct any timing problems by using the quantization function:

1. Look closely at the Redrum performance. You can see many timing inconsistencies because the events don't quite match up with the vertical lines (see Figure 4.26).

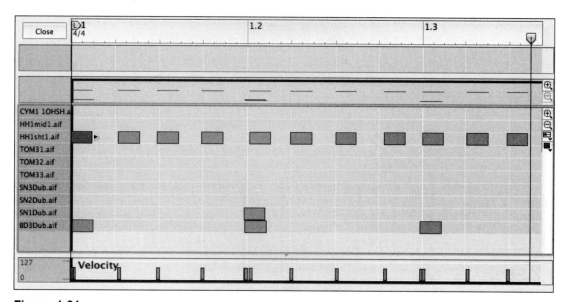

Figure 4.26
© Propellerhead Software AB.

2. Use the Pointer tool to click and drag a box around the Redrum events to select them all. You also can press Ctrl+A (Windows) or Command+A (Mac).
3. Select the note value used to quantize. Start by selecting the Quantize tool in the Tool Window. Next, select a 1/4-note value. This means that Reason will nudge each note to its nearest quarter note.
4. Just below the Quantize menu is the Amount menu. This option determines the amount of quantization that will occur when the process is performed. By default, it is set to 100%, which means that the events will be moved completely to the nearest quarter note. This setting is fine for this demonstration, but you can try different values to achieve a different effect. This feature can help to prevent your music from feeling too robotic or unnatural.
5. Click on the Apply button to quantize your performance. Alternatively, press Ctrl+K (Windows) or Command+K (Mac).
6. Look at the performance again. You can see the events have been nudged left and right toward their closest quarter note (see Figure 4.27). Click Play and listen to the corrected timing.

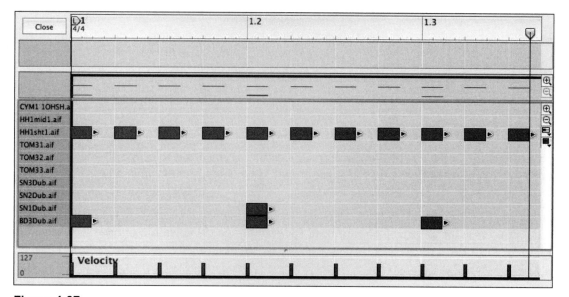

Figure 4.27
© Propellerhead Software AB.

TIP: You can also quantize while you are recording a performance. Just to the right of the main transport buttons is the Q Rec button, which, when activated, automatically quantizes your events while recording your performances. To dig into this function a little more, try activating it and recording a new Redrum pattern like the one you created at the beginning of this section.

Adding Velocity

Now that the timing has been corrected, you can add some dynamics to the performance by using the velocity edit lane, which appears below the drum edit lane (see Figure 4.28). This editor can increase or decrease the amount of velocity assigned to a recorded MIDI note. It is a great tool to use if you find that you didn't press the keys hard enough when recording your performance. In this exercise, you edit the velocity of your Redrum pattern with the Pencil tool:

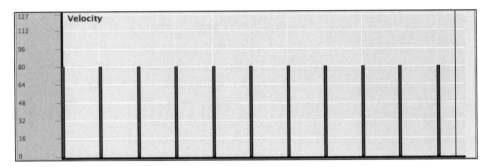

Figure 4.28
© Propellerhead Software AB.

1. With the velocity edit lane open, select the Pencil tool.
2. Click and drag downward on the velocity of the first MIDI event. Notice that as you drag down, decreasing the velocity, the color of the MIDI event changes from a dark red to a light pink (a darker color for higher velocities, a lighter color for lower velocities).
3. Use the Pencil tool on a couple of other MIDI events to alter their velocities. Try alternating between MIDI events to create a more interesting sequence (see Figure 4.29).

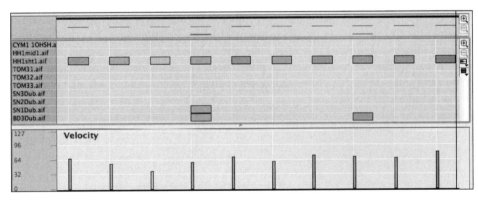

Figure 4.29
© Propellerhead Software AB.

Universal Edits: Edits made in the velocity edit lane are universal. That means a velocity edit you make to a MIDI event affects all the other MIDI events that occur at that same time location within a clip. The significance of this is illustrated in the following example.

Looking back at Figure 4.28, you can see all the MIDI events used to create the drum pattern. Notice how two separate MIDI events occur at the same time on each beat. For example, on the downbeat of bar 1, you see a kick drum MIDI event and a hi-hat MIDI event lined up vertically, which means that they trigger at the same time.

Now use the Pencil tool again to edit the velocity of the downbeat of bar 1. As you make a change to the velocity, notice that both of the MIDI events change in color. That means the velocities of the hi-hat and the kick drum are being altered simultaneously.

This situation can become a problem because each drum sample's velocity should be independent of the other. So how do you combat this problem? Well, there are a few things you can do:

► You can record on separate note lanes for each drum sound. For example, you can create one note lane dedicated to the kick drum and another for the snare, and so on.
► You can use the Velocity knobs on the Redrum interface to decrease each channel's sensitivity to different velocities.
► You can use the Explode option of the Extract Notes to Lanes tool.

However, there is another way to accomplish this goal: Simply select the note that you want to edit with the Selector tool, switch to the Pencil tool, hold down the Shift key, and set a new velocity for the single note.

In addition to the Pencil tool, the Line tool can also be used to edit the velocities of a performance. You access the Line tool by first selecting the Pencil tool and then holding down the Ctrl (Windows) or Option (Mac) key. Try the following:

1. Select the Line tool.
2. Click and drag horizontally across the velocities of a few events.
3. Release the mouse, and the velocities should change accordingly (see Figure 4.30).

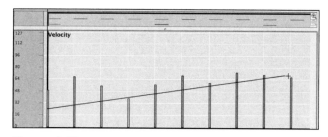 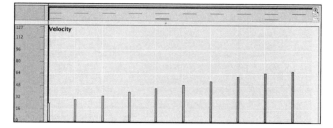

Figure 4.30
© Propellerhead Software AB.

4. Start at the beginning of the Redrum pattern, and then click and drag from left to right in an upward motion diagonally across the velocity edit lane until you reach the end of the pattern. Release the mouse, and you have now created a fantastic crescendo (see Figure 4.31).

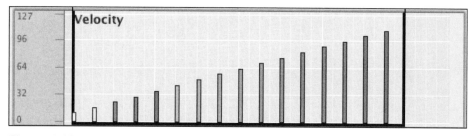

Figure 4.31
© Propellerhead Software AB.

Sequencing Written Data

The Reason Sequencer screen can also be used to draw in events and MIDI data quite easily. This section shows you the following:

▷ How to draw and erase events with the Key and REX Lane Editors
▷ How to draw in controller information

Drawing and Erasing Events

Drawing in events in the Sequencer screen is quite easy. Often, you might find it most efficient to write complicated performances that would otherwise be difficult to learn and execute perfectly in a live keyboard performance. It's also a handy way to write in performances when you do not have a MIDI keyboard available, which is the case for many traveling musicians. When inspiration hits, drawing in sequences is a real lifesaver.

Let's begin by drawing in a SubTractor sequence with the Key Lane Editor. Get yourself ready by starting a new Reason song and creating an instance of SubTractor. Also, make sure you set your right locator to bar 2. Then do the following:

1. Using the Pencil tool, click and drag a clip between bars 1 and 2.
2. Double-click on the clip to switch to Edit mode. The Key Lane Editor should open by default (see Figure 4.32).

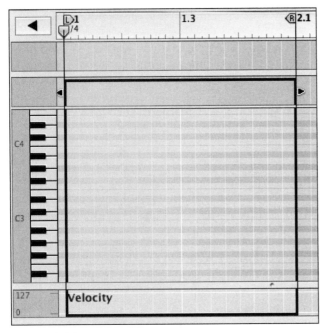

Figure 4.32
© Propellerhead Software AB.

3. Use the horizontal zoom tools (found at the lower-left corner of the Sequencer screen) to zoom in on the individual beats of bar 1.
4. You are going to write in an 1/8 note sequence, so select 1/8 from the Snap menu (see Figure 4.33). Also make sure that Snap to Grid is activated.

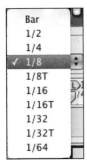

Figure 4.33
© Propellerhead Software AB.

5. Select the Pencil tool and draw in an 1/8-note sequence. For the sake of simplicity, you might want to try something as simple as a C major arpeggio (C-E-G), as shown in Figure 4.34.
6. Click Play. You'll hear the sequence play back in perfect time. At this point, you can try drawing in some different velocities for effect.
7. Press Ctrl+E (Windows) or Command+E (Mac) to switch to Song view.

> **TIP:** After writing your sequence, you can easily shift the events around by using the Selection tool. Try selecting the sequence and then clicking and dragging on individual events to change their event and time locations. When you're doing this, notice that you can move the events left and right only by 1/8-note increments. The reason is that the Snap value is set to 1/8. If you want to make finer adjustments, try changing the Snap value to 1/16 for 1/16 notes.

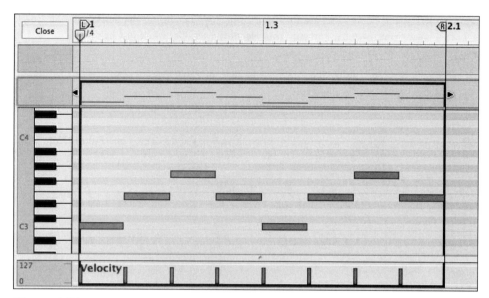

Figure 4.34
© Propellerhead Software AB.

Duplicating MIDI Events

After performing or drawing in MIDI events, you can very easily duplicate those MIDI events to create a repetition. While there are a few ways to do this you can use the mouse and a key command to duplicate the events and place them anywhere you want.

Let's look at the first method by using the current song, selecting the SubTractor track, and following along:

1. Use the Selector tool to click and select the SubTractor clip.
2. Open the Edit menu and choose Copy. Alternatively, press Ctrl+C (Windows) or Command+C (Mac).
3. Open the Edit menu and choose Paste. Alternatively, press Ctrl+V (Windows) or Command+V (Mac). This pastes the copied events immediately after the original selected events (see Figure 4.35).

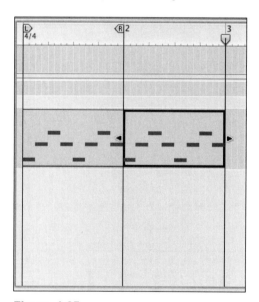

Figure 4.35
© Propellerhead Software AB.

Now let's look at the other way of doing this:

1. Use the Selector tool to select your clip.
2. Hold down the Ctrl (Windows) or Option (Mac) key as you click and drag the events to the right.
3. Release the mouse button. The events should now be duplicated and placed where you released the button.

For the next example, you'll use Dr. Octo Rex and the REX Lane Editor. Prepare for this example by clicking on the SubTractor in the Reason Rack screen and selecting Dr. Octo Rex Loop Player from the Create menu. This places the Dr. Octo Rex just below the SubTractor, with its default patch already loaded. Then do the following:

1. Expand the Dr. Octo Rex Programmer by clicking the triangle in the lower-left corner of Dr. Octo Rex.
2. Click on the Copy Loop to Track button to send the loop to its sequencer track.
3. Disable Loop Playback mode in the Dr. Octo Rex by clicking the Enable Loop Playback button in the upper right (the red light should turn off).
4. Double-click on the clip in the Dr. Octo Rex sequencer track to switch to Edit mode. You will see the REX Lane Editor. Notice that the velocity edit lane is also open.
5. Select the Eraser tool and erase a few REX slices by clicking on them.
6. Time to draw in a few events. Set your Snap value to 1/16 so that you can draw 1/16 notes.
7. Select your Pencil tool and draw in a few REX slices in the same area that you erased earlier (see Figure 4.36).

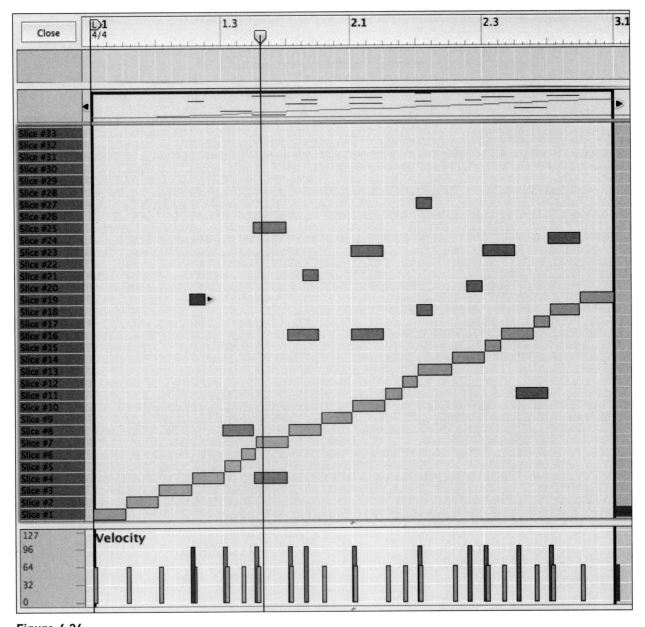

Figure 4.36
© Propellerhead Software AB.

8. Click Play. The REX loop should now sound rhythmically different.

Resizing Events

As you edit your MIDI data in either of the lanes, you might want to resize the events that you have either drawn in or performed live. This is very easy to do. Try the following:

1. Switch back to the SubTractor track.
2. Double-click on the clip to switch to Edit mode.
3. Use the Selector tool to draw a marquee around a few of the events to select them.
4. With the Selector tool still active, navigate to the end of the selected MIDI events. Notice that the Selector tool changes to an icon with two arrows pointing in opposite directions. This icon is used to resize the events.
5. Click and drag to the right. The MIDI events start growing in length (see Figure 4.37).

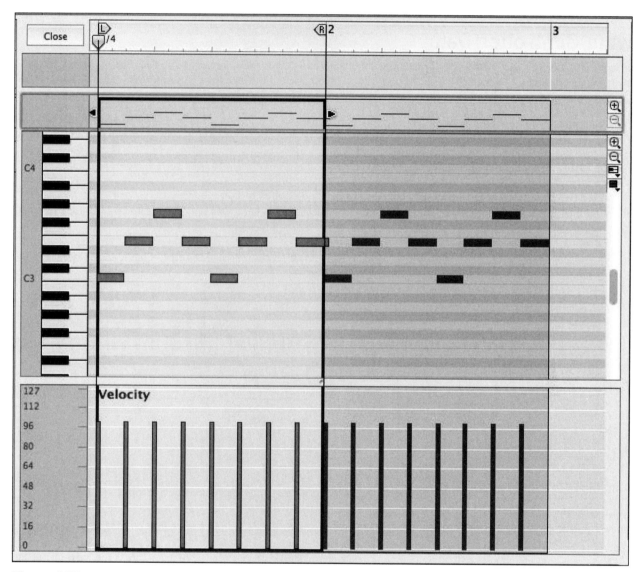

Figure 4.37
© Propellerhead Software AB.

6. Release the mouse. The events should now be resized (see Figure 4.38).

NOTE: Individual MIDI events as well as groups of events can be resized.

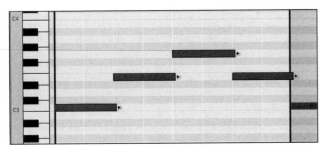

Figure 4.38
© Propellerhead Software AB.

Drawing Controller Data

Reason's Sequencer screen is also a great way to draw in data that controls the various parameters of each Reason device, which is done via the Note Lane Performance Parameter Editor. Although it's covered briefly in this chapter, you will find oodles of info on controller data and automation in Chapter 12.

This section continues to use the setup from the preceding section and shows you how to draw in controller data for the Dr. Octo Rex modulation wheel. Before beginning the exercise, locate the Filter Freq to Mod Wheel Amount knob (labeled F. Freq) on Dr. Octo Rex's programmer. Use your mouse to turn down this control to about nine o'clock. Now the modulation wheel will control the filter frequency in a useful way. Then follow these steps:

1. Select the Dr. Octo Rex sequencer track and double-click its clip to switch to Edit mode.
2. Click on the Note Lane Performance Parameter button and select Mod Wheel. This opens the editor you're going to work with (see Figure 4.39).

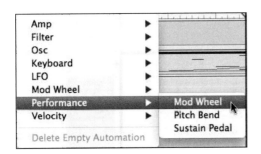
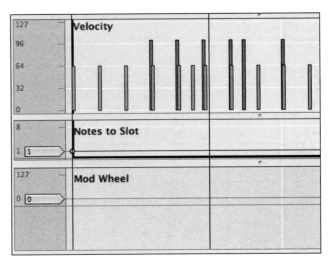

Figure 4.39
© Propellerhead Software AB.

3. At this point, you are almost ready to write in your controller data. Before you begin, select 1/64 from the Snap menu. This allows you to make very fine changes to the controller data.
4. Select your Pencil tool and begin to draw in some controller data for the modulation wheel (see Figure 4.40).

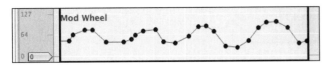

Figure 4.40
© Propellerhead Software AB.

The ReGroove Mixer

Even with all the sequencing tips and tricks you've learned throughout this chapter, you may end up finding that your sequences lack the feeling or vibe you're trying for. As a result, your first few songs in Reason might end up sounding a little stale and robotic. Never fear. Propellerhead has brought forth a great feature that will get your songs and sequences grooving in no time. I give you the ReGroove Mixer (see Figure 4.41).

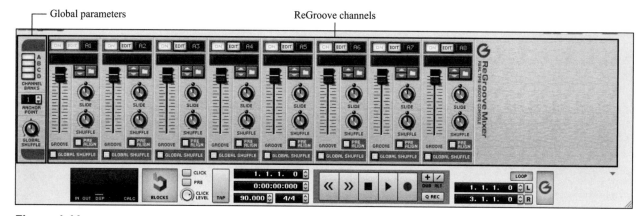

Figure 4.41
© Propellerhead Software AB.

The ReGroove Mixer functions in a fashion similar to an audio mixer, except in this case the ReGroove Mixer is mixing the "feeling" or grooves between 32 accessible channels. There are several templates and tools to help you achieve the kind of feeling that you want for your Reason songs, so stop dreaming and start driving. To begin, click on the ReGroove Mixer button in the Transport panel to launch it.

Let's examine the basic layout of the ReGroove Mixer. Looking back at Figure 4.41, you can see that the ReGroove Mixer is divided into two sections:

▷ **Global parameters:** These appear on the far-left side of the ReGroove interface.
▷ **ReGroove channels:** These sliders, knobs, and buttons occupy the rest of the interface.

The global parameters affect the entire ReGroove interface and include the following:

▷ **Channel Banks:** These buttons enable you to access the four available banks of eight ReGroove channels each, giving you a total of 32 possible grooves within a Reason song.
▷ **Anchor Point:** This tool enables you to set when ReGroove should begin to play back your programmed grooves. A good use for this tool is a song that has a one-bar pickup, with the song beginning at bar 2. In this case, you would want to set the Anchor Point to 2.
▷ **Global Shuffle:** This knob enables you to introduce a shuffle or swing feel to all the ReGroove channels. Additionally, it is used in combination with the Shuffle button found on the Matrix, RPG-8, and Redrum interfaces. Simply activate them and use the Global Shuffle knob to swing the patterns that are playing back from any of these Reason devices.

The ReGroove channels enable you to affect the individual channels of the ReGroove Mixer. They include the following options:

▷ **On:** This turns the ReGroove Channel on and off.
▷ **Edit:** This opens the Groove settings in the Tool Window. You'll revisit this feature later.
▷ **Channel number:** This displays the bank and channel number of the ReGroove channel.
▷ **Patch name:** This displays the name of the patch used in a ReGroove channel.
▷ **Groove Patch Browser:** These buttons are used to find grooves by making use of the Patch Browser.
▷ **Slide:** This knob is used to slide notes back and forth in ticks.
▷ **Shuffle:** This knob introduces a swing feeling, much like Global Shuffle, except this time it applies to an individual channel.
▷ **Pre Align:** This button activates the Pre Align feature, which applies a rigid quantization to any incoming notes before they are grooved. Note that this is a nondestructive function.
▷ **Groove Amount:** This slider determines how strongly the selected groove patch will be applied to the MIDI sequence. It works in combination with the Groove settings in the Tool Window.
▷ **Global Shuffle:** This button links a ReGroove channel to the Global Shuffle knob.

And finally, before getting into using ReGroove, let's go over the parameters of the Groove settings of the Tool Window (see Figure 4.42).

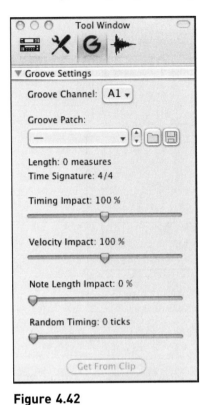

Figure 4.42
© Propellerhead Software AB.

▷ **Groove Channel:** This menu enables you to navigate between the different channels of the ReGroove Mixer.

▷ **Groove Patch:** This displays the name of the selected groove. To the right are the Browse and Save buttons, which are used to locate and import or save grooves to use in ReGroove.

▷ **Length/Time Signature:** These parameters are used to display the length and time signature of a loaded groove.

▷ **Timing Impact:** This slider determines how much the timing of a loaded groove will affect your sequences. The greater the value, the closer the sequence will be to the original timing of a loaded groove. Also note that this works in combination with the Groove Amount slider in the ReGroove Mixer, which serves as a means to scale back the timing impact as the sequence plays back.

▷ **Velocity Impact:** This slider determines how much the velocity of a loaded groove will affect your sequences.

▷ **Note Length Impact:** This slider determines how much the note length of a loaded groove will affect your sequences. Note that this works only with grooves that have note lengths embedded within, which does not include drum grooves.

▷ **Random Timing:** This slider randomizes the timing of your groove in tick measurements.

▷ **Get From Clip:** This neat feature extracts the groove from a selected MIDI clip and places its parameters into the Groove settings. Let's say you come up with a killer groove on your own and you'd like to use it in another song. You can use this button to extract the groove and then save it using the Save button.

Now that you're familiar with the parameters of ReGroove, let's dive in and see how it works.

Getting Started with ReGroove

Let's start off with something simple, like assigning sequencer tracks to the ReGroove Mixer. To really feel the impact of ReGroove, I suggest using a basic drum sequence. Assuming that you have this ready to go, let's begin.

First, you have to assign a sequencer track to a ReGroove channel, which is easily accomplished by navigating to the note lane of a sequencer track, clicking on the Select Groove menu, and selecting a ReGroove channel to assign to this track to (see Figure 4.43).

Pretty easy, huh? As you will find throughout the rest of this book, Propellerhead has really made a great effort to make this program easy and intuitive to understand and use.

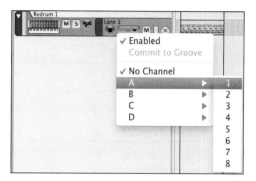

Figure 4.43
© Propellerhead Software AB.

CAUTION: Looking at Figure 4.43, you can see the Commit to Groove option. Selecting this option applies whatever adjustments you've made with the ReGroove Mixer to your sequence. I don't suggest using this option unless you're absolutely sure that this is what you want to do with your sequence.

Now that your sequencer track has been assigned to a ReGroove channel, you're ready to explore the limitless possibilities of ReGroove.

Applying Groove to Your Sequence

At first listen, you won't hear any difference in your sequence because you haven't made any adjustments to your ReGroove channel. So let's try a couple of quick parameter adjustments to demonstrate how this works. You might want to turn on the Click function to really feel the impact of the adjustments.

Adjust the Slide knob to the left or right to hear the difference in the sequence. Remember that this parameter has a range of +/−120 ticks, which is really not that much; however, the results will be heard. On the left side of Figure 4.44 is the sequence without any adjustments. The center image is the sequence with the Slide knob adjusted to −120, and the right side is the sequence with the Slide knob adjusted to +120.

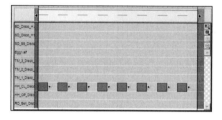 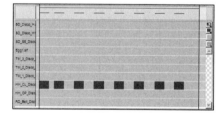 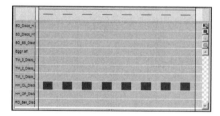

Figure 4.44
© Propellerhead Software AB.

Now let's look at the Shuffle knob. Try adjusting this to the left or right to hear the difference in the groove. This effect is much more pronounced; you'll certainly hear it as soon as you make some adjustments. The left side of Figure 4.45 displays the original sequence; the center displays the sequence with the Shuffle knob set to 35%, and the right side displays the sequence with the Shuffle knob at 70%. As you can see, there's quite a difference.

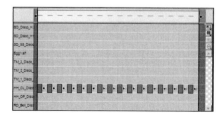 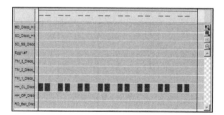 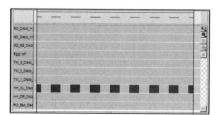

Figure 4.45
© Propellerhead Software AB.

> **NOTE:** If you activate the Global Shuffle button, the LED above the Shuffle knob on the ReGroove channel will turn off, indicating that it is no longer changing the swing of the sequence. However, the Slide knob will still work even with the Global Shuffle button active.

> **TIP:** At any time you can click the On button on any ReGroove channel to bypass the ReGroove effect to hear how your sequence sounds without it.

Working with ReGroove Patches

After you've done some experimenting with the parameters in the preceding section, I'm willing to bet you've come up with some pretty nasty little grooves with shuffle and slide galore. Well, strap yourself in because it's time to show you how to use the provided ReGroove patches. As with nearly all the Reason devices, you'll find that Propellerhead has included a feast of ReGroove patches that you can be sure will give your sequences something original. Before you begin, it would be a good time to set the Slide and Shuffle knobs to their default values and set the Groove Amount slider to 50%. You can also start playing your sequence back in a loop because you're going to preview these grooves in real time.

Navigate over to the Groove settings in the Tool Window and click on the Folder icon to launch the Patch Browser window. Then click on the Reason Factory Sound Bank icon in the upper-left corner and double-click on the ReGroove Patches folder. When you're done, you should see a window that looks like Figure 4.46.

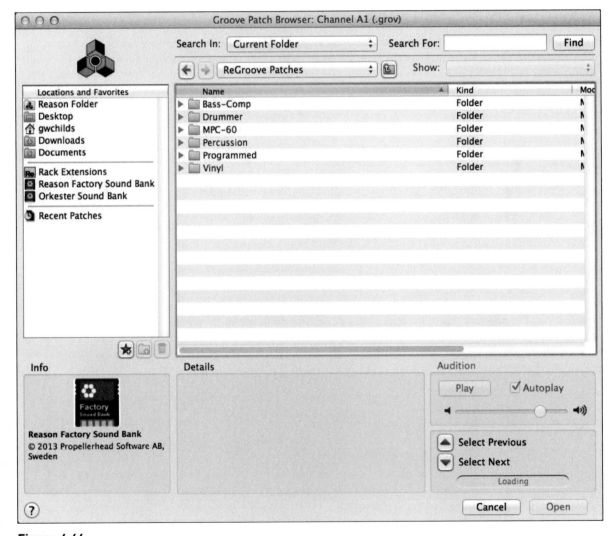

Figure 4.46
© Propellerhead Software AB.

As you can see, Reason supplies a healthy dose of groove patches to play with, including the following:

▷ **Bass-Comp/Drummer/Percussion:** These grooves were recorded live by studio musicians, analyzed, and then extracted into individual groove patches. Don't be confused, though; they don't contain audio, simply the timings and velocities of what they originally played.

▷ **Programmed:** These grooves were programmed by studio musicians to emulate well-known drum programming grooves for use in hip-hop or pop music.

▷ **MPC-60:** These grooves were extracted from an Akai MPC-60, which is probably the most important drum machine ever, because it had a timing and feel that have never really been duplicated.

▷ **Vinyl:** These grooves were captured from vinyl groove record samples. The samples were then analyzed and extracted into individual groove patches. You had better believe there's some funk to be had here.

Assuming your sequence is playing now, use the Patch Browser to preview patches by simply clicking on them one time. When you do, the sequence will play with the patch applied to it. Pretty cool, huh? So when you're thoroughly versed in what the patches feel like and you find one you like, go ahead and click OK. For this demonstration, my money's on the Bobby B patch, located in the Vinyl folder.

After the patch is imported, you can use the Groove Amount slider to adjust the amount of groove you'd like to hear while the sequence is playing back. A setting of 50% works fine for me, but you might find that you need that extra little kick, so use whatever's comfortable.

At this point, I'm going to show you what the sliders do in the Groove settings of the Tool Window, starting with the Timing Impact slider. Looking at Figure 4.47, on the left is my sequence without any groove, the center is the sequence with the Timing Impact set to 100%, and the right is the sequence with the Timing Impact slider set to 200%. As stated, you can use the Groove Amount slider to scale back this effect.

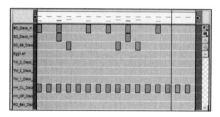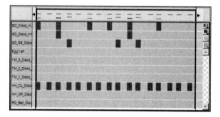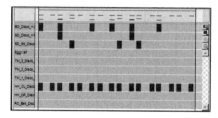

Figure 4.47
© Propellerhead Software AB.

I'm going to leave the Timing Impact slider at 100%, so you can see the Velocity Impact slider. Looking at Figure 4.48, you can see the sequence with 100% Timing Impact and 100% Velocity Impact on the left and 100% Timing Impact and 200% Velocity Impact on the right.

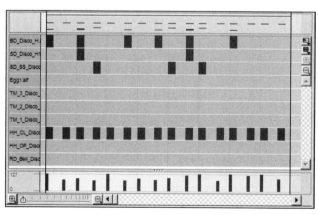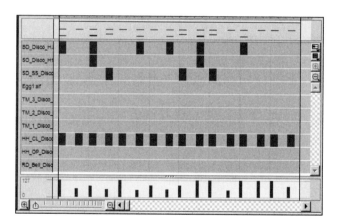

Figure 4.48
© Propellerhead Software AB.

Next up is the Note Length Impact slider, but because I'm not using a synth-based sequence, like a lead or bass line, this slider will have little or no impact on this drum sequence. So let's move down to the Random Timing slider and introduce some randomization to the timing of this groove. Looking at Figure 4.49, you can see the sequence with 100% Timing Impact and 100% Velocity Impact and no Random Timing on the left, whereas on the right, you can see the sequence with Random Timing set to 36 ticks. Because this has a range of only 120 ticks, it does not create a huge difference, but you can still see and hear the results.

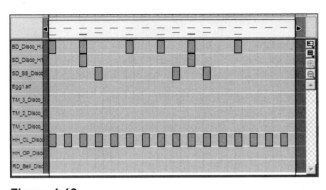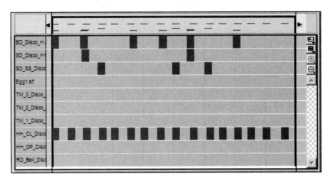

Figure 4.49
© Propellerhead Software AB.

Additional ReGroove Tips

Wow, there's a lot under the hood when you really start to look at the ReGroove Mixer in Reason. And believe it or not, there are some additional features that you should be aware of:

▷ **Initialize Channel:** Let's say you want to wipe the slate clean. Just right-click on any ReGroove channel and select Initialize Channel.

▷ **Copy/Paste:** These options are handy if you want to lock in the same groove between two instruments, such as drums and bass. Simply right-click on the ReGroove channel with the groove you want and select Copy Channel. Then go to the channel where you want to paste the groove to and select Paste Channel.

▷ **Commit to Groove:** As mentioned earlier in this chapter, this option is a destructive edit that applies your ReGroove settings to the selected sequencer track. This option can be found in the Select Groove menu on your sequencer track. Although this is a neat shortcut, remember that it actually alters the placement of the MIDI notes in the sequence, so be sure that you are happy with it.

Recording an Audio Performance

Now that you have taken a close look at the MIDI features of Reason 7, it's time to change direction a bit and look at the audio side of the Sequencer screen. This is a newer feature that's quite exciting because previously, Reason users had to use other digital audio workstation (DAW) applications to record their guitars, drums, and vocals. As of Reason 6, however, you can do all your recording in one application. This section of the chapter covers the following topics:

▷ Creating an audio track
▷ Recording a simple audio performance
▷ Editing the performance

Let's begin by creating an audio track in Reason. Start a new song and select Create Audio Track from the Create menu. When you're done, you should have a setup similar to that shown in Figure 4.50.

As you can see, an audio track looks quite a bit different from the tracks you've used throughout this chapter. Obviously, there are a few commonalities, such as the Mute/Solo buttons and the Record Enable buttons, but there are a few new buttons that you may not be very familiar with. Let's quickly review the layout.

The first button to take note of is the Monitoring button, which is the button with a speaker icon on it. When activated, this button enables you to listen to the incoming signal on your audio track. This button is active by default whenever an audio track is created and will automatically turn itself off whenever you're playing back your audio performance. If you want to alter the behaviors of the monitoring functions, you can do so within the Audio tab of the Preferences window.

The next button is Select Audio Input, which is located just to the left of the meter. This button enables you determine if your audio track will be a stereo or a mono track and which inputs on your audio interface will be used to record your performance. Looking at Figure 4.51, you can see that I have selected to record a mono track and I will be using Input 1 on my audio interface.

The final new button to take note of is the Tuner button. It is a real helper for guitarists and bassists because it provides a means to keep your instruments in tune before you begin to record your audio performance. Simply plug in your guitar or bass, activate the tuner, and play a string. Reason will detect the pitch and tell you whether or not you're in tune (see Figure 4.52).

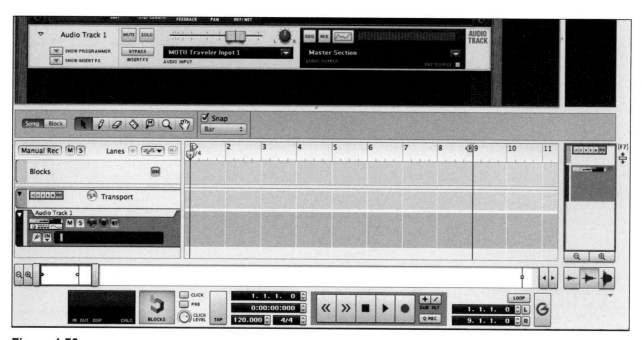

Figure 4.50
© Propellerhead Software AB.

Figure 4.51
© Propellerhead Software AB.

Figure 4.52
© Propellerhead Software AB.

You're now ready to record your first audio track in Reason. Assuming that you have a strong signal from your audio interface to Reason, do the following:

1. In the Transport panel, make sure that the Loop section is deactivated. Set the right locator to bar 9. This will provide you with eight empty measures to record a quick loop. Also make sure that both Click and Pre are turned on so that you will have a full measure count in and a metronome to play against. Finally, make sure that you set the tempo to one you're comfortable playing. If this is your first time, I suggest 90 BPM.

2. Click the Stop button twice to send the position indicator back to measure 1. Now click on the Record button to start recording. The position indicator should begin moving to the right and will start recording audio data.

3. When the sequencer starts recording data, either sing or play a very simple melody or chord progression until the position indicator reaches measure 9. Click Stop on the Transport panel or press the spacebar on your computer keyboard to stop the recording. Notice that there is now audio data displayed as a waveform on the Song view of the Sequencer screen (see Figure 4.53).

Editing Your Audio Performance

At this point, you have recorded your audio performance. Now it's time to push forward into the editing capabilities of Reason, which offers a variety of interesting options that are both easy to use and execute.

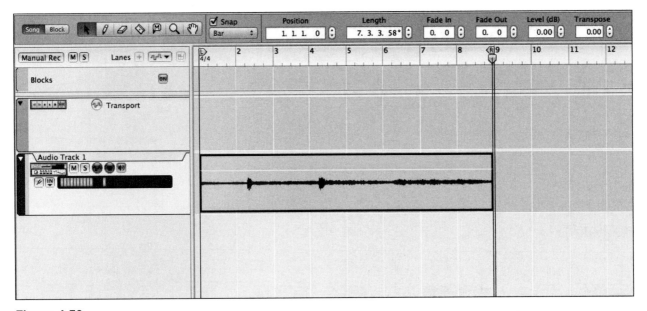

Figure 4.53
© Propellerhead Software AB.

Normalization and Reverse

The first edit you can make on your audio performance is a function known as *Normalization*. This is a very handy editing feature for boosting the volume of a recording that sounds a little too quiet for your song. Normalization is a function that examines the entire waveform and locates the loudest point within the performance as a point of reference. The volume of that point is then increased to 0 dB (full scale), and the rest of the waveform is adjusted accordingly.

To normalize your audio performance, do the following.

1. Select the audio clip by clicking on it.
2. Select Normalize Clips from the Edit menu.

In Figure 4.54, notice the original clip on the left, followed by the processed clip on the right.

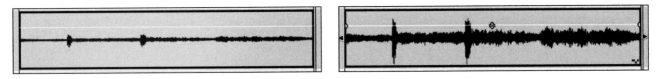

Figure 4.54
© Propellerhead Software AB.

> **CAUTION:** Although normalizing your audio has its advantages, just be aware that while normalizing increases the volume of your recorded performance, it also increases the volume of the noise within your performance. If you have a particularly noisy recording, you might want to skip normalizing it.

Reversing your audio performance is a surefire attention-getting element within a song. Does it contain a subliminal message? Does it tell you where John buried Paul? Does it contain a recipe for an awesome batch of cookies? Who knows? But some of the best-known rock recordings have a reverse audio element in them. A great example is "Are You Experienced" by Jimi Hendrix. The whole rhythmic element of that song is based on a reverse strum of the guitar. Back then, it was a rather complicated task to create this texture. In Reason, it's a snap.

To reverse your audio performance, do the following:

1. Select the audio clip by clicking on it.
2. Select Reverse Clips from the Edit menu.

In Figure 4.55, notice the original clip on the left, followed by the reversed clip on the right.

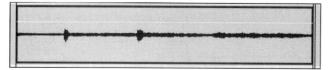

Figure 4.55

© Propellerhead Software AB.

Transpose, Level, and Fades

When you select an audio clip in the Reason Sequencer screen, you'll see some additional displays appear in the Inspector: Fade In, Fade Out, Level (dB), and Transpose (see Figure 4.56).

Figure 4.56

© Propellerhead Software AB.

The Fade In and Fade Out displays are very useful. They are used to create fade-ins and fade-outs with ease. Let's take a quick tour through these tools:

▷ **Fade In:** This display is used to create a fade for the beginning of an audio clip in your song. It allows you to make adjustments in increments of 1/16 notes and ticks. Simply use the spin controls or double-click in the setting to make your adjustments. Try making some adjustment, and you'll see that the audio clip updates its appearance in real time.

▷ **Fade Out:** This display does exactly the opposite, creating a fade-out for the end of any selected audio clip in your Reason song.

▷ **Level (dB):** This display enables you to adjust the overall volume of your selected audio clip.

▷ **Transpose:** This display enables you to alter the tuning of a selected audio clip in increments of semitones and cents. It has a range of +/−12 semitones. Try selecting a clip of audio, such as a vocal or guitar line, and use the Transpose display to raise and lower the pitch to hear the result. Just as a point of interest, you should also see the Calc indicator in the Transport Panel working to recalculate the audio clip as it's being transposed.

> **TIP:** Another way to make fade and level edits to your clips is to use the set of handles located at the start (fade in), middle (level), and end (fade out) of any selected clip of audio in your Reason song. Simply click and drag the handles to create your fade and level adjustments graphically.

Comp Editing

Aside from some of the editing features you might normally find on other DAWs, one of Reason 7's secret weapons is the ability to comp tracks. Say you've recorded a couple of takes of the same vocal or guitar part for your song. Listening to both takes, you find that although you don't like either of the entire takes, you like elements of both. A perfect solution to this dilemma is comping, which makes it possible for you to extract elements of different takes and combine them into a single complete audio performance. Comping is a fairly common practice in modern recordings because it allows the musician/producer to quickly create tracks and keep the creativity flowing.

Let's push forward and explore some basic comping to give you an idea of what can be accomplished. Figure 4.57 shows a simple audio track that we're going to comp. I have recorded two takes of the same guitar riff and switched to Edit mode in the Reason Sequencer screen. You can see that one take is grayed out, whereas the other is active. This is a perfect starting point.

1. Press Ctrl+E (Windows) or Command+E (Mac) to switch to Comp mode.
2. Click on the Single Take button (it looks like a speaker, with an arrow pointing away from it) to audition one of the comp layers.
3. You're now ready to make the first cut. Take it really easy here because this is your first comp edit. With Snap set to Bar, select the Razor tool, navigate to bar 2 of the grayed-out take, and click, hold, and drag from bar 2 to bar 3 to create two cut markers. When you're done, you should have an edit similar to the one in Figure 4.58.
4. At this point, you could create some more cut markers by clicking on either take with the Razor tool. If you switch to a finer Snap value, you can create cuts up to a 1/64 note resolution. Looking at Figure 4.59, you can see that I've made 1/8 note cuts to create a unique guitar part.

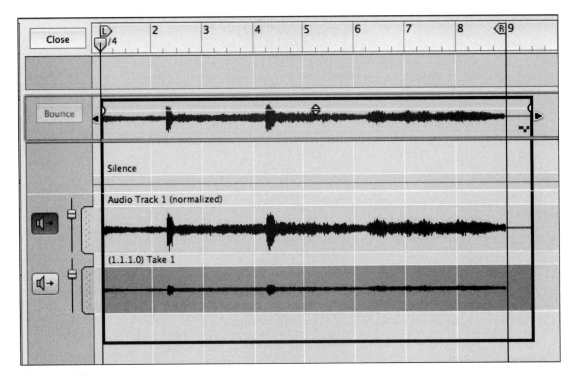

Figure 4.57
© Propellerhead Software AB.

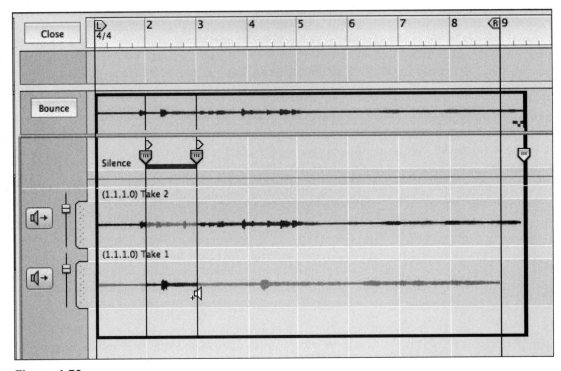

Figure 4.58
© Propellerhead Software AB.

Another possibility is to click and drag the cut markers even more to fine-tune the comped audio performance. Just make sure to switch to the Selector tool before you begin.

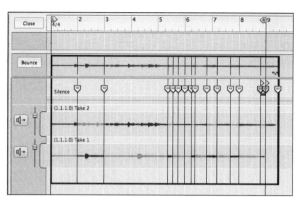

Figure 4.59
© Propellerhead Software AB.

> **TIP:** While creating a comped audio performance, you may find that you need to smooth out the transitions between different cut markers. This is easily done by creating a crossfade. To do this, simply click on any cut marker to select it; a handle appears just above the marker. Click and drag to the right, and Reason creates a crossfade between the different takes, similar to Figure 4.60.

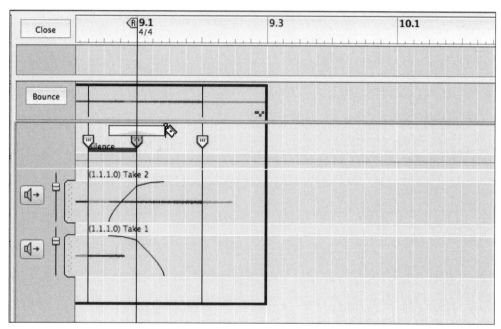

Figure 4.60
© Propellerhead Software AB.

Spectrum EQ

Of course, after a bit of audio editing, it's pretty fair to say that you're going to want to EQ your audio track a little as well. Although you could go to the Mix screen to start EQing your work, you could also use the EQ button, shown in Figure 4.61 to access the Spectrum EQ. Or, even better, press the F2 button. This visual EQ system controls the mixer EQ in a fun, versatile way, and also lets you see the spectrum image of the incoming signal in real time. Keep in mind that the Spectrum EQ is the exact same EQ on the actual Reason mixer. The Spectrum EQ window, however, gives you a much more intuitive way of tweaking the EQs on the mixer. And it provides a very powerful spectrum analyzer to boot!

One thing that is extremely cool about the Spectrum EQ is that once its window is activated and visible, it will continue to jump with you from track to track, displaying the spectral analysis of each track. An easy way to see this in action is to press F2 and then select a few different lanes in the Sequencer screen, as shown in Figure 4.62. By moving between tracks and viewing which track frequencies are strong or soft, you can see and hear which frequencies on one track are competing with frequencies on another track. An example would be removing some lower frequencies on a bass drum so that you can feel the lowest frequencies of a kick drum.

Figure 4.61
© Propellerhead Software AB.

Figure 4.62
© Propellerhead Software AB.

While displaying a track, you can use the Spectrum EQ to dial in the frequencies of your audio track by using either the dedicated low-pass filter (LPF) and high-pass filter (HPF), which are also available on the Reason mixing board. You may also enable the dedicated EQ, as shown in Figure 4.63 for your audio or instrument track. Go ahead and try enabling the HP filter now!

Figure 4.63
© Propellerhead Software AB.

The HPF cuts low frequencies so that only the high frequencies can pass through. A lot of the time, I'll start with the HPF when I begin EQing a vocal track, as lower vocal frequencies are often unwanted and tend to have frequencies that clash with bass and drums. If you drag the small orange circle toward the right, you will begin to see and hear, if your audio track is playing, how the HPF kills those low signals (see Figure 4.64).

When I'm working with male vocals or electric guitar, I'll often use the LPF to cut the high frequencies as well. Electric guitar harmonics, when higher frequencies are activated, can be extremely uncomfortable for a listener. And male vocals never tend to have too many high frequencies, anyway. Cutting these frequencies can end up killing additional, unwanted room noise that the vocal mic picked up, and even get rid of smacks and mouth noises. Enable the LPF now and try it on your own stuff. (See Figure 4.65.)

Of course, there may be some frequencies that seriously don't work. For example, maybe there's some sibilance you want to get rid of. Why not enable the EQ? With the EQ enabled, you get additional frequency bands that can be used to shelve, peak, or just about any other EQ possibility you can think of. Try this: Hold down the Alt (Windows) or Option (Mac) key while dragging the blue circle/band up or down. Notice how this changes the shape of the curve you're working with? It adjusts the EQ (see Figure 4.66). Using this method, you can boost very specific frequencies or cut them. It's up to you.

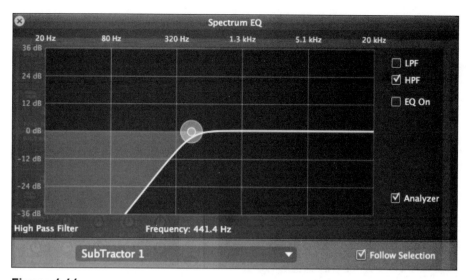

Figure 4.64
© Propellerhead Software AB.

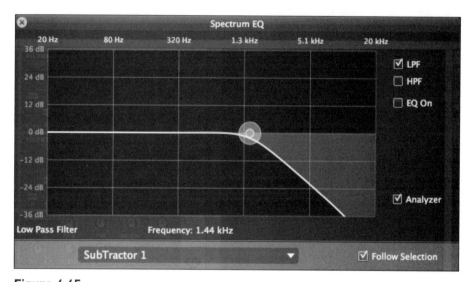

Figure 4.65
© Propellerhead Software AB.

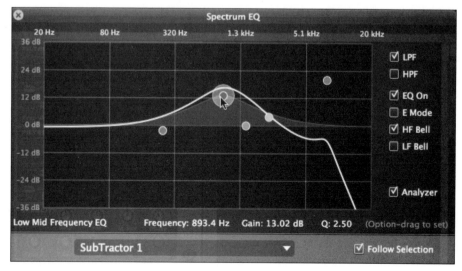

Figure 4.66
© Propellerhead Software AB.

Finally, the gray and red circles, by default, act as low and high shelves. But, when you place them in the high-frequency bell (HF Bell) or low-frequency bell (LF Bell) graph, you can use these bands to boost specific frequencies as well (see Figure 4.67).

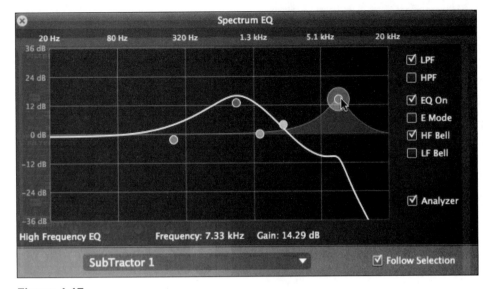

Figure 4.67
© Propellerhead Software AB.

Using Spectrum EQ really can make the production cycle much quicker and more efficient, and yield better-sounding results. It's much smoother than having to jump back and forth to the mixer, and it keeps you in the loop visually and aurally.

Moving On

Throughout this chapter, you have witnessed the ins and outs of the Reason Sequencer screen. I'm betting you'll agree that there is a lot under the hood of this baby. Be sure to read Chapter 12, which takes an in-depth look at automation and revisits the Sequencer screen.

5

Kong: Close-Up

W HEN IT COMES TO PROVIDING CREATIVE AVENUES FOR BEAT CREATION, Propellerhead Software has not been known to rest on its laurels. Way back when, with Reason 5, the company decided to push the creative envelope and introduce Kong (see Figure 5.1). *Kong* is an electronic musician's dream machine because it includes a desirable feature set of sampling, physical modeling, and effects, all wrapped up in an interface that looks and feels similar to the popular Akai MPC series of drum machines.

Figure 5.1
© Propellerhead Software AB.

When you first create an instance of Kong, the first parts of the interface you see are the Pad section and the dedicated drum control (see Figure 5.2). Additionally, you see the Patch Browser buttons, the pitch and modulation wheels, and the master level. As you will learn later in this chapter, this is just the first half of the interface. For now, let's concentrate on the basics and work our way out from there.

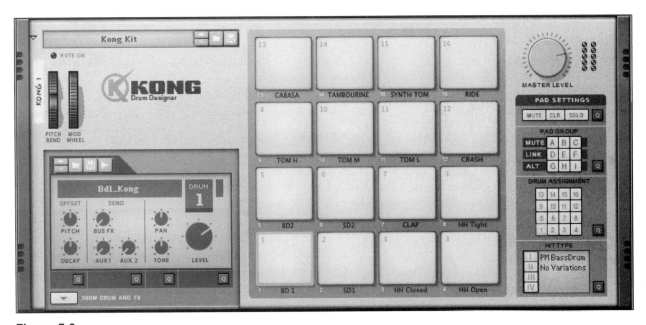

Figure 5.2
© Propellerhead Software AB.

Browsing and Loading Patches

When you first create an instance of Kong, a default drum kit is loaded. After a while, you'll certainly want to try different drum kits, so navigate to the upper-left corner of the interface, where you can browse the drum patches (see Figure 5.3).

Figure 5.3
© Propellerhead Software AB.

Click on the browser window or on the folder button located directly below it to open the Patch Browser window (see Figure 5.4).

When the Patch Browser window is open, you can locate and load any of the available Kong patches by opening the Kong Patches folder, found in the Reason Factory Sound Bank. When you do this, you can select between standard Kong kits and the same Kong kits mapped out specifically for keyboards. Try a simple kit now to familiarize yourself with the Kong interface. Open the Club Kits folder and select the Downtempo kit. Click on the OK button in the Patch Browser, and the kit loads itself into the Kong interface.

The Pad Section

In the Pad section of the Kong interface, you graphically trigger the individual sounds in a loaded Kong kit. Looking back at Figure 5.2, you can see that there are 16 individual pads arranged in groups of four. You can trigger these sounds by using any of the following methods:

▷ Clicking on them with your mouse
▷ Using a controller keyboard
▷ Using the onscreen piano keys (press F4 on your computer keyboard)

> **TIP:** The individual Kong pads are mapped in a similar fashion to Redrum, which starts at C1 and ends at D#2 on your keyboard.

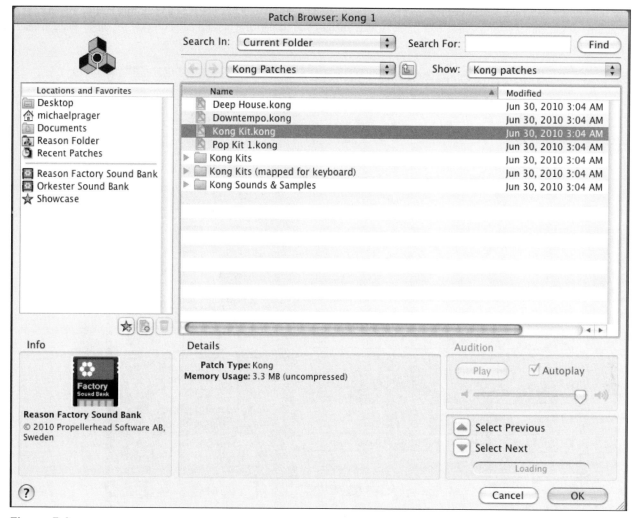

Figure 5.4
© Propellerhead Software AB.

All of Kong's pads are *velocity sensitive,* which means that they respond and sound differently depending on how hard or soft you trigger them from your keyboard. Additionally, you can use your mouse to achieve the same effect by clicking from the bottom (softest) to the top (hardest) on each pad.

To the right of the Pad section is the Pad Settings panel, which houses various parameters that allow you to assign the pads, edit them, and remap them (see Figure 5.5).

Figure 5.5
© Propellerhead Software AB.

Let's look at each of these, starting with the Mute, Clear, and Solo buttons:

▷ The Mute button mutes any selected Kong pad. When you click the Mute button, it and the selected Kong pad turn bright red.

▷ The Clear button deactivates all assigned solos and mutes to the Pad section. For example, if you had both of the kick drum pads muted, you could click the Clear button to unmute both with one click.

▷ The Solo button works in the opposite way of the Mute button, isolating the drum sample that you want to hear on its own. Select a pad, click the Solo button, and all the other pads turn bright red, whereas the selected pad shows as a bright green hue.

Just to the right of the Mute, Clear, and Solo buttons is the Pad Mute/Solo Quick Edit Mode button. If you click this button, the area of the Pad section you are editing launches into Quick Edit mode, which enables you to perform several edits quickly for all 16 pads instead of one pad at a time (see Figure 5.6).

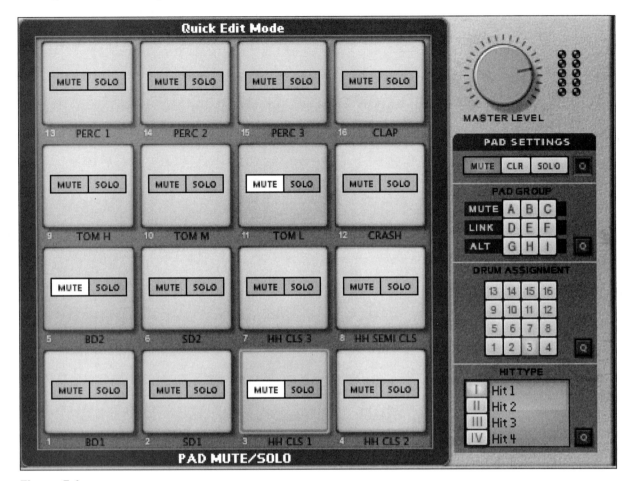

Figure 5.6
© Propellerhead Software AB.

Next down from the Mute, Clear, and Solo buttons are the pad groups (see Figure 5.7). You use these to assign different play parameters to your selected Kong pads. Using these buttons effectively can give a much more realistic effect to your drum samples, and they also allow you to be a lot more creative with your sequencing.

Figure 5.7
© Propellerhead Software AB.

You can use mute groups to have one pad mute the sound of another pad assigned to the same group. For example, say you have an open hi-hat sample on pad 7 and a closed hi-hat sample on pad 8. You can assign both of them to a mute group so that when you play the open hi-hat sample, you can use the closed hi-hat sample to mute it, which is exactly how it would sound on an acoustic drum kit.

Try the following exercise. Make sure you're still using the Downtempo Kong kit before you begin.

1. Select pad 12, which is a crash cymbal.
2. Click on mute group A to assign pad 12 to it.

3. Select pad 4, which is a closed hi-hat.
4. Click on mute group A to assign pad 4 to it.
5. Play pad 12 and then pad 4. You should hear the crash cymbal abruptly end.

Link groups enable you to combine or link several pads together so they are triggered simultaneously. To get a better idea of how this feature works, try the following exercise:

1. Select pad 13, which is a shaker type sound.
2. Click on link group D to assign pad 13 to it.
3. Select pad 6, which is a snare drum.
4. Click on link group D to assign pad 6 to it.
5. Play either pad 13 or pad 6, and you'll hear both of them played back at once.

Alt groups enable you to create a randomization effect between grouped pads. This is certainly one of the more creative groups that Kong offers. Try the following exercise to see how they work:

1. Select pad 1, which is a kick drum, and assign it to alt group G.
2. Select pad 5, which is another kick drum, and assign it to alt group G.
3. Select pad 9, which is a high tom, and assign it to alt group G.
4. Select pad 13, which is a shaker sound, and assign it to alt group G.
5. Play any of the four assigned pads, and Kong randomly plays any of the four sounds.

The Drum Assignment buttons enable you to assign the drum sounds of Kong to any of the 16 individual pads (see Figure 5.8). I'll get into this topic later in this chapter when I show you how to build your own drum kit with Kong.

Figure 5.8
© Propellerhead Software AB.

The Hit Type section enables you to assign one of four hit types to a single Kong pad (see Figure 5.9). This is another feature that probably won't make a whole lot of sense this early in the chapter, but it will shortly.

Figure 5.9
© Propellerhead Software AB.

The Drum Control Panel

Kong's Drum Control Panel enables you to assign specific sounds to each selected Kong pad, as well as mix the loaded sound with send effects, panning, tone, and volume (see Figure 5.10). Additionally, you can sample your own sounds into Kong from these controls, making for a very powerful drum-sampling machine.

Figure 5.10
© Propellerhead Software AB.

In this section, you can select new sounds for any selected pad, edit it, and save it using the available Browse and Save buttons. Although each Kong pad has its own series of controls, you cannot view them until you select one of the pads by clicking on it with your mouse. Click on the BD1 pad and look at the available parameters:

▷ **Select Previous Drum Patch/Select Next Drum Patch:** These buttons enable you to select new samples one by one from within a selected directory. For example, if you have selected the kick drum Kong pad, the Select Previous Drum Patch and Select Next Drum Patch buttons allow you to select a new kick drum patch. Also note that you can click on the naming parameter in the Drum Control Panel and select a new drum patch from a pop-up list.

▷ **Browse Drum Patch:** This button enables you to launch the Kong Drum File Browser, which makes it possible to search for, preview, and import new samples into your Kong kit.

▷ **Save:** This button enables you to save your sample.

▷ **Sample:** This button launches the sampling function so you can record your own sounds into a Kong kit.

▷ **Pitch:** This knob enables you to change the pitch of the selected Kong pad.

▷ **Decay:** This knob is used to change the decay of a selected Kong pad. This feature is especially useful if you have a cymbal sound with a very long decay or sustain.

▷ **Bus FX:** This knob is used to send a signal from a selected Kong pad to one of several provided bus effects. I will discuss this feature further later in this chapter.

▷ **Aux1/Aux2:** These knobs are used to send signals from a selected Kong pad to Kong's auxiliary outputs (labeled Aux Send Out on Kong's rear panel).

▷ **Pan:** This knob is used to set the placement of the selected Kong pad in the stereo field.

▷ **Tone:** This knob is used to alter the tone, or equalization, of the selected Kong pad.

▷ **Level:** This knob sets the level of the selected Kong pad.

Just below each of these controls is a series of Quick Edit buttons that allow you to see and edit various parameters for all 16 pads simultaneously instead of one pad at a time (see Figure 5.11). Clicking one of the buttons marked with a Q calls up the Quick Editor. The Quick Editor is an X-Y Cartesian plot that overlays on each pad, and the parameters change depending on the selected Quick Edit mode. Clicking a different Quick Edit Mode button changes the parameter options, and clicking the active Quick Edit Mode button again switches off the Quick Editor and returns the pads to their normal operation.

▷ **Drum Pitch/Decay Offset Quick Edit Mode:** This Quick Edit button makes changes to pitch and decay offset using an X-Y controller on each pad.

▷ **Drum Sends Quick Edit Mode:** This Quick Edit button makes changes to the Bus FX send and Aux Send knobs. However, unlike Quick Edit 1, this Quick Edit button makes its changes with individual adjustments for each knob instead of an X-Y controller.

▷ **Drum Pan/Level Quick Edit Mode:** This Quick Edit button makes changes to the pan and level using an X-Y controller on each pad.

▷ **Drum Tone/Level Quick Edit Mode:** This Quick Edit button makes changes to the tone and level using an X-Y controller on each pad.

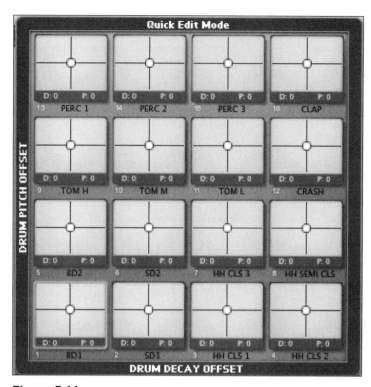

Figure 5.11
© Propellerhead Software AB.

The Drum Module and FX

There's a whole other layer to the complexity of Kong, which is the included Drum Module and FX section (see Figure 5.12). In this section, you select the type of synthesis that will generate your drum sounds and the real-time effects to enhance them further.

Figure 5.12
© Propellerhead Software AB.

Click on the Show Drum and FX button to display this section and let's start exploring.

The Drum Module

At the far left is the Drum Module, where the sound of Kong is generated. Kong provides three types of synthesis to produce sounds:

▷ **Samples:** Kong supports several digital audio formats, including WAV, AIFF, SoundFonts, and REX files.
▷ **Physical modeling:** This type of synthesis is used to generate sounds by mathematically simulating or emulating an acoustic kick drum, snare drum, and toms.
▷ **Analog modeling:** This type of synthesis is used to generate sounds by mathematically simulating or emulating classic analog kicks, snares, hi-hats, and toms.

Let's look at these and discuss each drum module in depth, starting with the NN-Nano.

The NN-Nano Drum Module

The NN-Nano is a drum sampler based off the NN-XT sampler (see Figure 5.13). This module is used to import or record samples and provides several creative editing options that can make your drums sound as realistic or synthetic as you would like. Note that when you're using the Downtempo kit, every pad uses the NN-Nano.

Figure 5.13
© Propellerhead Software AB.

Let's explore the various parameters of the NN-Nano, starting with the Sample Map display.

The Sample Map

Using the Sample Map display, you can select or edit samples and map their hit type to a selected Kong pad (see Figure 5.14). The NN-Nano supports multiple hit samples, which enables you to create either realistic or synthetic samples for your Kong kit because each sample is assigned to one of four different hit types. All the nuances and sonic characteristics of the sampled instrument can be accurately mapped in the NN-Nano.

Let's discuss the individual parameters:

▷ **Sample scroll controls:** These buttons are used to select new samples one by one from within a selected directory.
▷ **Browser:** This button is used to launch the Sample Browser, which makes it possible to search for, preview, and import new samples.
▷ **Sample:** This button launches the sampling function so you can record your own sounds.
▷ **Add Layer:** This button is used to add a layer to a selected sample hit. For example, you could have a kick drum on hit 1 and then use the Add Layer button to add a layer with a cowbell sample onto it.
▷ **Remove Layer:** This button removes any selected layer.
▷ **Edit Sample:** This control is used to launch the Sample Editor for any selected sample.
▷ **Hit:** This control is used to select one of four available hit types.

Figure 5.14
© Propellerhead Software AB.

▷ **Sample:** This control displays the name of the loaded sample. You can select a new sample by double-clicking here, and you can preview the loaded sample by Alt-clicking (Windows) or Option-clicking (Mac) on the sample.

▷ **Velocity (Graphical):** This control is used to display and edit the mapped velocity of a loaded sample in a graphical way. Simply click and drag from either the left or right corner of a selected sample to assign its low- or high-velocity value.

▷ **Level:** This displays the amplitude of a selected sample.

▷ **Velocity (Numeric):** This is used to display and edit the mapped velocity of a loaded sample in a numeric way. Simply click and drag up or down to assign its low- or high-velocity value.

▷ **Alt:** This control is used to alternate between different layers in the same hit. For example, if you have three snare samples loaded onto one hit, you can assign them to the Alt function to create the alternate effect. It helps to introduce some randomization to your loaded sample.

▷ **Pitch:** This control is used to assign a pitch to a selected sample.

▷ **Hit Name:** This control is used to assign a new name to a selected hit.

The Global Parameters

The NN-Nano also includes a wide assortment of synth parameters that you can assign to your selected sample (see Figure 5.15). These parameters are global, which simply means that they affect all the hits in a selected Kong pad equally.

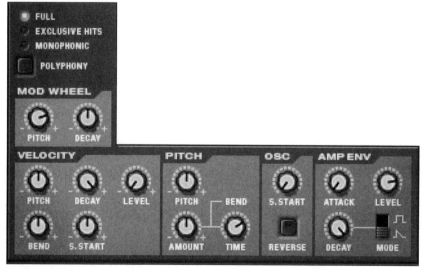

Figure 5.15
© Propellerhead Software AB.

The Polyphony controls determine how many voices can be heard simultaneously from a selected hit. NN-Nano offers three choices:

▷ **Full:** This is the full polyphony setting, which means that all hits can be heard with full polyphony.

▷ **Exclusive Hits:** When this control is selected, any played hit abruptly cuts off any other audible hits, while maintaining full polyphony in the currently played hit.

▷ **Monophonic:** When this control is selected, only one hit is heard at a time, with only one voice of polyphony.

The Mod Wheel parameters enable you to assign both pitch and decay to Kong's modulation wheel. They can offer some creative textures because the mod wheel is a lively sounding effect best served in a live environment.

The Velocity parameters allow you to edit the following parameters of your hits based on the amount of velocity used:

▷ **Pitch:** The velocity modifies the pitch for a sample hit.
▷ **Decay:** The velocity modifies the decay time for a sample hit.
▷ **Level:** The velocity modifies the level for a sample hit.
▷ **Bend:** The velocity modifies the pitch bend effect. This is similar to the Bend parameter featured in Redrum.
▷ **Sample Start:** The velocity modifies the starting time for the sample hit.

You can use the Pitch parameters to set the global pitch and create a pitch bend effect for your hits. For example, you could load a crash cymbal and have it pitch bend up or down over a specific amount of time. The parameters are as follows:

▷ **Pitch:** This knob sets the global pitch for your hits.
▷ **Amount:** This knob sets the amount of pitch bend. A positive value causes the pitch to bend down, whereas a negative value has the opposite effect.
▷ **Time:** This knob determines the amount of time given to the pitch bend effect.

The Oscillator (OSC) parameters enable you to determine the sample start time. Additionally, you can use NN-Nano to reverse the playback of your samples by clicking the Reverse button. Reversing playback creates a fantastic backward sound to your loaded samples.

The Amp Envelope (AMP ENV) parameters assign global envelope parameters to the amplitude of your hits. The parameters are as follows:

▷ **Attack:** This parameter sets the attack to your hits.
▷ **Level:** This knob sets the amplitude of your hits.
▷ **Decay:** This knob is used to determine the decay of your hits after they've been triggered. The Decay parameter includes two additional parameters, Gate and Trig. When Gate is selected, the Decay knob assigns the minimum decay to your hit, with the decay stage starting when the Kong pad is released. When Trig is selected, the decay stage begins as soon as you strike the pad, even if you continue holding the pad.

Nurse Rex

Now that you're done touring NN-Nano, let's change the drum module by selecting pad 1 and clicking the down-facing arrow located at the upper-left corner. A pop-up menu allows you to select from a list of nine drum modules (see Figure 5.16). Select the Nurse Rex Loop Player module, and you're ready to begin.

Figure 5.16
© Propellerhead Software AB.

Nurse Rex (see Figure 5.17) is a light version of the Dr. Octo Rex loop player device, which is covered in Chapter 6, "Dr. Octo Rex: Close-Up." This drum module loads REX files and enables you to assign the slices to any Kong pad.

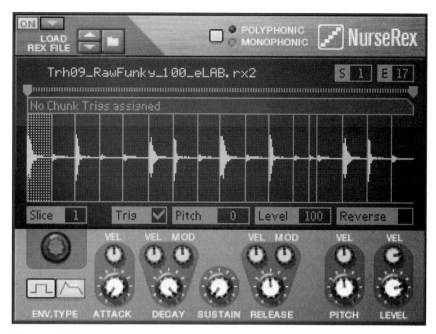

Figure 5.17
© Propellerhead Software AB.

Loading REX Files

After you create an instance of Nurse Rex, the first thing you should do is load a REX file. You do this by clicking on the Browse Loop button, located in the upper-left corner of the module. This launches the REX File Browser, where you can navigate, browse, and select your REX file. The best way to do this is as follows:

1. Click on the Reason Factory Sound Bank icon in the REX File Browser.
2. Double-click on the Dr Rex Drum Loops folder to display its contents.
3. You can browse through this entire folder, which contains subfolders with loops of various styles. For the sake of simplicity and time, select the file Acs01_StrghtAhead_130.rx2, located in the root Dr Rex Drum Loops folder.
4. Click OK, and the loop is loaded into Nurse Rex.

Now that you have loaded a REX file, play the associated Kong pad to hear the loop play back. By default, the REX file plays back in its entirety without stopping until it reaches the end of the file. This is known as Loop Trig mode, which is one of the four available hit types for Nurse Rex (see Figure 5.18).

Figure 5.18
© Propellerhead Software AB.

Loop Trig mode is governed by a pair of start and end points in the Waveform display. You can alter the range of these points by clicking or dragging up or down in the display or simply clicking and dragging the start and end points to the left or right on the ruler along the Waveform display. For example, you could set the start point to 3 and the end point to 3, which would cause Nurse Rex to simply play the third slice of the REX file when triggered.

Chunk Trig mode is a hit type that makes it possible to assign individual slices of a loaded REX file to multiple Kong pads. This is a really great feature because you can use a single drum module to feed several Kong pads at one time, which saves CPU and memory resources. Here's how to do it:

1. Select Chunk Trig as the hit type on pad 1.
2. Click the Quick Edit mode or Q button under the Drum Assignments section.
3. Set pad 2 to drum 1 by clicking on the 1. Then set its hit type to Chunk Trig.
4. Set pad 3 to drum 1 by clicking on the 1. Then set its hit type to Chunk Trig.
5. Set pad 4 to drum 1 by clicking on the 1. Then set its hit type to Chunk Trig.

After you've made your edits, your Kong setup with Nurse Rex should look like Figure 5.19. Play the pads now, and each pad will play a specific chunk of the REX file. At this point, you can set the size of the chunks by clicking and dragging between them to the left or right and come up with some wild combinations.

Figure 5.19
© Propellerhead Software AB.

Slice Trig mode is made to assign a single slice or multiple slices of a REX file to a single Kong pad. Select pad 1, select Slice Trig as the hit type, and then play the pad. You should now hear only a single slice playback, which is the first slice by default. If you want to select a different slice, you must deselect the first slice by clicking on the Trig parameter to deactivate it (see Figure 5.20).

Figure 5.20
© Propellerhead Software AB.

At this point, you can select another slice by clicking on it with your mouse and then selecting the Trig parameter to set it as the slice that the Kong pad will trigger (see Figure 5.21).

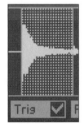

Figure 5.21
© Propellerhead Software AB.

In addition to triggering a single slice, you can also choose multiple slices. Select the Trig parameter, and the Kong pad will alternate between each of the slices (see Figure 5.22). Here's how to do it using pad 1:

1. Hold down Ctrl (Windows) or Command (Mac) key and use your mouse to select multiple slices.
2. Select the Trig parameter.
3. Play the Kong pad. Nurse Rex alternates between the various slices (see Figure 5.22).

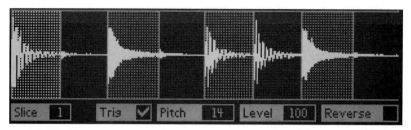

Figure 5.22
© Propellerhead Software AB.

Stop mode enables you to abruptly stop a REX file while playing back in either Loop Trig or Chunk Trig mode. If you want to do this, just assign one of the other available Kong pads to drum 1 and set its hit type to Stop. Now play the REX file with the first Kong pad and use the other assigned pad to stop it.

The Waveform Display Parameters

The Nurse Rex Waveform display offers a variety of parameters that can be assigned to each slice of a loaded REX file (see Figure 5.23):

Figure 5.23
© Propellerhead Software AB.

▷ **Slice:** This enables you to select any slice of a REX file by clicking and dragging up or down.
▷ **Trig:** This is used to assign a slice to be triggered when the Slice Trig hit type is selected.
▷ **Pitch:** This alters the pitch of a single REX slice.
▷ **Level:** This alters the amplitude of a single REX slice.
▷ **Reverse:** This assigns a reverse playback effect to a single REX slice.

The Panel Parameters

Nurse Rex offers a wide assortment of real-time parameters to twist up and turn your REX file around, which can produce some very eclectic and creative results (see Figure 5.24). Note that these parameters are global, meaning they affect the entire REX file.

Figure 5.24
© Propellerhead Software AB.

▷ **Envelope Type:** This toggles between Gate mode, which is set by the Decay parameters, and ADSR (Attack/Decay/Sustain/Release) mode.
▷ **Attack:** This is used to set the attack when ADSR mode is selected. The attack sensitivity can be modulated by using the included Velocity parameter.
▷ **Decay:** This is used to set the decay when the ADSR mode is selected. The decay sensitivity can be modulated by using the included Velocity parameter or the Mod parameter, which is linked to the modulation wheel.
▷ **Sustain:** This is used to set the sustain when the ADSR mode is selected.
▷ **Release:** This is used to set the release when the ADSR mode is selected. The release sensitivity can be modulated by using the included Velocity parameter or the Mod parameter, which is linked to the modulation wheel.
▷ **Pitch:** This is used to alter the pitch of the REX file and can be modulated by using the included Velocity parameter.
▷ **Level:** This is used to alter the level of the REX file and can be modulated by using the included Velocity parameter.

> **TIP:** You can assign each Kong pad to a different hit type when you're using Nurse Rex. For example, pad 1 can be set to a Loop Trig hit type, while pads 2 and 3 can be set to Slice Trig, and finally pad 4 can be set as a Stop. Don't be afraid to jump in and try different combinations of hit types with Nurse Rex. You may find just what your music needs to give it that creative edge you've been looking for.

Physical Bass, Snare, and Tom Tom Modules

The physical Bass, Snare, and Tom Tom modules are drum sounds based on the principles of physical modeling, which is a form of sound synthesis that mathematically emulates the inner workings of an instrument. In the case of these drum modules, physical modeling is used to emulate the characteristics of the acoustic kick, snare, and tom tom drums (see Figure 5.25). Before you begin this section, select pad 1 and then change the drum module to either the Bass, Snare, or Tom Tom module.

  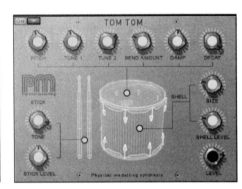

Figure 5.25
© Propellerhead Software AB.

Several parameters are shared between these modules, which you'll explore throughout the next couple of sections. For example, there is a Level parameter on each of the drum modules, and it performs the same task on each: adjusting the level of the audio signal sent from the module to the FX section, which you'll read about later in this chapter.

The Drum Head and Shell Parameters

Each of the drum modules shares similar parameters, such as the drum head and shell parameters, which affect the overall tone characteristics of the drums. These parameters include the following:

- ▷ **Pitch:** This knob sets the pitch for all the drum modules.
- ▷ **Tune 1 and Tune 2:** Available on the Bass and Tom Tom modules, these knobs alter the harmonics of the drum, which is similar to adjusting the screws on the sides of an acoustic drum.
- ▷ **Tune:** Available on the Snare module, this knob adjusts the tension of the snare head.
- ▷ **Bend:** Available on the Bass and Tom Tom modules, this knob creates the natural pitch bend of an acoustic drum when struck hard.
- ▷ **Damp:** This knob sets the damping for all the drum modules.
- ▷ **Decay:** This knob sets the decay for all the drum modules.
- ▷ **Shell Level:** Available on the Bass and Tom Tom modules, this knob enables you to introduce the sound of the shell into the mix.
- ▷ **Shell Size:** Available on the Tom Tom module, this parameter adjusts the length of the shell. Think of it like those drum kits you've seen with very long, deep toms.
- ▷ **Edge Tune:** Available on the Snare module, this parameter sets the tuning of the head. Note that this works only when hit type 4 is selected.
- ▷ **Snare Tension:** Available on the Snare module, this parameter adjusts the tension of the snare, which is located on the bottom of an actual snare drum.
- ▷ **Bottom Pitch:** Available on the Snare module, this parameter adjusts the bottom head of the snare drum.
- ▷ **Bottom Mix:** Available on the Snare module, this parameter adjusts the amount of the bottom head you'll hear in the mix.

The Beater and Stick Parameters

The Beater and Stick Parameters are used to emulate the beater sound of the kick drum and the stick sound of the snare and toms. These parameters have a very pronounced effect, and there are several variations.

▷ **Density:** Available on the Bass module, this parameter adjusts the "make" of the beater. For example, a rubber beater produces a much different sound than a traditional fabric-style beater.

▷ **Tone:** Available on the Bass and Tom Tom modules, this knob adjusts the tone.

▷ **Beater Level:** Available on the Bass module, this knob adjusts the level of the beater hit in the mix.

▷ **Stick Level:** Available on the Snare and Tom Tom modules, this knob adjusts the level of the stick hit in the mix.

The Synth Bass, Snare, Tom Tom, and Hi-Hat

The synth Bass, Snare, Tom Tom, and Hi-Hat modules are the complete opposite of their physical counterparts (see Figure 5.26). These modules are used to emulate the electronic characteristics of the analog drums of the 1980s, such as the Roland TR-808 and Simmons electronic drum kits.

Figure 5.26
© Propellerhead Software AB.

Drum Parameters

As with the physical modules, the synth drum modules share many common parameters, such as the Level parameter. Let's explore them further:

▷ **Pitch:** This parameter adjusts the pitch of the drum.

▷ **Tone:** Available on the Bass module, this parameter adjusts the tone of the drum.

▷ **Attack:** Available on the Bass module, this parameter adjusts the attack of the kick sound.

▷ **Decay:** This parameter adjusts the decay time of all the drum modules. In addition, the parameter also offsets the Noise Decay setting on the Bass, Snare, and Tom Tom modules, as well as the Harmonic Decay setting on the Snare module.

▷ **Harmonic Balance:** Available on the Snare module, this parameter adjusts the mix between the base tone and the harmonic tone.

▷ **Harmonic Frequency:** Available on the Snare module, this parameter adjusts the harmonic frequency.

▷ **Harmonic Decay:** Available on the Snare module, this parameter adjusts the decay of the harmonic tone.

▷ **Click Frequency:** Available on the Bass module, this parameter adjusts the click frequency.

▷ **Click Resonance:** Available on the Bass module, this parameter adjusts the resonance of the click sound.

▷ **Click Level:** Available on the Bass module, this parameter adjusts the click volume.

▷ **Bend Amount:** Available on the Bass and Tom Tom modules, this parameter sets the amount of pitch bend by assigning an upper pitch.

▷ **Bend Time:** Available on the Bass and Tom Tom modules, this parameter adjusts the time it takes from the pitch set by the Bend Amount setting to reach the original pitch.

▷ **Noise Tone:** Available on the Snare and Tom Tom modules, this parameter sets the tone of the noise element in the sound.

▷ **Noise Decay:** Available on the Snare and Tom Tom modules, this parameter sets the decay of the noise element in the sound.

▷ **Noise Mix:** Available on the Snare and Tom Tom modules, this parameter sets the level of the noise element in the sound.

The Synth Hi-Hat

The final drum module discussed here is the synth Hi-Hat module (see Figure 5.27). This module emulates the classic sounds and textures of the 808 and 909 hi-hats.

▷ **Pitch:** This knob sets the pitch of the hat sound.

▷ **Decay:** This knob sets the decay of the hat.

▷ **Level:** This knob adjusts the level of the hat.

▷ **Click:** This knob adjusts the level of the click in the hat sound.

▷ **Tone:** This knob adjusts the overall tone of the hat.

▷ **Ring:** This knob is used to introduce a resonance into the hat sound to create a metallic ring tone.

Figure 5.27
© Propellerhead Software AB.

Kong Routing and FX

In addition to all the groovy sounds and editing parameters, Kong also sports a complex yet versatile array of routing parameters to help make your drums sound their best. From here, you can specify how to route your drum module through the insert effects, bus effects, and master effects.

In Figure 5.28, you can see that, by default, the Kong drum modules are routed to two separate insert effects. Just as a reminder, an insert effect processes the entire dry signal that's fed to it. That processed signal is fed to the Master FX/Output. Additionally, Kong supports a single Bus FX slot that is fed a dry signal by using the Bus FX knob on the Drum Control panel. This gives you a very solid mix of drums and effects.

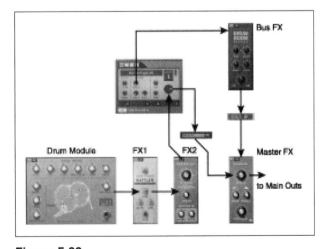

Figure 5.28
© Propellerhead Software AB.

Kong also offers bonus routing possibilities by making use of the Drum Output menu at the bottom of the FX1/2 Slots (see Figure 5.29).

The last point of interest here is that you can specify how much processed signal is sent from the Bus FX slot to the Master FX slot by using the Bus FX To Master FX knob at the bottom right of the Kong interface.

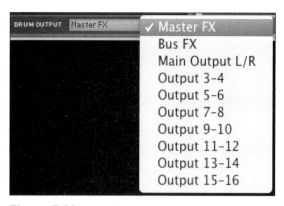

Figure 5.29
© Propellerhead Software AB.

Kong Effects

Now that you have a better understanding of the routing potential of Kong, let's look at the real-time effects that come with it. As stated, there are two insert slots and a bus slot. Additionally, there's a master effect slot, which is used as an insert to process the entire signal when routed to the master outputs.

The effects I want to discuss here are the generator effects, which include the Noise effect and the Tone effect. These effects enable you to enhance the Kong pads by introducing additional tones and textures to the samples and synth percussion sounds generated by Kong. They can be used as insert effects on both insert slots.

Noise Effect

Using the Noise effect, you can introduce a digital noise tone into your Kong pads (see Figure 5.30). This is a fantastic effect for adding more crispness to your hi-hat or snare sounds.

Figure 5.30
© Propellerhead Software AB.

The Noise effect has the following parameters:

▷ **Hit Type:** The Noise effect can be assigned to any or all hit types on a Kong pad. For example, if you were to load up a physical Snare module, you could use this parameter to assign a noise to any of the four hit types associated with that module.
▷ **Pitch:** This sets the pitch of the noise.
▷ **Attack:** This alters the attack time of the noise.
▷ **Decay:** This alters the decay of the noise.
▷ **Reso:** This assigns the resonance to the noise.

- ▷ **Sweep:** This assigns the start pitch of the noise sweep.
- ▷ **Click:** This sets the noise's click level.
- ▷ **Level:** This sets the level of the generator.

Tone Effect

The Tone effect generates a synth tone via an oscillator, which is then mixed with the sound generated by a Kong pad (see Figure 5.31).

Figure 5.31
© Propellerhead Software AB.

The Tone effect has the following parameters:

- ▷ **Hit Type:** The Tone effect can be assigned to any or all hit types on a Kong pad.
- ▷ **Pitch:** This sets the pitch of the tone.
- ▷ **Attack:** This alters the attack of the tone.
- ▷ **Decay:** This alters the decay of the tone.
- ▷ **Bend Decay:** This alters the decay of the pitch bend effect.
- ▷ **Bend:** This parameter assigns the pitch of the generated tone.
- ▷ **Shape:** This parameter alters the shape or tone of the generator.
- ▷ **Level:** This parameter sets the level of the generator.

The next effects covered are the FX modules, which are similar to the standard real-time themed effects you'll find all over the Reason interface.

Drum Room Reverb Effect

The Drum Room Reverb effect creates a reverberation, or echo, to any audio that's fed through it (see Figure 5.32). Think of it as the ambience effect that works great with just about any drum sound, especially snares and tom toms.

The Drum Room Reverb effect includes the following parameters:

- ▷ **Size:** This adjusts the size of the room.
- ▷ **Decay:** This adjusts the decay of the reverb effect, which is also known as the *tail*.
- ▷ **Damp:** This adjusts the dampening of the high frequencies in the reverb.
- ▷ **Width:** This adjusts the width of the reverb's stereo field.
- ▷ **Dry/Wet:** This adjusts the ratio between the dry unprocessed sound and wet processed sound.

Figure 5.32
© Propellerhead Software AB.

Transient Shaper Effect

The Transient Shaper effect bears a lot of similarities to a compressor effect (see Figure 5.33). However, unlike a traditional compressor, this effect just alters the loudness of the beginning section of the audio that it's processing, which is called the *transient*.

Figure 5.33
© Propellerhead Software AB.

The Transient Shaper effect includes the following parameters:

▷ **Attack:** This parameter alters the amplitude of the attack on the transient.
▷ **Decay:** This parameter alters the decay time of the effect.
▷ **Amount:** This parameter determines the level of the effect.

Compressor Effect

The Compressor effect is typically used to level out audio signals that are too loud in the mix and are in danger of digitally clipping (see Figure 5.34). You also can use this effect to make your drum sounds stand out in the mix by increasing the perceived loudness without actually increasing the amplitude of the sound.

Figure 5.34
© Propellerhead Software AB.

The Compressor effect has the following parameters:

▷ **Amount:** This sets the sensitivity of the compressor.
▷ **Attack:** This is used to alter the attack of the compression effect.
▷ **Release:** This sets the release of the compression effect.
▷ **Make Up Gain:** This compensates for any volume lost by the compression effect.

Filter Effect

The Filter effect enables you to create a tonal sweeping effect on your Kong pads (see Figure 5.35). It's a commonly heard yet effective sound in electronic music.

Figure 5.35
© Propellerhead Software AB.

The Filter effect has the following parameters:

▷ **Frequency:** This assigns the cutoff frequency.
▷ **Resonance:** This assigns the volume applied to the frequencies around the cutoff.

▷ **Filter Type:** This changes the filter type. You can choose between Low Pass (low frequencies pass through the filter), Band Pass (mid frequencies pass through the filter), or High Pass (high frequencies pass through the filter).

▷ **MIDI Trig Amount:** This determines the amount that a MIDI note will trigger the filter effect.

▷ **MIDI Trig Decay:** This sets the decay time of the MIDI controlled envelope.

Parametric EQ Effect

The Parametric EQ effect is used to alter the equalization, or tonal qualities, of the signal fed through it (see Figure 5.36).

Figure 5.36
© Propellerhead Software AB.

The Parametric EQ effect has the following parameters:

▷ **Frequency:** This assigns the center frequency to alter.

▷ **Gain:** This determines the gain of the center frequency.

▷ **Q:** This sets the bandwidth around the frequency. From here, you can create a nice, round EQ curve, or a curve for surgical boosting or cutting of frequencies.

Ring Modulator Effect

The Ring Modulator is a unique effect. It produces a pronounced and distinctive sound that makes the hairs on the back of your neck stand up. Basically, the Ring Modulator effect (see Figure 5.37) takes the input of your audio and multiplies it with another signal called a *sine wave*. This produces a very metallic tone that's perfect for special percussion effects.

The Ring Modulator effect has the following parameters:

▷ **Frequency:** This assigns the frequency of the sine wave.

▷ **Amount:** This assigns the amount of sine wave applied to the original signal.

▷ **MIDI Trig Amount:** This determines the amount that a MIDI note will trigger the Ring Modulator effect.

▷ **MIDI Trig Decay:** This sets the decay time of the MIDI-controlled envelope.

Rattler Effect

The Rattler effect (see Figure 5.38) is another unique effect in that it emulates the character of the snare strand assembly and applies it to other drum sounds. Imagine having a snare on your tom toms or kick drum. The Rattler effect will get the job done.

The Rattler effect includes the following parameters:

▷ **Snare Tension:** This assigns the tension of the snare.

▷ **Tone:** This alters the tone of the snare effect.

▷ **Decay:** This is used to set the decay of the ring of the snare.

Figure 5.37
© Propellerhead Software AB.

Figure 5.38
© Propellerhead Software AB.

▷ **Tune:** This tunes the snare.
▷ **Level:** This assigns the volume of the overall effect.

Tape Echo Effect

The Tape Echo effect emulates the characteristics of a classic type of delay that was generated via infinite loops of tape (see Figure 5.39). This created a very distinct sound, and that sound is now a part of Kong.

The Tape Echo effect includes the following parameters:

▷ **Time:** This sets the amount of time between echoes.
▷ **Feedback:** This assigns the number of echoes.
▷ **Wobble:** This emulates the wobbling of the tape speed. That means the frequency of each echo will be tonally unique.

Figure 5.39
© Propellerhead Software AB.

▷ **Frequency/Resonance:** These set the cutoff frequency and resonance of the tape echoes. Think of these knobs as a filter for the delay.

▷ **Dry/Wet:** This adjusts the ratio between the dry unprocessed sound and wet processed sound.

Overdrive/Resonator Effect

The Overdrive/Resonator effect is a dual effect of sorts (see Figure 5.40) because it includes an overdrive/digital distortion effect and a resonator. Put these effects together, and you've got a mean, growling snare or kick.

Figure 5.40
© Propellerhead Software AB.

The Overdrive/Resonator effect includes the following parameters:

▷ **Drive:** This assigns the amount of distortion.

▷ **Resonance:** This assigns the amount of resonance.

▷ **Size:** This determines the size of the resonance chamber.

▷ **Model:** This toggles between the different resonance bodies.

Kong Connections

Press the Tab key to swing the Rack screen around and you'll see all the Kong control voltage (CV) and audio connections available (see Figure 5.41).

Figure 5.41
© Propellerhead Software AB.

Audio Outputs

Kong includes three different kinds of audio outputs:

▷ **Main outputs:** Located to the far right of the interface are the main outputs. Kong supplies a pair of master outputs as well as an individual output for every Kong pad. That means you have a virtually endless supply of routing possibilities.

▷ **Aux outputs:** Located to the far left of the interface are a pair of stereo aux outputs. These are used to send the signal of any or all of Kong's pads to an external audio effect device. For example, you could route the snare pad of a Kong kit to an instance of the RV7000 by making use of the first or second pair of aux outputs. Once this is done, simply use the Aux 1 or Aux 2 knob in the Drum Control panel of any selected Kong pad.

▷ **External outputs:** This pair of outputs is used to send audio from Kong (including audio that's routed into Kong to an external Reason device) to an external effect. These outputs are used in combination with the external inputs to create an insert effect loop with other Creative or Studio effect devices.

Audio Inputs

In addition to a variety of audio outputs, Kong also supplies a couple pairs of audio inputs. Both pairs are located at the bottom left and center on the rear panel of the Kong interface:

▷ **Audio inputs:** These are the standard audio inputs for Kong. From here, you can route the outputs of other Reason devices and send them through the Bus FX and Master FX.

▷ **External inputs:** These inputs are used in combination with the external outputs to insert an external effects device into the Kong audio signal chain.

Here's a quick example showing how to use Kong's inputs and outputs. Looking at Figure 5.42, you can see that there is an instance of Kong, Dr. Octo Rex, and the Malström. You can also see the following connections:

▷ The left output of Dr. Octo Rex is connected to the left audio input of Kong, which routes to Kong's Bus FX and Master FX.

▷ The left external output of Kong is routed to the Shaper/Filter A input of the Malström. Activate these sections on the Malström interface, and you can achieve some sonically wild results.

▷ The right output of Dr. Octo Rex is routed to the Filter B input of Malström.

▷ The main outputs of Malström are routed to the external inputs on Kong, which routes to Kong's Master FX.

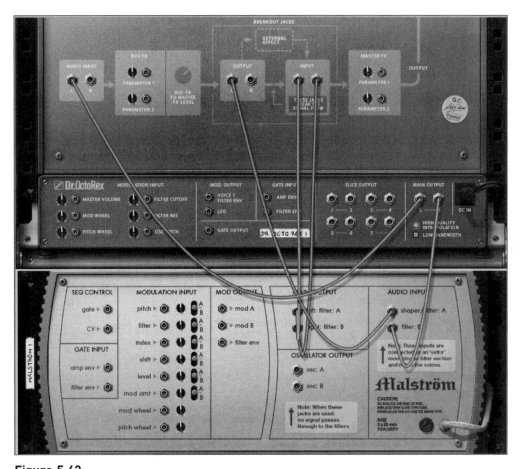

Figure 5.42
© Propellerhead Software AB.

CV Inputs/Outputs

Kong sports a wide variety of CV inputs and outputs, which are used to route control voltage information to and from Kong to any other Reason device. Let's begin with the gate inputs and outputs.

Gate Inputs/Outputs

The gate inputs and outputs are found on every Kong pad and are used to trigger other Reason devices with the outputs and/or have other Reason devices trigger the individual pads. Try this quick exercise to see how they work:

1. Create an instance of Redrum.
2. Write in a quick bass drum sequence.
3. Press the Tab key to view the back of the Reason Rack screen.
4. Connect the Gate Out of Redrum's channel 1 and route it to the Gate In on any Kong pad.
5. Play the Redrum sequencer, and you should now hear both Redrum and Kong play the same sequence.

Modulation Inputs

Kong includes a number of CV inputs that are used to modulate its various parameters by routing the modulation output of any Reason device to it. For example, you could route from the modulator outputs of Malström to Kong's Volume modulation input.

Here are the available Kong modulation inputs:

▷ **Volume:** Routing a CV connection to this input modulates Kong's volume.
▷ **Pitch:** Routing a CV connection to this input modulates Kong's pitch wheel.
▷ **Mod Wheel:** Routing a CV connection to this input modulates the modulation wheel.
▷ **Bus Effects:** These CV inputs are used to modulate two specific parameters of loaded effects in Kong's Bus FX slot, called Parameter 1 and Parameter 2. For example, if you have a Compressor effect loaded into the Bus FX slot, the Parameter 1 input is used to control the Attack parameter of the Compressor effect and Parameter 2 input is used to control the Release parameter.
▷ **Master Effects:** These effects operate just like the bus effects, except they are routed to the Master FX slot on the Kong interface.

Sequencer Control

The final set of CV inputs is the sequencer control inputs. These inputs are used to route sequencer information from another Reason device with a sequencer, such as Matrix and Thor, to Kong. That way, you can run both devices together with the same rhythm. Just remember that the CV input of the sequencer control is used to dictate which Kong pad will be triggered (which note), whereas the gate input of the sequencer control is used to trigger the note on/off and velocity of Kong.

Moving On

As you have seen throughout this chapter, Kong is an amazing drum machine capable of much sonic goodness, yet with an incredibly easy-to-understand interface. Be sure to really dig into this Reason device and create your own Kong kits.

Dr. Octo Rex: Close-Up

O NE OF THE MORE UNUSUAL DEVICES IN THE REASON RACK SCREEN IS THE DR. OCTO REX LOOP PLAYER (see Figure 6.1). Dr. Octo Rex is a RAM-based sample playback device based on the ReCycle! technology created by Propellerhead Software. Dr. Octo Rex can import specially prepared digital audio loops, called REX files, and play them back at just about any tempo.

Figure 6.1
© Propellerhead Software AB.

Dr. Octo Rex can import the following file formats:

▷ **REX.** A mono file format supported by the Mac platform
▷ **RCY.** A mono file format supported by the PC platform
▷ **RX2.** A stereo file format supported by both Mac and PC platforms
▷ **DREX.** A patch format that stores Dr. Octo Rex settings, including references to ReCycle! loops

> **TIP:** If you're a long-time Reason user, you might have noticed that Dr:rex is no longer listed as one of the Reason devices. That's because Dr. Octo Rex has replaced Dr:rex. Thankfully, you'll find throughout this chapter that all the Dr:rex features are found in Dr. Octo Rex. I'm sure that Dr:rex had a nice retirement party, though. And don't worry: If you have any songs created with previous versions of Reason that contain Dr:rex, they will open just fine in Reason 7, with Dr. Octo Rex substituted for Dr:rex.

A New Reason to ReCycle!

Propellerhead Software began to make its mark in the audio industry in 1994 by releasing a sample-editing software product called ReCycle! (see Figure 6.2). This program enabled musicians to edit digital audio loops on their computers and export them to hardware samplers in a format that would allow the tempo to be varied while not affecting the pitch. It was a real breakthrough because musicians could now use the same loops in different songs and styles and keep everything in the original pitch and matching tempo.

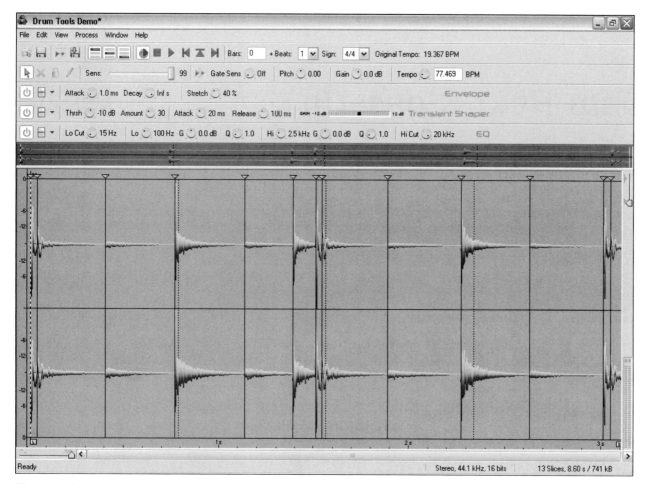

Figure 6.2
© Propellerhead Software AB.

The ReCycle! file export format is the REX file (short for ReCycle! Export). A REX file is a single audio file that contains a number of smaller separate audio files, or *slices*. The audio file is automatically sliced on the transients, or attacks, of the waveform. The REX file can then be imported into a digital audio/MIDI sequencing program, and the audio loop will instantly work at any tempo. Not only that, but if you were to change the tempo of your song, the REX files would instantly speed up or slow down to match that new tempo.

REX files became an adopted format for many digital audio programs, such as Cubase and Logic. Since the introduction of the REX format, many companies have begun releasing new REX format titles and also reissuing older audio loop titles. At the time of this writing, there are literally thousands of audio loops available in the REX format.

> **NOTE:** Yep, in this chapter, we'll also be covering how to create your own loop files…in Reason. ReCycle! is now a part of Reason, and that means lots of loop making for us all.

In 2000, when the release of Reason 1.0 was announced, it seemed only right that Propellerhead would incorporate its REX technology into this program because it's all about remixing and loops. With that, I give you the subject of this chapter, Dr. Octo Rex!

A Guided Tour of Dr. Octo Rex

Now that you have a basic idea of what Dr. Octo Rex is and the technology behind it, you can begin your tour of the Dr. Octo Rex interface. Create an instance of it and then expand the Programmer so you can view the entire interface.

Getting Sound into Dr. Octo Rex

By default, Dr. Octo Rex automatically loads eight loops into its interface across eight different triggers, or "slots," which are incredibly useful when you are trying to get to know this fantastic loop machine. If you'd like to hear the preloaded loop, click the Run button. Dr. Octo Rex will play and repeat the loop until you either click the Run button again or click the Stop button in the Transport panel. Additionally, you can preview any of the loaded loops by clicking on their corresponding slot numbers (1 through 8). However, you'll soon want to start trying new sounds and textures, so let's discuss how to load sounds into Dr. Octo Rex by loading a DREX patch file.

In the middle of the Dr. Octo Rex interface is its file browser (see Figure 6.3). Start by clicking on the folder icon. This brings up the Patch Browser so you can begin to audition and load sounds (see Figure 6.4).

Figure 6.3
© Propellerhead Software AB.

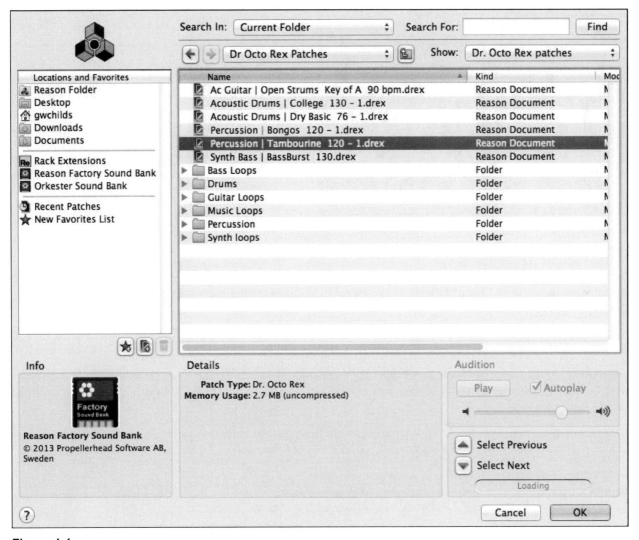

Figure 6.4
© Propellerhead Software AB.

When the Patch Browser opens, you might not see any sound files to audition. If this is the case, click on the Reason Factory Sound Bank (on the left, under Locations). Now you'll see four different folders:

▷ Dr. Octo Rex Patches
▷ Dr. Rex Drum Loops

▷ Dr. Rex Instrument Loops
▷ Dr. Rex Percussion Loops

For this example, double-click on the Dr. Octo Rex Patches folder. From any of these folders, you can select a DREX patch to import into your Dr. Octo Rex device. For example, you could open the Drums, Acoustic Drums, and Pop folders, and then select a DREX patch you want to import into a Dr. Octo Rex style drum loop.

> **NOTE:** The auditioning feature plays loops at the tempo at which your Reason song is set.

After selecting your patch, click the Patch Browser's OK button or just double-click the patch file to load it into Dr. Octo Rex. Notice also that the name of the REX file in the patch is now displayed in the Dr. Octo Rex Waveform display (see Figure 6.5).

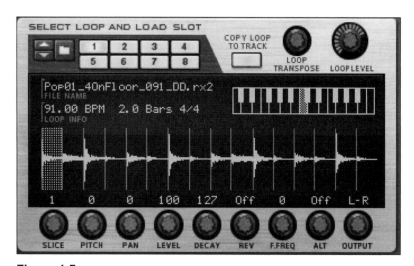

Figure 6.5
© Propellerhead Software AB.

After a patch file is imported into Dr. Octo Rex, the slices that make up the REX file are mapped out over the C1 octave of your keyboard. This enables you to preview each slice of a loaded REX file by arming the sequencer track and playing any keys in the C1 octave of your keyboard (C1, C#1, D1, D#1, E, and so on).

You can also preview the slices of any of the other REX files in the DREX file by clicking on its Notes to Slot button, which is the red LED located just to the left of each slot in the Dr. Octo Rex interface.

If you'd rather listen to the entire REX file play back, just click on the Run button, located at the top-right corner of the Dr. Octo Rex interface. This will play back the selected REX file indefinitely until you click the Run button again, click another Loop Slot button, or click Stop in the Reason Sequencer screen.

While the Loop Playback section of Dr. Octo Rex is playing, you can switch between different slots in real time. If you want to specify how quickly Dr. Octo Rex changes between different selected slots, you can select one of three options on the far-left side of the interface:

▷ **Bar.** The REX file will change slots at the end of the nearest completed bar.
▷ **Beat.** The REX file will change slots at the end of the nearest completed beat.
▷ **1/16.** The REX file will change slots at the end of the nearest completed 1/16 note.

Selecting Different REX Files in a Patch

As you'll come to find throughout this book, there's very little that Reason can't do when it comes to creative thinking and sound design. For example, let's say you load a DREX patch and you like the REX files loaded onto all the slots except for slot 8. It's easy to select another REX file by simply clicking on the name of the REX file in slot 8 and selecting Open Browser from the pop-up menu (see Figure 6.6).

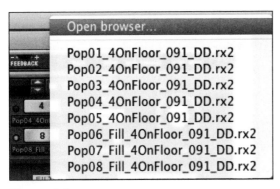

Figure 6.6
© Propellerhead Software AB.

At this point, the Patch Browser will open, and you can use it to locate, preview, and import a new REX file into slot 8.

Polyphony

Toward the bottom of the Dr. Octo Rex Programmer is the Polyphony parameter (see Figure 6.7), which determines the number of REX slices your MIDI keyboard can play simultaneously. Dr. Octo Rex contains a large polyphony potential that ranges from 1 to 99. You can change the polyphony by clicking on the increase/decrease controls to the right of the display or by clicking and dragging in the display itself.

Figure 6.7
© Propellerhead Software AB.

The Polyphony control assigns the number of voices that can be played simultaneously. Because each slice in a REX file is assigned to a key on your MIDI keyboard, you can resequence loops using the REX Lane Editor in the Reason sequencer. This will give you a chance to reinterpret the loop by introducing a new groove and feel that includes playing multiple slices simultaneously.

The Synth Parameters

The Dr. Octo Rex Programmer is the main section, where you can edit REX loops with ease. Here, you can accomplish everything from transposition to pitching and panning each slice in a loaded REX file. Just to review, a REX file contains a number of different slices of audio, which are compiled and seen as one file. The sliced nature of the REX files makes them ideal for editing.

The Waveform Display

In the Dr. Octo Rex Waveform display (see Figure 6.8), you can see the REX file split in a slice-by-slice view along with the original tempo of the loop. Above the waveform and to the right, Dr. Octo Rex displays the default pitch of the REX file. The default pitch for any REX file loaded into Dr. Octo Rex is C. Every aspect of the REX file can be edited, with the help of the parameter knobs above and below the Waveform display. Let's take a look at them.

Located just above the Waveform display are a few of Dr. Octo Rex's play parameters (see Figure 6.9).

▷ **Select Slice by MIDI.** This checkbox allows you to select each REX slice with a MIDI controller, such as a keyboard or drum machine. If you select this checkbox and click Play, you'll see the slice selector move across the loop from left to right in accordance with the MIDI note that is being played. Above this is the Note On indicator light, which lets you know when Dr. Octo Rex receives any kind of MIDI signal, whether from a controller or a keyboard.

▷ **Follow Loop Playback.** When this checkbox is selected, Dr. Octo Rex will display the currently triggered REX file in the Waveform display. This will change as a new REX file from a different slot is selected.

▷ **Copy Loop to Track.** This button sends the MIDI notes that are assigned to each slice of a selected REX file to Dr. Octo Rex's sequencer track. If you select the Dr. Octo Rex sequencer track and click on the Switch to Edit Mode button, you will see each of these MIDI notes displayed in the REX Lane Editor.

▷ **Loop Transpose.** This knob alters the pitch of the entire REX file. The range of this parameter is +/−12 semitones.

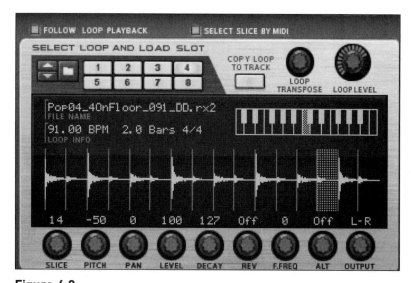

Figure 6.8
© Propellerhead Software AB.

Figure 6.9
© Propellerhead Software AB.

> **TIP:** After you click the Copy Loop to Track button to send the REX slices to the Reason sequencer, you might hear a strange flange or phaser sound as you play back your song. This is due to the fact that while the Reason sequencer is playing back your REX file from the sequencer track, it is also playing back the REX file from the Dr. Octo Rex interface. This happens because the Enable Loop Playback parameter is activated. This parameter is located just above the Run button. Deactivate this parameter, and your REX file should sound just fine.

Below the Waveform display, you'll find the following parameters to edit the REX file (see Figure 6.10).

Figure 6.10
© Propellerhead Software AB.

▷ **Slice.** This knob allows you to select each slice in the Waveform view by clicking and dragging the mouse up or down.
▷ **Pitch.** The Pitch knob transposes each slice in a REX file. Each slice can be adjusted up or down, giving you a possible pitch range of eight octaves. This effect is great for creating some interesting rhythmic ideas or mapping the pitches in a chromatic effect.
▷ **Pan.** The Pan knob adjusts the stereo position for any slice in the REX file. For example, you can set slice 1 to –64, or hard left while setting slice 3 to 63, or hard right. This setting can create a very cool stereophonic effect, especially when you combine it with the Pitch knob.
▷ **Level.** This knob changes the volume of an individual slice in a REX file. By default, each slice is set to 100, which is moderately loud. This allows for some interesting dynamic changes that can affect the overall feel of the REX file when used creatively.
▷ **Decay.** The Decay knob adjusts the length of each slice in a REX file. By default, each slice is set to 127, which is the maximum length. When adjusted, each slice can be shortened to create a gate effect of sorts.

▷ **Reverse.** Using this knob, labeled "Rev," creates a reverse effect on an individual slice in a REX file. This is really cool for drum samples in particular.

▷ **Filter Frequency.** This knob, labeled "F.Freq," is used to offset the cutoff frequency of the Filter section the selected slice. The Filter section is covered later in this chapter.

▷ **Alt.** This knob is used to create a natural feel for your loaded REX files. You accomplish this by assigning individual slices of a REX file to one of four groups. These groups then randomize each time the REX loop plays. For example, say you have a REX file with four different snare slices. You can use the Alt knob to assign all the snare slices to Alt Group 1. Each time the loop plays (using the Loop Playback function), the snare slices will be shuffled with each other, making the loop sound just a bit different each time it plays. Slices assigned to Alt groups will also be randomized when using the Copy Loop to Track function.

▷ **Output.** This knob allows you to assign the individual slices of a REX file to one of five pairs of outputs on the back of the Dr. Octo Rex interface.

TIP: One of my favorite features in Dr. Octo Rex is Slice Edit mode, which you access from the Dr. Octo Rex Programmer (see Figure 6.11, button shown in the lower-right corner). When it is selected, you can edit the slices of a loaded REX file by using the Pencil tool directly on the Waveform display. Select any of the slice editing parameters by clicking on its name in the Waveform display, and you can edit the individual slices. This powerful feature makes it possible to simply draw in your edits rather than use the knobs of the individual slice parameters, which can be a little cumbersome at times.

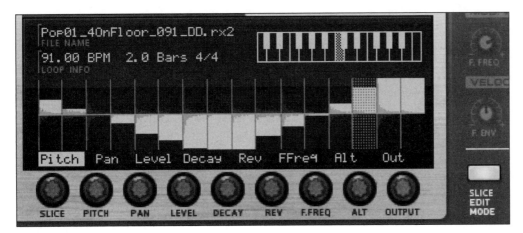

Figure 6.11
© Propellerhead Software AB.

The Oscillator Pitch Section

The Oscillator Pitch section can adjust the overall pitch of the REX loop statically with knobs to adjust the octave and fine tuning. You can even assign the Dr. Octo Rex Filter Envelope to dynamically affect the pitch of your REX loop (see Figure 6.12).

Figure 6.12
© Propellerhead Software AB.

▷ **Env. A.** The Envelope Amount (Env. A.) knob is used to assign a determined amount of the Dr. Octo Rex Filter Envelope to modulate the pitch of the REX loop. This creates a dynamic pitch-shifting effect based on the amount of Filter Envelope applied to the oscillator.

▷ **Oct.** The Oct knob enables you to transpose the entire REX file up or down an octave at a time and has an eight-octave range.

▷ **Fine.** The Fine knob adjusts the overall pitch of the REX file in cents, which are hundredths of a semitone. With a range of +/−50 cents, this is for making extremely minor adjustments to the overall pitch.

> **TIP:** In the lower-right section of the main panel of the Dr. Octo Rex interface is the Global Transpose parameter. It affects the overall pitch of all the REX files loaded in an instance of Dr. Octo Rex. It has a range of +/−1 full octave.

The Filter Section

To the right of the Waveform display lies Dr. Octo Rex's Filter section (see Figure 6.13). By shaping the overall tone of the REX file, you can generate incredible filter sweeps that hurt the ears and shatter speakers. The filter can then be modified with an envelope and finally be assigned to the modulation wheel for dynamic control. Now let's look at the filter.

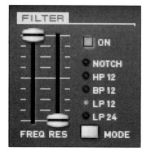

Figure 6.13
© Propellerhead Software AB.

Whenever Dr. Octo Rex is loaded into the Reason Rack screen, the filter is already activated. It can be turned off and on by simply clicking on the Filter button located at the top of the Filter section. Once the filter is activated, you can select one of five filter modes by clicking on the individual names or by clicking on the Mode button:

- ▷ **Notch.** This filter can be thought of as the opposite of a band pass filter. It rejects the mid frequencies while allowing the high frequencies and low frequencies to pass through. Although not the most dramatic filter effect, it still has a place in the mix for making minor changes to a sample.
- ▷ **HP 12.** This mode filters out the low frequencies while letting the high frequencies pass through. It has a roll-off curve of 12 dB per octave.
- ▷ **BP 12.** This mode filters out both the high and low frequencies, leaving the mid frequencies alone to be toyed with. With a roll-off curve of 12 dB per octave, the BP 12 can be used effectively on instrument loops, such as a guitar loop or possibly hi-hat-heavy percussion loops.
- ▷ **LP 12.** This filter allows low frequencies to pass through, whereas high frequencies are filtered out. It is similar to the 24 dB low pass (introduced next), but the roll-off curve is not as strong because it has a range of only 12 dB per octave. This makes the LP 12 a perfect solution for creating a filter sweep that is low but not low enough to blow up your speakers.
- ▷ **LP 24.** Like the LP 12, this filter allows low frequencies to pass through while filtering out high frequencies. To top it off, this low-pass filter has an intense roll-off curve (approximately 24 dB per octave), which produces a greater emphasis on the low frequencies.

A filter typically has two controls:

- ▷ **Cutoff frequency.** The cutoff frequency (or *filter frequency* or *cutoff filter*, as it is also called) specifies where the filter will function in the frequency spectrum. It is a popular parameter used to create the "sweeping" effect that you hear so often in electronic music. When the frequency is used to alter a filter, it opens and closes the filter in a specific frequency range. For example, if the cutoff frequency is set to the highest position possible and is in LP 12 mode, the entire frequency spectrum will pass through. Likewise, if the cutoff is set to a lower position and the cutoff frequency is set in the LP 12 mode—say, between the middle and bottom—the resulting sound will contain a majority of low-end signal because only the lower end of the frequency spectrum can pass through.
- ▷ **Resonance.** Resonance, on the other hand, is a parameter that modifies the filter's sound. It is used to emphasize the frequencies around the Filter Frequency slider. When used in different positions, the Resonance slider can filter out different frequencies or create fantastic bell tones. For example, in High Pass mode, if the cutoff slider is set to the maximum potential and the resonance is set to the minimum potential, the resulting sound will be extremely treble heavy with minimal bass. However, if the Resonance slider is in the middle position, the very high frequencies around the cutoff frequency will be boosted even more. If the resonance is set to its highest potential while the Filter Frequency slider is set to its lowest potential and the filter is in LP 12 mode, the

resulting signal will be extremely bass heavy (or inaudible, depending on your monitoring setup). As the cutoff filter moves up, the bass frequencies will be dynamically enhanced by the resonance, and the resulting sound will have the neighbors pounding at your door immediately afterward.

TIP: As stated, make sure to keep an eye on the Audio Out Clip indicator, which is at the bottom left of the Transport panel, especially when you start fiddling with the filters found on just about every synth and sound module in Reason. You not only can distort your signal, but also run the risk of damaging your speakers and, more importantly, your ears.

To the right of the Filter modes is the Filter Envelope (see Figure 6.14). An envelope is used to modify specific synth parameters, including pitch, volume, and filter frequencies. By using an envelope creatively, you can control how these parameters are modified over a specific amount of time. But before you get ahead of yourself, take a look at the essential controls of the Filter Envelope.

Figure 6.14
© Propellerhead Software AB.

▷ **Amount.** This slider is used to determine the extent to which the Filter Envelope will affect the Filter Frequency. By default, the Amount slider is set to 0.

▷ **Attack.** When a sound's envelope is triggered, the Attack parameter, labeled "A," determines the length of time before the envelope reaches its maximum value.

▷ **Decay.** Once the maximum value is reached, the Decay parameter, labeled "D," determines the length of time it takes for the value to drop to the level determined by the Sustain value.

▷ **Sustain.** The Sustain setting, labeled "S," determines the level at which the falling value rests at the end of the decay stage.

▷ **Release.** The Release parameter, labeled "R," determines how long it will take for the value to fall to 0 after a Note Off message has been received (such as when a key is released or at the end of the playback of a REX slice).

A Filter Exercise: The following is a filter exercise that should help you start brewing a few ideas. Before you begin, start a new Reason song and create an instance of Dr. Octo Rex.

1. Load a REX loop with a lot of kick drum in it. For example, choose something from the House folder in Dr. Rex Drum Loops. After loading the REX loop into Dr. Octo Rex, click the Run button so you can listen and edit at the same time.

2. Select the LP 12 Filter mode and adjust the Frequency Filter slider to a 25 and the Resonance to about 75. This should produce a very low-end, bass-heavy sound.

3. Raise the Filter Envelope's Amount slider to about 50. This should start to change the timbre of the sound immediately.

4. Now try working with a different combination of Filter Envelope parameters. For example, to create a percussive loop, set the Attack, Decay, and Release to 0. Then move the Sustain slider up and down until you reach a desired effect. Click on the Run button to stop playing the loop.

5. To make this loop appear in the Reason sequencer, click on the Copy Loop to Track button. The corresponding MIDI notes should appear in the Dr. Octo Rex track. Turn off Enable Loop Playback and click Play in the Reason sequencer to hear your loop.

The LFO (Low-Frequency Oscillator)

Directly beneath Dr. Octo Rex's filter, you will find the low-frequency oscillator (LFO), shown in Figure 6.15. An LFO is capable of generating waveforms with a low frequency (well below the range of human hearing), hence the name LFO. An LFO's purpose is to modulate a parameter, such as a filter or another oscillator. That means the LFO itself is never actually heard, just its effect on other synth parameters.

Figure 6.15

© Propellerhead Software AB.

To hear the effect of the LFO, you must first adjust the Amount knob, located to the right of the Rate knob. Once this parameter is turned up, you can start to explore the functions of the LFO.

KEEPING IT IN SYNC

No "boy band" jokes, please. The LFO can run in either free time or synchronized time that is determined by the master tempo of the Transport panel. To activate the synchronization, click on the Sync button, located directly above the Waveform selector (see Figure 6.16). This will sync the Dr. Octo Rex LFO with the Reason master tempo. At this point, you can follow it up by assigning both a waveform shape and a destination for the LFO.

Figure 6.16

© Propellerhead Software AB.

WAVEFORMS: TAKE YOUR PICK

Six types of waveforms can be applied to your LFO. You can select them by clicking on them with the mouse or by using the Wavef. button at the bottom of the waveform list.

Let's discuss the differences between these individual waveforms:

▷ **Triangle.** This creates a smooth up and down vibrato.
▷ **Inverted Sawtooth.** This creates a cycled ramp-up effect.
▷ **Sawtooth.** This creates a cycled ramp-down effect.
▷ **Square.** This makes abrupt changes between two values.
▷ **Random.** This creates a random stepped modulation. Also known as sample and hold.
▷ **Soft Random.** This is exactly the same as the previous waveform, but with a smoother modulation curve.

DESTINATION: ANYWHERE

After selecting an LFO waveform and rate/amount, you're ready to choose which parameter will be modulated by the LFO. LFO modulation can be applied to three destinations. Again, you can click directly on each one or cycle through them by clicking the Dest button.

▷ **Osc.** This sends the LFO modulation effect to the overall pitch of the REX loop. Depending on which waveform is selected and how much LFO is assigned to the oscillator, it can produce a very neat up-and-down effect.

▷ **Filter.** This sends the LFO modulation to the Filter section of Dr. Octo Rex. This can produce a tempo-based filter sweep effect if the Sync button is activated.

▷ **Pan.** This sends the LFO modulation to the Stereo Pan setting of Dr. Octo Rex. When synced, this will create a tempo-based stereophonic effect.

The Amp Envelope

Creating an audible sound takes two basic actions: the generation of the sound and its amplification. So far, this chapter has focused on the generation of sound in Dr. Octo Rex. Modulation of the amplification aspect is covered by Dr. Rex's Amp Envelope feature (see Figure 6.17).

Figure 6.17
© Propellerhead Software AB.

▷ **Level.** This slider controls the volume of Dr. Octo Rex.

▷ **Attack.** When a sound's envelope is triggered, the Attack parameter, labeled "A," determines the length of time before the envelope reaches its maximum value.

▷ **Decay.** Once the maximum value is reached, the Decay parameter, labeled "D," determines the length of time it takes for the value to drop to the level determined by the Sustain value.

▷ **Sustain.** After the value begins to drop, the Sustain parameter, labeled "S," determines the level where the falling value rests.

▷ **Release.** The Release parameter, labeled "R," determines how long it will take for the value to fall to 0 after a Note Off message has been received (such as when a key is released or at the end of the playback of a REX slice).

The Velocity Section

The Velocity section (see Figure 6.18) allows you to assign certain filter and amplification parameters to be modified according to the velocity at which each note (or slice) is played. Remember, *velocity* refers to how hard the note is played on your keyboard. Whether you play it hard or soft, these assignable parameters will respond according to their settings. If you are not using a controller keyboard, you can draw the velocity data in via the Reason sequencer.

Figure 6.18
© Propellerhead Software AB.

▷ **F. Env.** When this parameter is set to a positive value, different velocities control the Amount knob of the Filter Envelope. A negative value has the opposite effect.

▷ **F. Decay.** When this parameter is set to a positive value, different velocities control the Decay parameter of the Filter Envelope. A negative value has the opposite effect.

▷ **Amp.** When this parameter is set to a positive value, the velocity controls the amount of volume. A negative value has the opposite effect.

Pitch Bend and Modulation

The Pitch Bend Range and Modulation controls are located below and above the Velocity section, respectively (see Figure 6.19).

Figure 6.19
© Propellerhead Software AB.

GET IT IN PITCH

The Dr. Octo Rex Pitch Bend Range is similar to Pitch controls on hardware synths; it bends the pitch of the whole loop up or down. You can click on the up and down buttons or just click and drag in the field itself to change the range. For kicks, try selecting 24, which is equivalent to 24 semitones, or two octaves. Then click the Preview button. While the file is playing, use a keyboard controller with a pitch-shifting wheel or just click and drag up or down on the Bend wheel to hear the pitch shifting at work.

MODULATION

Modulation is the "secret sauce," or essential ingredient, in any form of artistic electronic music. It can be used to effectively change the timbre of a signal. The common modulation wheel found on most typical synthesizers can be assigned to a number of different synth parameters. When assigned, the modulation wheel then makes modifications in real time to the played note according to the selected parameter and its assigned value.

The modulation wheel has three parameters that can be assigned to it (see Figure 6.20):

Figure 6.20
© Propellerhead Software AB.

> **F. Freq.** This is assigned to the cutoff filter (labeled "Freq") of the Dr. Octo Rex Filter section. When a value is assigned to this knob, the cutoff filter's value decreases or increases as the modulation wheel is used.
> **F. Res.** This is assigned to the Resonance control of the Filter section. Depending on where it is set, the Resonance control increases or decreases while the modulation wheel is in use.
> **F. Decay.** This is assigned to the Decay slider of the Filter Envelope. Depending on where it is set, the envelope decay increases or decreases.

The whole point of electronic music is to experiment and deviate from the norm. The modulation wheel is a useful tool for accomplishing that goal.

Make It Punchy! Here's a quick DIY tutorial on using the modulation wheel with its three parameters. Before beginning this exercise, start a new Reason song and create an instance of Dr. Octo Rex.

1. In the Filter section, by default, the Filter mode should be set to LP 12 mode, which is fine for this exercise. Now set the Filter Frequency slider to about 25 and set the Resonance slider to 75.
2. Click the Run button to hear your REX file in action with the active filter.
3. In the Filter Envelope, set the Amount slider to 100%. Then set the Attack, Decay, Sustain, and Release parameters to 0.
4. In the Modulation Wheel section, set the F. Freq knob to 32, the F. Res knob to −32, and the F. Decay knob to −64.
5. Use the modulation wheel with your mouse or MIDI keyboard. Notice how the filter opens up as it is activated. Also notice how the Decay amount increases.

Dr. Octo Rex Connections

Press the Tab key to swing the Rack screen around, and you'll see all the Dr. Octo Rex control voltage (CV) and audio connections available (see Figure 6.21).

Figure 6.21
© Propellerhead Software AB.

Audio Quality in Dr. Octo Rex

In the lower-right corner of the back panel are two parameters that affect the quality of your loops (see Figure 6.22):

Figure 6.22
© Propellerhead Software AB.

▷ **High Quality Interpolation.** When this parameter is activated, Dr. Octo Rex plays back the REX file with a more advanced interpolation algorithm, resulting in a higher-quality audio signal. The difference is most noticeable in loops containing a lot of high-frequency data, such as a hi-hat track. This enhanced audio quality does come at the price of a bit of extra work for your processor.

▷ **Low Bandwidth.** This parameter removes some of the high end from the playback of a REX file to relieve the burden on your CPU. The difference is especially evident in loops with a lot of hi-hat or Latin percussion. If, on the other hand, your loops are mostly low-frequency data, or if they've been put through a low-pass filter, you'll be less likely to hear the difference.

Audio Outputs

The rear panel of Dr. Octo Rex offers two types of audio outputs.

▷ **Main outputs.** These are used as the main outputs of Dr. Octo Rex. All the loaded REX files are automatically routed to these outputs.

▷ **Slice outputs.** These outputs are available for routing individual slices of loaded REX files in an instance of Dr. Octo Rex. This is done by making use of the Output parameter on the Waveform display editor on the front panel of the interface. Simply select the slice you want and assign it to one of four pairs of stereo outputs.

CV Outputs

Three CV outputs are available to you on the rear panel of the Dr. Octo Rex interface:

▷ **Filter Envelope.** This is a modulation output that sends modulation information from the first voice of polyphony of a REX file played through the Filter Envelope to any modulation input on another Reason device. For example, you could route this output to the Gate CV input of the ECF-42 filter. Every time the REX file plays back, the first voice of polyphony will trigger the Gate parameter of the ECF-42.

▷ **LFO.** This is another modulation output that sends modulation information from the LFO of Dr. Octo Rex to the CV inputs of any other Reason device.

▷ **Gate Output.** This is an output that sends out a gate signal for every slice of a REX file.

Gate Inputs

Two CV inputs receive gate information from another Reason device and can be used to trigger two different envelopes: the Filter Envelope and the Gate Envelope. In this case, you could have the Gate Output of a Redrum channel trigger the Filter Envelope or Gate Envelope as a sequence plays back. Or, you could use the Curve CV output of an instance of the Matrix to trigger either of these two envelopes.

Modulation Inputs

To the far left of the rear panel are all the modulation inputs of Dr. Octo Rex. In this case, however, you'll see that there are not only inputs, but also input knobs to the left that specify how intense or subtle the modulation effect will be.

▷ **Master Volume.** Routing a CV connection to this input modulates the master volume of Dr. Octo Rex.

▷ **Mod Wheel.** Routing a CV connection to this input modulates the modulation wheel. You can edit this even further by assigning any or all three of the modulation destinations on the front panel.

▷ **Pitch Wheel.** Routing a CV connection to this input modulates the pitch wheel.

▷ **Filter Cutoff.** Routing a CV connection to this input modulates the Filter Frequency parameter of the Filter section.

▷ **Filter Resonance.** Routing a CV connection to this input modulates the Resonance parameter of the Filter section.

▷ **OSC Pitch.** Routing a CV connection to this input modulates the pitch of the loaded REX file.

Creative Uses for Dr. Octo Rex with the Reason Sequencer

The key to enjoying a long, creative, and fruitful future with Dr. Octo Rex and Reason is to try different combinations and ideas. Remember, anything can be routed into anything in Reason. This section provides a few tips and tricks to fire up the synapses and get the creative juices flowing.

Before you begin these exercises, make sure you start a new Reason song and create an instance of Dr. Octo Rex. Finish preparing yourself by locating a new REX file or a DREX patch from the Reason Factory Sound Bank and loading it into Dr. Octo Rex.

Cut It Out!

Although many folks like a good, predictable, four-on-the-floor beat in dance music, it is a good idea to introduce some variations from time to time. One of those variations includes the deletion of different slices from a REX file to give it an entirely different feel.

Recall that a REX file contains two types of information to do its magic. The first type is digital audio information, which you see in the Waveform view of Dr. Octo Rex as a series of slices. The other type of information is the corresponding MIDI notes that accompany each digital audio slice. When you click the Copy Loop to Track button on the Dr. Octo Rex interface, it copies the MIDI notes to its track on the sequencer. After recording the MIDI tracks, you can simply open the appropriate editor in the sequencer and remove a few of the MIDI notes so that the corresponding audio slices will not play back.

Start by clicking on the Switch to Edit Mode button on the Reason sequencer. Because this is a Dr. Octo Rex track, the sequencer will automatically know which editor to open—in this case, the REX Lane Editor. At this point, you should see all the MIDI notes lined up in zipper fashion (see Figure 6.23) as they move upward diagonally from left to right. To the far left of the notes is a list of numeric names for each slice. Depending on the length of the loop, up to 92 slices can be displayed here. Navigate your mouse to Slice 1 in the Slice list and notice that the Selector tool becomes a Speaker tool, which enables you to preview a slice by clicking on the slice name. You can also click and hold on the name of any slice in the list and drag your mouse up or down to preview the slices one by one.

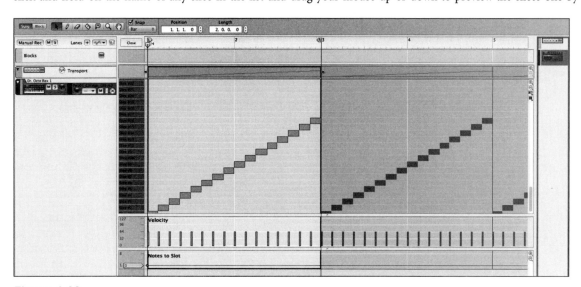

Figure 6.23
© Propellerhead Software AB.

At this point, listen to each slice and decide which sound you want to remove from your loop. For example, you will probably want to keep the kick drum to keep a steady beat, but you can remove the snare or hi-hat sounds. Locate each of the sounds that you want to remove and then select them. Click Delete to get rid of them or use the Eraser tool.

When you're finished, play the loop and see how you like the results. Getting a sound you like might take a lot of experimenting. Remember, you can always go back to the original loop by using the Copy Loop to Track button in Dr. Octo Rex or the Undo edit function.

Write Your Own Grooves

Aside from erasing MIDI notes, you also can rewrite your REX file groove in a couple of ways.

▷ Draw in a new sequence using the slices.
▷ Use a MIDI controller to record a new sequence.

Using the Pencil tool, you can redraw the MIDI notes that are connected to the different slices in your Dr. Octo Rex module. This task is easier than it sounds, but it will take a little practice.

1. Start a new Reason song and load an instance of Dr. Octo Rex.
2. Load a new REX file into Dr. Octo Rex and click on the Copy Loop to Track button to send the MIDI notes of the REX file to the Reason sequencer.
3. Click on the Switch to Edit Mode button. You should now see the REX Lane Editor.
4. Find the sounds for which you want to draw notes by clicking on the slices of the REX file.
5. Open the Edit menu and choose Select All to highlight each MIDI note in the editor. Then press the Delete key to erase all the notes. As you can see in Figure 6.24, you have a clean palette to work with.
6. Create a two-bar loop so that you can work quickly. In the Transport panel, set your left locator to bar 1 and the right locator to bar 3. Make sure that the loop function is on by clicking on the Loop On/Off button in the Transport panel. Click the Stop button twice in the Transport panel to send the position indicator back to the beginning of the sequence. Click Play. You should now have a two-bar template to work with.
7. Choose the note value that you want to draw in. Because this is probably your first time doing this, I suggest using something simple like an 1/8 note. To do this, just select 1/8 from the Snap pull-down menu of the Sequencer toolbar (see Figure 6.25). Select the Pencil tool, and you can begin to draw in your MIDI notes.
8. Start with Slice 1 and draw in an 1/8 note at the beginning of each 1/4 note in bar one (1, 2, 3, and 4). (See Figure 6.26.) Click Play. You should now hear the first slice play four times.

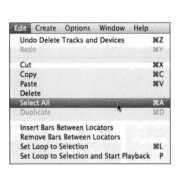
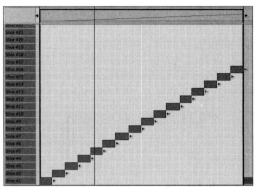
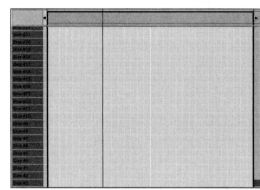

Figure 6.24
© Propellerhead Software AB.

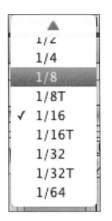

Figure 6.25
© Propellerhead Software AB.

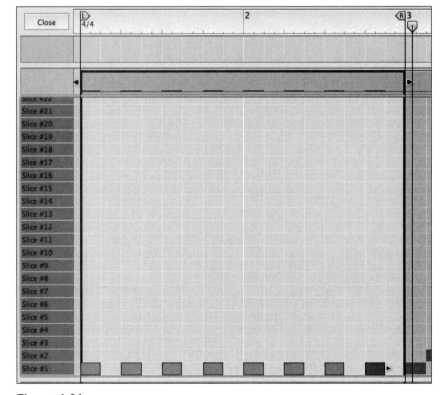

Figure 6.26
© Propellerhead Software AB.

9. Choose a few more slices and draw them in. As you can see in Figure 6.27, you can make a simple yet effective rhythm with just a few slices. Try it on your own with different note values, and you'll be on your way to a groove.

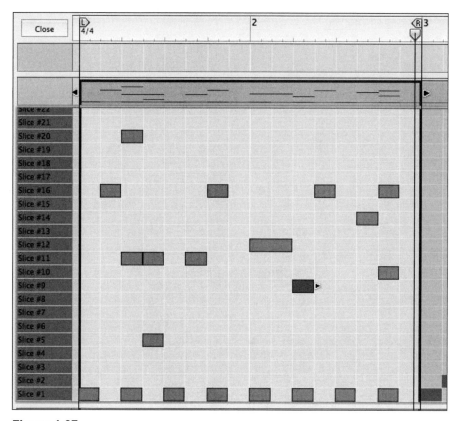

Figure 6.27
© Propellerhead Software AB.

> **TIP:** If you've sequenced in other programs, you might be accustomed to seeing a Key Edit window that looks more like
> Figure 6.28. As you learned in Chapter 4, "The Reason Sequencer: Close-Up," Reason also has a Key Edit window called the Key
> Lane. You can draw in your new REX grooves using either the REX Lane Editor or the Key Lane Editor by selecting them in the
> upper-right corner of the sequencer (see Figure 6.29).

You can also input data into the Reason sequencer live (covered in Chapter 4). Just make sure that your Dr. Octo Rex track is activated and ready to accept live MIDI data. You do so by making sure the Record Enable button is turned on for Dr. Octo Rex in the Track List (see Figure 6.30). Using your MIDI keyboard, you can now play Dr. Octo Rex in much the same way that you would play a drum machine with a MIDI keyboard. Any REX file loaded into Dr. Octo Rex is mapped across a MIDI keyboard, starting with C1 on your keyboard corresponding to Slice 1 in Dr. Octo Rex.

Just click Record. You can record a new performance of the REX file.

Creating Your Own REX Files

As of Reason 7, it is no longer necessary to own ReCycle!. The ability to create REX files now resides directly in Reason. This saves several steps toward REX file creation and it is very easy to create a loop library of your own. In this section, let's take a look at how to make your own REX Files.

Just so we can make a REX file that is truly your own, let's go ahead and start from a new Reason project with nothing in it. (If you have something that you'd like to keep from what we've been working on so far, make sure to save it before you proceed.)

1. In a new Reason session, create a Redrum drum machine. Then click the Patch Browse button, shown in Figure 6.31. This will open the Patch Browser, of course.

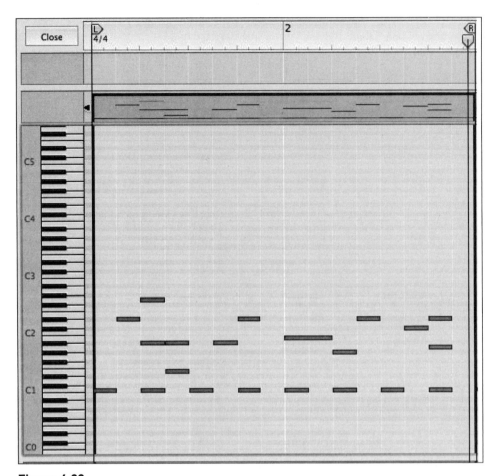

Figure 6.28
© Propellerhead Software AB.

Figure 6.29
© Propellerhead Software AB.

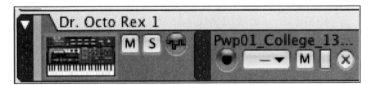

Figure 6.30
© Propellerhead Software AB.

2. In the Reason Patch Browser, you should already be in the Redrum Drum Kits folder of the Reason Factory Sound Bank. Double-click on the Chemical Kits directory, and then double-click on the Chemical Kit 01.drp, as shown in Figure 6.32. This will load a drum patch in to Redrum.

3. Use Redrum to make a drum beat. To do this, simply select a drum channel—let's say channel 1 (kick drum), as shown in Figure 6.33. Then press the space bar to start the Reason sequencer, which in turn will start the Redrum drum sequencer. Use the buttons 1–16 to draw in drum beats. Once your channel 1 drum sounds good, select another channel and draw in beats. Keep doing this until you have a drum beat that is enjoyable to your ears!

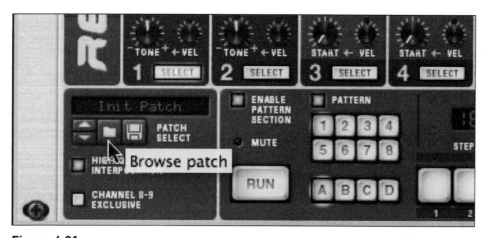

Figure 6.31
© Propellerhead Software AB.

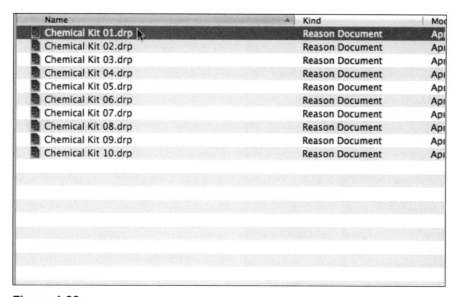

Figure 6.32
© Propellerhead Software AB.

4. Press F7 to switch to the Sequencer screen. In this screen, set your left loop point at measure 1 and your right loop point at measure 2. This will tell Reason how long you want your loop to be. See Figure 6.34.

5. Stop the sequencer with the space bar and select Bounce Mixer Channels from the File menu. In the browser that appears, select the Redrum mixer channel. Also select Loop as the Range to Bounce To value. This tells Reason to render only what's between your loop points. Finally, select Bounce to New Tracks in Song. (See Figure 6.35.) You may also want to select the Mute Original Channels option. This will mean that the Redrum track will be muted once the audio loop is rendered and will not play on top of the copy of the loop that you'll be adding to the arrangement.

6. After the rendering takes place, you'll notice a new audio clip in the sequencer. Double-click this audio clip to go into Inline Edit mode. In this mode, you'll see several, small arrows all over the audio, as shown in Figure 6.36. These arrows designate slices. Slices are what REX files are based on. By cutting up several transients, or hits, in the audio file, Dr. Octo Rex will eventually be able to play a loop back at any speed, as will Reason. In fact, if you try changing the project tempo now, you'll notice that the audio loop will speed up or slow down based on your chosen tempo. The pitch, however, will not change.

7. Before you create your REX loop, you may want to change the name of the track that you're going to convert to a REX loop. This will cause the REX loop, once rendered, to be labeled with the name of your choosing for the loop. Names like "Nasty Beat (132)" are fine because they let you know the original tempo of the loop, while also letting you know the original tempo of the loop. You can change the label of the track label by clicking the track in the sequencer and then typing over the existing name, as shown in Figure 6.37.

8. Now, to make a REX loop. Right-click on the audio clip and choose Bounce > Bounce Clip to REX Loop from the menu that appears. The Tool Window opens and displays your REX file in the Song Samples screen, as shown in Figure 6.38.

Figure 6.33
© Propellerhead Software AB.

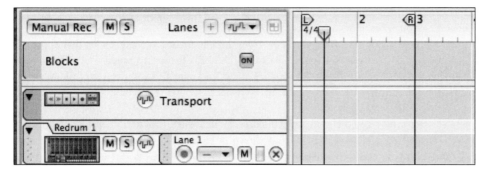

Figure 6.34
© Propellerhead Software AB.

9. With the REX file selected, you'll notice that there are options at the bottom of the Song Samples screen for things you can do with it. The first, and funnest option is the To Rack button, shown in Figure 6.39. This places the REX file in a Dr. Octo Rex automatically for you. Try this now!

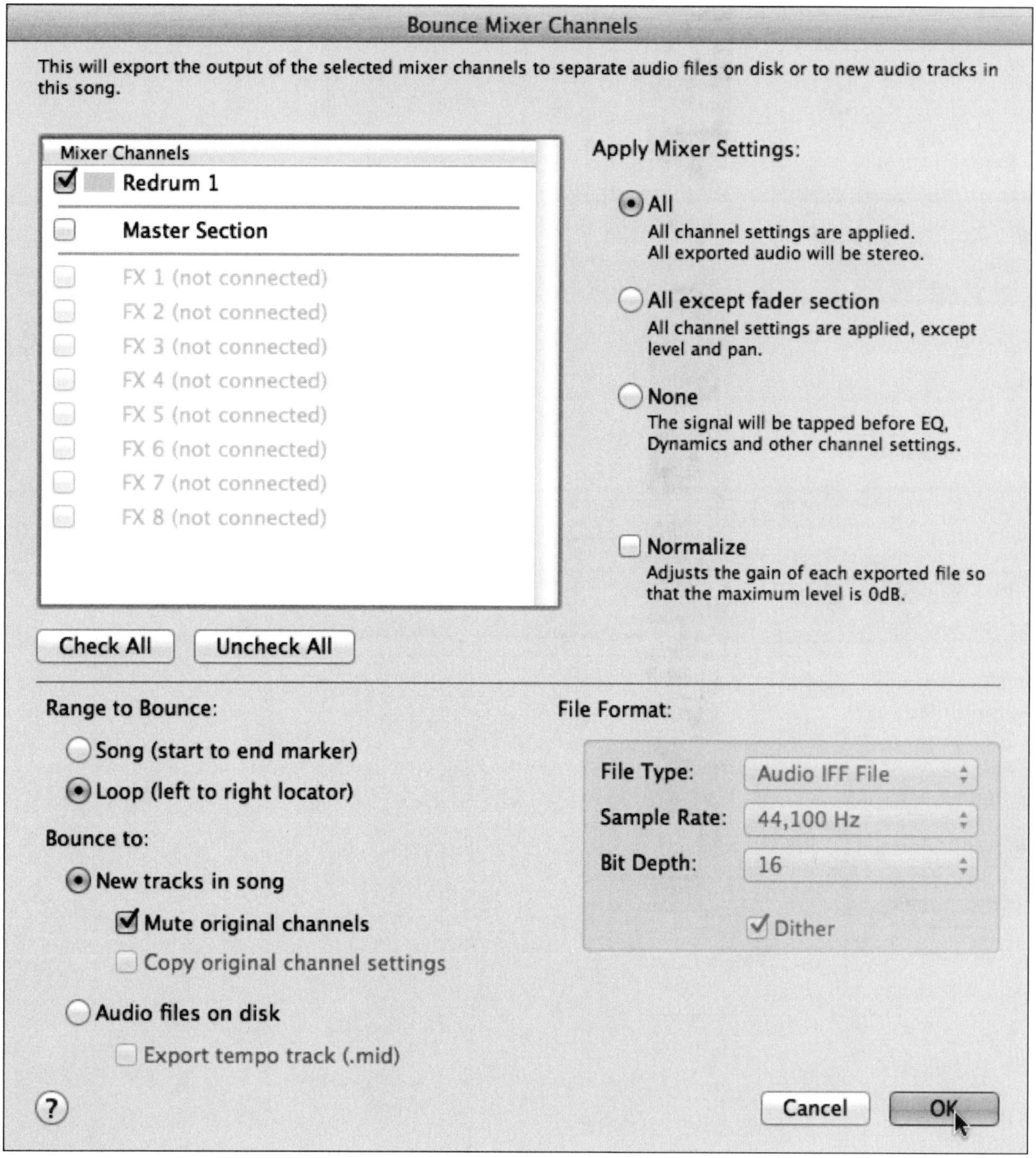

Bounce Mixer Channels

This will export the output of the selected mixer channels to separate audio files on disk or to new audio tracks in this song.

Mixer Channels

☑ Redrum 1

☐ Master Section

☐ FX 1 (not connected)
☐ FX 2 (not connected)
☐ FX 3 (not connected)
☐ FX 4 (not connected)
☐ FX 5 (not connected)
☐ FX 6 (not connected)
☐ FX 7 (not connected)
☐ FX 8 (not connected)

[Check All] [Uncheck All]

Apply Mixer Settings:

◉ **All**
All channel settings are applied.
All exported audio will be stereo.

○ **All except fader section**
All channel settings are applied, except level and pan.

○ **None**
The signal will be tapped before EQ, Dynamics and other channel settings.

☐ **Normalize**
Adjusts the gain of each exported file so that the maximum level is 0dB.

Range to Bounce:
○ Song (start to end marker)
◉ Loop (left to right locator)

Bounce to:
◉ New tracks in song
  ☑ Mute original channels
  ☐ Copy original channel settings
○ Audio files on disk
  ☐ Export tempo track (.mid)

File Format:

File Type:	Audio IFF File ⇕
Sample Rate:	44,100 Hz ⇕
Bit Depth:	16 ⇕
	☑ Dither

(?)   [Cancel] [OK]

Figure 6.35
© Propellerhead Software AB.

10. If you decide you'd like to add this loop to a personal REX/Loop collection, click the Export button, shown in Figure 6.40. By exporting to a file on your computer, you can make this loop available to any songs you currently have or create later. I highly recommend this route. As you've seen throughout this chapter, REX files in Dr. Octo Rex can be manipulated in many strange ways. So many, in fact, that you can completely disguise the original recording. Try exporting now. Make sure and create a file in a directory that you'll visit a lot. Take mental note of it!

There you go! REX files are really easy to create in Reason. What's also wonderful is that REX files can be used in more than just Reason. Pro Tools, Ableton Live, and even Logic Pro all support REX files. So, if you're using more than one DAW, you can bring some stuff over and have some fun.

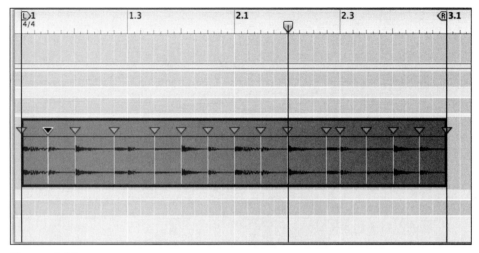

Figure 6.36
© Propellerhead Software AB.

Figure 6.37
© Propellerhead Software AB.

Figure 6.38
© Propellerhead Software AB.

Figure 6.39
© Propellerhead Software AB.

Figure 6.40
© Propellerhead Software AB.

Moving On

As you have seen in this chapter, Dr. Octo Rex is a Reason device that takes looping to a whole new level. Next, you are going to delve into the first of Reason's three virtual synths: the Malström!

7

The Malström: Close-Up

Wᴴᴇɴ Rᴇᴀsoɴ 2.0 ʜɪᴛ ᴛʜᴇ ᴍᴀʀᴋᴇᴛ ɪɴ 2002, Propellerhead introduced a new virtual synth, based on an original form of synthesis, called the Malström (see Figure 7.1). With its handsome graphical interface and unbelievable synthesis prowess, it is likely to quickly become a permanent fixture in your Reason songs.

Figure 7.1
© Propellerhead Software AB.

Graintable Synthesis

Malström's uniqueness stems from the method by which it generates sound, called *graintable synthesis*, which is essentially a combination of granular and wavetable synthesis. To better understand how this works, you need to understand these two forms of synthesis.

In *granular synthesis*, sound is generated by a specific number of short, adjacent audio segments, called grains. Grains can be generated either by using a mathematical formula or by using a sample. These grains are usually 5–100 milliseconds long and are spliced together to form a sound. Altering the order of slices or modifying the individual properties of each slice can change the overall sound.

Wavetable synthesis is based on the playback of a set of single cycle waveforms. Wavetable synthesis offers a few key benefits, such as the capability to sweep through the wavetable at any speed without affecting the pitch, and quickly accessing specific points of the stored waveform data.

These two sound-generation techniques are very similar because they access stored audio data. Wavetable synthesis is always bound to a full periodic cycle, and the length of the audio segment is determined by the wavetable. With granular synthesis, the length of the audio segment is arbitrary and determined by a length parameter.

> **NOTE:** For modern-day examples of both granular and wavetable synthesis, check out the Native Instruments Reaktor virtual synth.

As stated, graintable synthesis is a combination of these two forms of synthesis and works in the Malström as follows:

1. The oscillators of the Malström play sampled sounds that have been preprocessed in a complex manner and cut into individual grains. From this point on, these converted samples are called graintables.
2. These graintables are made up of periodic sets of waveforms that, when combined, play back the original sounds.
3. At this point, the graintable is treated in the same way as a wavetable. You have the ability to sweep through the graintable and single out any nuance of the graintable that you would like to manipulate. For example, you could extract a vowel out of a voice

graintable. The graintable can be manipulated further by incorporating the ability to "shift" the frequency region or "formant" without altering the pitch, which is a granular synthesis quality.

Tour the Malström

Now that you have learned the fundamentals of graintable synthesis, load an instance of the Malström and take a tour of the interface. Before you begin this section, start a new Reason song and load an instance of the Malström.

The Oscillator Section

The Malström has two oscillators from which to generate sound (see Figure 7.2). The Malström's oscillators are meant to perform two tasks:

▷ Play the loaded graintable.
▷ Generate a pitch.

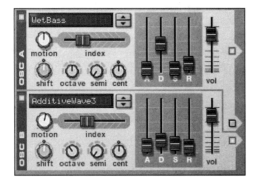

Figure 7.2
© Propellerhead Software AB.

When you create an instance of the Malström, a default patch will load and can be heard by playing your keyboard. This is a good, solid sound to begin touring the Malström, but you can click on the Patch Browser located in the upper-left corner of the Malström interface and load patches from the Reason Factory Sound Bank. As was the case with other Reason instruments, Malström patches are organized by their intended use, including the following:

▷ Bass
▷ Effects
▷ Mono synths
▷ Pads
▷ Percussion
▷ Poly synths
▷ Rhythmic

Of course, none of these presets is set in stone, so to speak. You can modify a poly synth patch to be used as a pad, or a mono synth patch to be used as a bass synth. You just have to learn your way around the Malström and understand how each part of the interface works.

With that thought in mind, let's continue onward by touring the individual sections of the Malström with a clean slate. Right-click on the interface and select Initialize Patch. This resets the Malström and gives you a good starting point.

After you activate either of the oscillators, the next task is to select a graintable from the display just to the right of the Osc A and Osc B power buttons. You can select a graintable either by using the scroll buttons of the graintable display or by clicking on the display itself. If you click on the display, a pop-up menu will appear, displaying a long list of available graintables from which to choose (see Figure 7.3).

Figure 7.3
© Propellerhead Software AB.

Organization of the Graintables: As you begin to explore the long list of more than 80 graintables, it's refreshing to see that Propellerhead has categorized these graintables by type. This arrangement makes it much easier when you're beginning to build a new patch from scratch or when editing a patch.

The graintable list is organized as follows:

- ▶ **Bass:** Six graintables
- ▶ **Effects:** 10 graintables
- ▶ **Guitar:** Five graintables
- ▶ **Misc:** Three graintables
- ▶ **Perc:** Five graintables
- ▶ **Synth:** 22 graintables
- ▶ **Voices:** 11 graintables
- ▶ **Wave:** 10 graintables
- ▶ **Wind:** 10 graintables

Setting the Oscillator Frequency

After selecting a graintable, you can alter the frequency of the oscillators by using a combination of three parameters (see Figure 7.4):

Figure 7.4
© Propellerhead Software AB.

▷ **Octave:** This alters the frequency of a graintable by octaves and has a range of seven octaves.
▷ **Semi:** This alters the frequency of a graintable by semitones and has a range of 12 semitones, or one full octave.
▷ **Cent:** This alters the frequency of a graintable by cents. With a range of one semitone, it is used to make very fine adjustments to a loaded graintable.

Altering the Oscillator Playback

After setting the frequency of a graintable, you can alter the playback of the oscillators by using the Motion, Index, and Shift parameters (see Figure 7.5).

Figure 7.5
© Propellerhead Software AB.

▷ **Index:** This is used to set the start point for the playback of the graintable. It has a range of 0–127.
▷ **Motion:** This is used to set the speed at which a graintable is played, according to its motion pattern. Turning the knob to the left slows down the motion of the graintable, whereas turning it to the right speeds it up.
▷ **Shift:** This alters the timbre or formant spectrum of a graintable. The formant spectrum is the overview that determines the overall character of a graintable. This is done by a procedure known as resampling. Using this parameter effectively creates a pitch-shift effect on the oscillator.

Motion Pattern: Each graintable in a patch has a preset motion pattern and speed. If you're setting the Motion parameter to any value higher than −63 or hard left, the graintable loops and follows one of two motion patterns:

▶ **Forward:** The graintable is played from beginning to end and then loops back to the beginning.
▶ **Forward/Backward:** The graintable is played from beginning to end and then from the end to beginning. It then starts over.

As stated, the Motion parameter can change the speed of the graintable but not the actual graintable itself.

The Amplitude Envelope

Each of the Malström oscillators has an individual envelope and volume knob to alter its amplitude (see Figure 7.6).

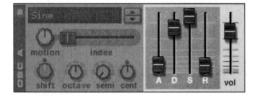

Figure 7.6
© Propellerhead Software AB.

▷ **Attack:** When an enveloped is triggered, the Attack parameter determines how long it takes for the envelope to reach its maximum value.

▷ **Decay:** Once the maximum value is reached, the Decay parameter determines how long it stays at the level before the value begins to drop.

▷ **Sustain:** After the value begins to drop, the Sustain parameter determines the level where the falling value should rest.

▷ **Release:** Once the value has been set at its rested value, the Release parameter determines how long it will take for the value to return to zero after the keys have been released.

Routing and Output

Once you have set the oscillator parameters, you can route the output of those signals to a combination of filter destinations. Looking at Figure 7.7, you can see that each oscillator points to the right, with a corresponding "routing" button that looks a lot like the standard power buttons you have been looking at throughout this chapter. To route the oscillators to their corresponding filters, just click on the available routing buttons.

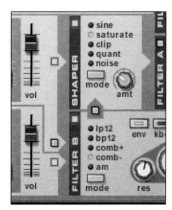

Figure 7.7
© Propellerhead Software AB.

The Output section of the Malström is simple, having only two adjustable parameters (see Figure 7.8).

Figure 7.8
© Propellerhead Software AB.

▷ **Spread:** This parameter is used to adjust the panning width of Osc A and Osc B. Turning this knob hard right creates a wide stereo field, in which Osc A is heard only in the left channel, whereas Osc B is heard in the right.

▷ **Volume:** This parameter adjusts the overall volume of the Malström.

The Filter Section

As any aspiring electronic musician knows, a filter is used to alter the overall character of a sound. The Filter section of the Malström does this tenfold by including additional filters and parameters that deviate significantly from most other filters (see Figure 7.9).

To activate Filter A or Filter B, click on their power buttons, found in the upper-left corner of each filter. Also, make sure that the appropriate oscillator is assigned to the desired filter.

Filter Types

Before altering the Resonance and Cutoff Frequency parameters, you must choose one of five filter types (see Figure 7.10).

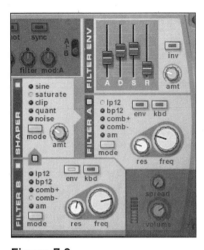

Figure 7.9
© Propellerhead Software AB.

Figure 7.10
© Propellerhead Software AB.

▷ **LP12:** This filter allows low frequencies to pass through it, while high frequencies are filtered out. This low-pass filter has a roll-off curve of approximately 12 dB per octave.

▷ **BP12:** This filter type filters out both the high and low frequencies, leaving the mid frequencies alone to be toyed with. With a roll-off curve of 12 dB per octave, the BP 12 can be used effectively on instrument loops such as guitar loops or possibly hi-hat-heavy percussion loops.

▷ **Comb +/−:** A comb filter is essentially a series of delays with very short delay times assigned to each delay instance, resulting in a detuned sound. The feedback of these delays is controlled by the Resonance parameter in each filter, and the delay time is controlled (inversely) by the Filter Frequency knob. The difference between the Comb+ and Comb− is the position of the delay peaks within the spectrum.

▷ **AM (Amplitude Modulation):** This filter produces a sine wave, which is then multiplied by the output of Osc A or Osc B. The resulting sound contains additional frequencies that are a result of the sum and difference of the two frequencies. Note that the Resonance knob controls the mix between the two signals. If this description sounds familiar, another way to think of this is as a ring modulator.

The Filter Controls

Once you have selected a filter type, you can then use the main controls of the filter to alter the character of the Malström patch (see Figure 7.11).

Figure 7.11
© Propellerhead Software AB.

▷ **Kbd (Keyboard Tracking):** When this is activated, it enables the filter to react differently the higher you play on the keyboard. If this parameter is deactivated, the filter effect will remain constant.

▷ **Env (Envelope):** When this is activated, the filter will be modulated by the Filter Envelope.

▷ **Freq (Cutoff Frequency):** This has two purposes, depending on which filter type is selected. When LP24, BP12, or Comb+/− is selected, this parameter acts as a cutoff frequency knob that specifies where the filter will function within the frequency spectrum. When the AM filter type is selected, the Frequency knob controls the frequency of the ring-modulated signal generated by the AM filter.

▷ **Res (Resonance):** This parameter has two purposes depending on which filter type is selected. When LP12, BP12, or Comb+/− is selected, this parameter emphasizes the frequencies set by the Freq knob. When the AM filter type is selected, the Resonance knob regulates the balance between the original and the modulated signal.

The Filter Envelope

The Filter Envelope is used to alter the characteristics of both Filter A and Filter B. The main parameters of the envelope match those of the oscillator envelopes, so there is no need to review how Attack, Decay, Sustain, and Release work (see Figure 7.12). The additional parameters for the Filter Envelope are as follows:

Figure 7.12
© Propellerhead Software AB.

▷ **Inv (Inverse):** This button is used to invert the individual parameters of the filter envelope. For example, say you are using the Attack parameter of the filter envelope and have assigned a value of 80, which produces a very slow attack. Activate the Invert button and the attack parameter is inverted, which means the attack will be much faster.

▷ **Amt (Amount):** This knob is used to assign the amount of envelope to the filters.

The Shaper

In addition to the obvious auditory goodies that the Filter section provides, take a moment to focus on the small but mighty Shaper. The Shaper is a *waveshaper*, which alters the waveform shape itself. This results in either a more complex, rich sound or a truncated distortion that rivals industrial music on a good day.

You activate the Shaper by clicking on its power button, located in the upper-left corner of the Shaper interface. Once it is activated, you can edit the waveshaping effect by selecting a mode and assigning an amount.

Let's look at the different shaping modes. You can select them by using the Mode button or by just clicking on the name of the desired mode itself (see Figure 7.13).

Figure 7.13
© Propellerhead Software AB.

▷ **Sine:** This creates a smooth sound.

▷ **Saturate:** This saturates the original signal, resulting in a rich, lush sound.

▷ **Clip:** This adds digital distortion to the signal.

▷ **Quant:** This truncates the signal and can be used to create a grungy 8-bit sound.

▷ **Noise:** This multiplies the original signal with noise.

> **TIP:** Located at the top of Filter B is a routing button that allows that filter to be sent to the Shaper, creating an interesting combination of sounds. For example, you can send Osc A to the Shaper and at the same time split and send Osc A to Filter B. Osc B will also be sent to Filter B and then routed to the Shaper as well. After both signals are combined and processed by the Shaper, the signal is then sent to Filter A and sent along to the outputs of the Malström.

The Modulator Section

Located above the Oscillator section is a pair of modulators, which are used to alter the character of the synth sound (see Figure 7.14). If this description sounds familiar, another way to think of these modulators is as low-frequency oscillators (LFOs). However, because the Malström is a synth unlike anything else in Reason, it's safe to say that these modulators go way above and beyond the call of duty when it comes to modulating the oscillators.

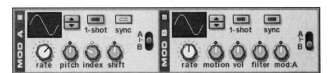

Figure 7.14
© Propellerhead Software AB.

> **TIP:** As with the SubTractor and Dr. Octo Rex, the Malström modulators do not produce sound on their own. Although they do generate a waveform and frequency, they are assigned to alter the character of Osc A and Osc B.

When an instance of the Malström is created, modulators A and B are active and ready to use. To deactivate either of these, click on their power buttons, which are located at the upper-left corner of each modulator.

Take a look at the source parameters of the Modulator section.

- ▷ **Curve:** This is used to select a modulating waveform. The selected waveform is shown in the Curve display window. You can either use the scroll buttons to select different waveforms or click and drag up and down on the display. There are more than 30 waveforms from which to choose, so it should keep you busy for a long time to come.
- ▷ **Rate:** This controls the speed of modulation. Turn the knob to the left to slow down the frequency or to the right to speed it up. Also note that if the Sync button is activated, the rate indicator is measured in note values (that is, 1/4, 1/8, and 1/16).
- ▷ **One Shot:** When activated, the One Shot parameter plays the modulation waveform a single time.
- ▷ **Sync:** This makes the modulator synchronize with the tempo of your Reason song.
- ▷ **A/B Selector:** This is used to select which oscillator the modulator will affect. You can select Osc A, Osc B, or both.

After selecting a modulation waveform, rate and a source, you can choose a destination parameter to be modulated. Note that both modulators have different destination parameters, so I will point them out along the way.

> **TIP:** The destination parameter knobs are bipolar. That means when the knob is in the middle position, there is no modulation effect, but turning the knob to the left or right increases the amount of modulation. To make it even more interesting, when the knob is turned to the left, the waveform of the modulator is inverted.

- ▷ **Pitch (Mod A):** This modulates the pitch parameter of Osc A, Osc B, or both.
- ▷ **Index (Mod A):** This modulates the index start position of Osc A, Osc B, or both.
- ▷ **Shift (Mod A):** This modulates the harmonic content of Osc A, Osc B, or both.
- ▷ **Motion (Mod B):** This modulates the motion speed of Osc A, Osc B, or both.
- ▷ **Level (Mod B):** This modulates the output amplitude of Osc A, Osc B, or both.
- ▷ **Filter (Mod B):** This modulates the cutoff filter of Osc A, Osc B, or both.
- ▷ **Mod:A (Mod B):** This alters the amount of modulation from Mod A.

The Keyboard Mode Parameters

The parameters covered in this section affect the overall sound of the Malström based on the way you play the synth (see Figure 7.15).

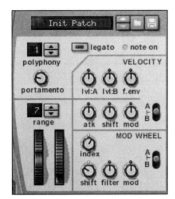

Figure 7.15
© Propellerhead Software AB.

Polyphony

Polyphony assigns the number of voices that can be played at one time. The Malström has a polyphony range of 1–16 voices, which is not a lot by comparison to the SubTractor or NN-19/XT synths. However, it is important to keep in mind that the Malström is a much more CPU-intensive virtual synth, and every voice takes a little more CPU power.

> **NOTE:** One feature that the Malström is missing is a Low Bandwidth button. There is no explanation why this feature is not included with the Malström, but perhaps the technology behind this synth wonder makes it impossible to support such a feature. I have run Malström with no problems on a pair of fairly slow computers. But keep in mind that the slower the computer, the more trouble you might have running the Malström.

Portamento

Portamento creates a sliding effect between played notes. The knob determines the amount of time it will take to slide from one note to another. It can be used with either monophonic or polyphonic patches and is a great tool for creating some interesting effects.

Legato

Legato is a commonly used parameter for playing monophonic patches, such as leads or bass lines. With the Legato parameter activated and Polyphony set to 1, press and hold down a note, and then press and hold another note. Notice that the new note has no attack because the Malström envelopes have not been retriggered.

Velocity Controls

The Malström is a velocity-sensitive synthesizer, as are the other Reason synths. The Velocity controls are used to affect different parameters of the Malström according to how much velocity is applied to individual notes.

> ▷ **Level A:** This parameter velocity controls the output of Osc A.
> ▷ **Level B:** This parameter velocity controls the output of Osc B.
> ▷ **Filter Envelope:** This parameter assigns the velocity control of the Filter Envelope.
> ▷ **Attack:** This parameter velocity controls the Attack parameter of Osc A, Osc B, or both.
> ▷ **Shift:** This parameter velocity controls the Shift parameter of Osc A, Osc B, or both.
> ▷ **Modulation:** This parameter velocity controls the amounts of Mod A, Mod B, or both.

Pitch Bend Wheel

The Pitch Bend wheel is an emulation of a standard pitch wheel found on most MIDI keyboards. Simply put, it is used to bend up and down the pitch of the played notes. The Range parameter, located just above the Pitch Bend wheel, controls the range of the pitch bend by up to +/− two octaves.

Mod Wheel

The Mod Wheel setting is used to control a number of available parameters:

▷ **Index:** This affects the graintable index of Osc A, Osc B, or both.
▷ **Shift:** This affects the Shift parameter of Osc A, Osc B, or both.
▷ **Filter:** This affects the Frequency filter of Filter A, Filter B, or both.
▷ **Modulation:** This alters the amount of modulation from Mod A, Mod B, or both.

CV Connections

Press the Tab key to flip the Rack screen around, and you'll see that the Malström has many connections that can be used to sequence with the Matrix, to modulate other devices, or to be modulated by other devices (see Figure 7.16).

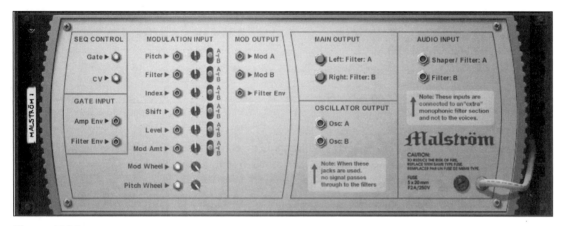

Figure 7.16
© Propellerhead Software AB.

Audio Outputs

The audio connections are used to output the signal from the Malström to the mixer. There are a couple of options:

▷ **Main outputs:** These are the main audio outputs of the Malström. They are taken from the outputs of the Filter section.
▷ **Oscillator outputs:** This second pair of outputs is taken directly from the outputs of Osc A and Osc B. If you connect these outputs to reMix, the main outputs will no longer work.

Audio Input

Another of the many lesser-known, yet equally mind-blowing, features of the Malström is its audio input capabilities. These inputs make it possible to route the audio output of any Reason device into the audio inputs of the Malström, which are then directly fed into Filter A and Filter B. Essentially, this makes the Malström an audio effect that is perfect for laying down some intense filter work on your loops, synths, and samples, or even your guitar!

For kicks, try the following exercise:

1. Create a new Reason song.
2. Create instances of the Malström and NN-19. Load a sample patch into the NN-19 and arm the sequencer track to receive MIDI.
3. Press the Tab key to flip the interface.
4. Disconnect the NN-19 from the mixer by selecting it and choosing Disconnect Device from the Edit menu.
5. Route the audio outputs of the NN-19 to the audio inputs of the Malström (see Figure 7.17).
6. With the NN-19 sequencer track selected and armed to receive MIDI, play a note on your MIDI keyboard, and you will hear the sample patch played through the filters of the Malström.

Seq Controls

The Seq (Sequencer) Control inputs are used to connect the Malström to a pattern-controlled device, such as the Matrix or Redrum. These inputs are as follows:

▷ **Gate:** This input is typically connected to the gate CV output of the Matrix or Redrum to receive Note On/Off messages.
▷ **CV:** This input is typically connected to the note CV output of the Matrix to receive note information.

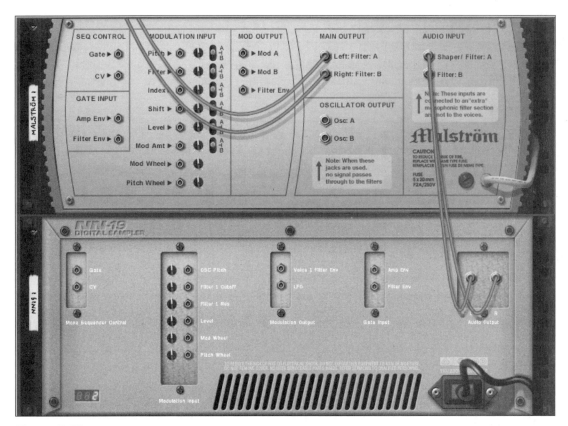

Figure 7.17
© Propellerhead Software AB.

Gate Input

The Gate inputs are used to receive gate information from either the Matrix or Redrum to trigger the amp envelope and filter envelope.

Modulation Input/Output

To the right of the Sequencer Control and Gate Input sections are the Modulation Input and Mod Output sections. The Modulation inputs can receive modulation output signals from any Reason device. The Curve CV output on the back of the Matrix is a good example of this. The Mod outputs send out modulation information to any Reason device. A commonly used connection is to connect any of the Mod outputs of the Malström to the Modulation inputs of the SubTractor or Thor.

Take a look at the various inputs:

- ▷ **Pitch:** This input is used to affect the pitch of Mod A, Mod B, or both.
- ▷ **Filter:** This input is used to affect the filter frequency of Mod A, Mod B, or both.
- ▷ **Index:** This input is used to affect the index of Mod A, Mod B, or both.
- ▷ **Shift:** This input is used to affect the shift of Mod A, Mod B, or both.
- ▷ **Level:** This input is used to affect the amplitude of Osc A, Osc B, or both.
- ▷ **Modulation Amount:** This input is used to affect the amount of modulation.
- ▷ **Modulation Wheel:** This input is used to affect the amount of mod wheel.
- ▷ **Pitch Wheel:** This input is used to affect the amount of pitch.

And now, take a look at the outputs:

- ▷ **Mod A:** This connection routes the output of Mod A to the modulation inputs of any other Reason device. Try connecting it to the FM Amount parameter of the SubTractor.
- ▷ **Mod B:** This connection routes the output of Mod B to the modulation inputs of any Reason device.
- ▷ **Filter Envelope:** This connection routes the output of the Filter Envelope to the modulation inputs of any Reason device.

Your First Malström Patch

Now that you have a pretty firm idea of how the Malström works, it's time to dig in and create your first customized Malström patch. This tutorial takes you through a step-by-step process of programming a bass synth patch that will be perfect for any ambient occasion.

Setting Up a Starting Point

Before you program your first Malström patch, it's important to find a good starting point. Writing in a sequence that's appropriate for the kind of patch you are going to create will make the programming process quicker and more efficient. For example, if you were going to create a pad sound, you would typically want to write in a sequence of long, sustained chords so you could hear the pad sound properly.

If you are planning to program a bass synth patch to be used in techno music, it's a good idea to write in a standard techno bass line in the Reason sequencer. Then set the sequencer to play the bass line over and over again in a loop. Then you can make real-time adjustments to the patch as the sequence is playing and program the patch to complement the style of music you are going to create with the patch.

Programming Your Malström Patch

In this tutorial, you are going to go build a bass patch by working with each section of the Malström interface. This tutorial serves as a good review tool to help you remember everything you have learned about the functionality of the Malström.

Programming the Oscillators

Let's start things off simple by working with Osc A and then add Osc B later. To hear the changes in real time, click Play on the transport bar. The two-bar loop should start playing continuously.

1. By default, the graintable of Osc A is set to a sine wave. Notice the organ-like tone that is produced.
2. Use the scroll buttons or click on the graintable box to display a list of available sounds. Choose the Wet Bass graintable.
3. Use the Index slider to set the start point of the graintable to 40. Notice how dramatically the overall tone and timbre of the graintable changes.

Let's also make a few adjustments to the Amplitude Envelope of Osc A. Set the parameters to the following values:

▷ **Attack:** 0
▷ **Decay:** 65
▷ **Sustain:** 0
▷ **Release:** 14 (for a short release)

And now, on to Osc B:

1. Activate Osc B and set its graintable to Synth: Additive Wave 3.
2. Set the Motion parameter to 7.
3. Set the Octave parameter to 3.
4. Set the Index slider to 48.

Let's make a few adjustments to the Amplitude Envelope of Osc B. Set the parameters to the following values:

▷ **Attack:** 12
▷ **Decay:** 25
▷ **Sustain:** 16
▷ **Release:** 10

Upon listening to the patch at this point, you will realize it lacks uniqueness. You can introduce such a quality by way of the modulators.

Programming the Modulators

As you read earlier in this chapter, the modulators are actually two separate LFOs. In this section of the tutorial, you are going to assign the modulators to manipulate Osc A and Osc B.

1. Activate Mod A and select the Sync button. This will lock up the modulation effect with the tempo of the Reason sequencer.
2. By default, the waveform of Mod A should be set to a sine wave. Leave it at this setting and set the Rate knob to 1/4, which means that the modulation effect will take place every 1/4 note.
3. Set the destination of Mod A to Osc A and Osc B by using the A/B selector to the right of the Mod A interface.
4. Assign a value of −24 to the Index knob. This should cause the Shift parameter of Osc A and Osc B to open and close in tempo.

Programming the Filter and Shaper

In this section of the tutorial, you are going to add the Shaper to Osc A to introduce a little distortion to the bass sound.

1. Activate both the Route Oscillator A to Shaper and Activate Shaper buttons.
2. Select Saturate Shaper mode by using the Mode button or by clicking on the name. You should immediately hear a strong distorted signal applied to Osc A.
3. Set the Shaper Amount knob to 39 to turn down the distortion effect.

Next, you'll route Osc B to Filter B and do some more damage:

1. Activate the Route Oscillator B to Filter B button. Filter B should already be activated and ready to use. Also note that the Env button is already active, which means that the Filter Envelope can be used at this time.
2. Set Filter mode to Comb– by using the Mode button or by clicking on the name.
3. Set the Resonance knob to 70.
4. Set the Frequency Filter knob to 99.

You can also assign Osc A to Filter B by clicking on the Route Osc A to Filter B button. I suggest not activating it for this tutorial because Osc A has a very strong signal of its own.

Additionally, you can route Filter B to the Shaper by clicking on the Route Filter B to Shaper button, which is located between Filter B and the Shaper sections. This will add a pleasant distortion to Filter B, which sounds pretty cool.

To finish with the Filter and Shaper sections, use the Filter Envelope on Filter B. Set the envelope parameters to these values:

- ▷ **Amount:** 32
- ▷ **Attack:** 38
- ▷ **Decay:** 59
- ▷ **Sustain:** 64
- ▷ **Release:** 10

Programming the Keyboard Mode Parameters

You're in the home stretch. You can finish this patch by making a few adjustments to the Keyboard Mode parameters of the Malström, as follows:

- ▷ **Polyphony:** By default, the Malström has Polyphony set to 8, and this setting is fine for a bass synth sound. You might even want to set Polyphony to 1 so that you can make this a monophonic synth.
- ▷ **Mod Wheel:** Set the A/B Selector to its default position. Assign a negative value to the Shift knob in the Mod Wheel section so it will decrease in value as the mod wheel is used. Assign a positive value to the Index knob in the Mod Wheel section.
- ▷ **Portamento:** Assigning a value of 34 to this parameter will create a sliding effect that sounds great with monophonic bass synths.

After all is said and done, your new bass patch should sound pretty awesome and work well with just about any form of electronic music. Just make sure to click on the Save Patch button to save your work.

For the bold explorers out there, I suggest some free-form experimentation. Sequence a short loop, start it playing, and then use your ears as you switch graintables and adjust the Motion, Shift, Index, Shaper, Modulation, and Filter parameters. You will quickly find that there are no upper (or outer) limits to what weird and wonderful sounds you can create.

Moving On

As you have seen in this chapter, the Malström is a true synthetic playground with nearly limitless creative possibilities. In the next chapter, you'll get to say hello to the synth god of thunder, Thor!

8

Thor: Close-Up

W HEN IT COMES TO GOING ABOVE AND BEYOND TO PLEASE THE HARD-CORE SYNTH FAN, Reason's centerpiece to the Device Rack is Thor (see Figure 8.1). And like the mythical god of thunder, Thor has more than enough power to give your songs that extra kick of dynamics with filters, effects, and, yes, a built-in step sequencer. In other words, you're going to love this synth.

Figure 8.1
© Propellerhead Software AB.

Polysonic: Many Synths

At first sight, you will certainly notice that Propellerhead has yet again coined a new phrase to describe this synthetic wonder, which is *polysonic*. If you ask the staff there, I'm sure that they've got a great PR sort of way to tell you how they came to call it such. But to me, polysonic suggests that Thor is not just one but rather a palette of different types of synthesis, mixed together to create truly unique sounds and textures. These forms of synthesis include the following:

▷ Subtractive

▷ Wavetable

▷ Phase modulation (PM)

▷ Frequency modulation (FM)
▷ Multi oscillation
▷ Noise

In addition, Thor sports an impressive step sequencer, real-time effects and filters, and an impressive modulation bus, all of which can be routed in a variety of ways. So in essence, this makes Thor a semi-modular synthesizer.

> **TIP:** I'm sure that upon your first look at Thor, you're thinking, "How am I going to figure this all out?" Well, the good news is that you've already read about most of the components that make up Thor. For example, the SubTractor is all about subtractive synthesis, whereas the Malström shares a similarity or two with wavetable. So worry not, brave readers; Thor is a piece of cake to navigate, as you will see throughout this chapter.

Take a Tour of Thor

You're now ready to push on and start exploring Thor, so I'm going to break it down and tackle each of the following sections step by step.

▷ **The Controller panel:** This is the first thing you see when you create an instance of Thor.
▷ **The Programmer:** This is where you tweak to your heart's content.
▷ **The Modulation Bus:** From here, you can create simple or complex modulation curves to control Thor's parameters in real time.
▷ **The Step Sequencer:** This is where you can create different patterns, such as melodies or modulation sources.

The chapter also covers the control voltage (CV) connections on the back of Thor. After you explore them, you'll apply what you have learned by building a few different patches.

The Controller Panel

Upon first loading an instance of Thor, you'll immediately see the Controller panel, which displays and controls Thor's performance parameters (see Figure 8.2). Obviously, this is just an abbreviated look for Thor because it's a very complex synth. The Controller panel is simply a way to load patches easily and begin playing with the real-time parameters, such as Portamento and Pitch.

Figure 8.2
© Propellerhead Software AB.

Because you've seen a few of these common parameters already in past chapters of this book, I'll just briefly list them, as there's no need for in-depth discussion.

▷ **Patch Browser:** This works exactly as in other devices.
▷ **Pitch Wheel:** No mystery here. There is also a Range setting above, which governs the amount of pitch (+/− 2 octaves).
▷ **Mod Wheel:** Although this is a common parameter, you'll find that there are several sources that can be routed to this wheel, making it quite versatile.
▷ **Master Volume:** This knob adjusts the overall amplitude of Thor.

Now let's dig into the more complicated parameters of Thor, starting with the keyboard modes. Although most of these parameters may seem a little common, like Portamento, Thor introduces some additional features that set it apart from anything you've learned about up to this point.

Thor includes two kinds of polyphony, as you can see from Figure 8.2.

▷ **Polyphony:** This is the standard polyphony that you've already read about in previous chapters. Thor supports a polyphony count of 0–32 voices.

▷ **Release Polyphony:** This is a unique type of polyphony that deals with the decay of your patches. Simply put, Release Polyphony manages the number of notes that are allowed to decay naturally after you release a note on your keyboard. It has a maximum value of 32, just like the regular polyphony. When set to its lowest value of 0, any notes played after released notes simply cut those released notes.

NOTE: Keep in mind that the greater the polyphony count, the more CPU you use.

In addition to the polyphony are the play modes, which you can select by clicking on them with your mouse or by using the Mode button. Let's discuss them in detail.

▷ **Mono Legato:** This simple monophonic mode does not retrigger the envelope.

▷ **Mono Retrig:** This monophonic mode does exactly the opposite, triggering the envelope even if another note is already held down.

▷ **Polyphonic:** When this mode is selected, Thor plays notes according to the number of polyphony and release polyphony that are assigned to it.

Moving to the right, the Portamento knob creates a sliding effect between played notes. The knob determines the amount of time it will take to slide from one note to another. It can be used with either monophonic or polyphonic patches and is a great tool for creating some interesting effects. There are three modes:

▷ **Off:** No Portamento effect.

▷ **On:** The Portamento effect happens no matter what notes you play on the keyboard.

▷ **Auto:** When this mode is selected, you hear the effect only when more than one note is played. However, if the mono modes are selected, Portamento will affect the legato notes.

The Trigger section dictates how Thor will be played:

▷ **MIDI:** Selecting this option tells Thor to respond only when receiving note information via MIDI.

▷ **Step Seq (Sequencer):** Selecting this option tells Thor to respond when receiving note information from the Step Sequencer.

▷ **Both:** You can select both the MIDI and Step Sequencer options to have Thor respond to either option.

To the right of the Trigger section are the Virtual controls, which consist of two knobs and two buttons (see Figure 8.3). This is a feature unique to Thor, as these knobs and buttons can be assigned to several parameters and can also be easily automated.

Figure 8.3
© Propellerhead Software AB.

All the assignments are handled by the modulation bus, which you'll read about later in this chapter. Note that you can easily label the different knobs and buttons simply by double-clicking on their corresponding labels and typing new names as needed.

In addition, the functions that you assign to the buttons can be assigned to MIDI notes to turn them off and on much more easily. For example, you could route them to the Delay and Chorus power switches and use MIDI notes to turn the effects off and on during a performance, thereby making the performance all the more dynamic. Just some food for thought, but I'll show you how to do this later.

The Programmer

The Programmer is where the real magic of Thor comes into play because there are so many different creative possibilities (see Figure 8.4). I could spend much more time than a book allows, but I'm going to leave that part to you. First things first, let's take a tour through this interface to better understand how everything works.

Figure 8.4

© Propellerhead Software AB.

Because this is a semimodular synth, I'm going to refer to each of these highlighted segments as modules, as that is in fact what they are. Each of these modules is routed or can be routed in a variety of different configurations to produce very different and complex sounds. To make things simple, I'm going to section off and explain each of the following modules:

  ▷ The oscillators
  ▷ The Mixer
  ▷ The filters
  ▷ The Shaper
  ▷ The Amplifier
  ▷ The LFO
  ▷ The envelopes
  ▷ The global parameters

> **TIP:** Because you have already read about a lot of the principles of synthesis, such as the definitions of an oscillator and envelope, I'm going to jump straight into touring the actual functions and features here to save time and get you working in Thor quickly.

The Oscillators

Thor has a total of three slots for oscillator modules, and each allows for six types of oscillators. You can select any of these oscillators by clicking on the pop-up menu arrow at the top-left corner of each slot:

  ▷ Analog
  ▷ Wavetable

▷ Phase Modulation
▷ FM Pair
▷ Multi Oscillator
▷ Noise

You also have the option to select Off to bypass a slot.

Oscillators share several common parameters, so let's get them out of the way first.

▷ **Oct (Octave):** The Octave knob sets the oscillator tuning to one of 10 possible octaves.
▷ **Semi:** This parameter alters the pitch in semitone increments.
▷ **Tune:** This fine-tuning knob adjusts in cents.
▷ **Kbd (Keyboard):** The Keyboard knob tells Thor how to interpret the pitch of each incoming MIDI message.
▷ **Waveform selectors:** Each oscillator can produce one of several different waveforms.
▷ **Sync:** Each of the oscillator modules can be synced. More on this later.

THE ANALOG OSCILLATOR

The Analog oscillator (Analog Osc) is the most common type of oscillator (see Figure 8.5). This module is similar in sound and style to that found in the SubTractor. There are four waveforms from which to select: Sawtooth, Pulse, Triangle, and Sine.

Figure 8.5
© Propellerhead Software AB.

You'll also notice that there is a Pulse Width knob (labeled PW), which affects just the pulse waveform.

THE WAVETABLE OSCILLATOR

The Wavetable oscillator (Wavetable Osc) is fashioned after the classic wavetable synths of the 1980s, such as the PPG Waveterm and Waldorf Wave (see Figure 8.6). Wavetable are compilations of different waveforms combined to create much different waveforms.

Figure 8.6
© Propellerhead Software AB.

You can choose from 32 wavetables here, ranging from the simplest (Basic Analog) to the more complex (Sax) to the actual original wavetables found in the classic PPG synth. This module also includes some exclusive parameters.

▷ **Position:** This knob determines at which point to sweep through the selected wavetable. You'll find that this alters the timbre of the wavetable drastically.
▷ **X-Fade:** The X-Fade option is used to smooth the transition between waveforms found within a wavetable.

PHASE MODULATION OSCILLATOR

The Phase Modulation oscillator (Phase Mod Osc) is unique in that it uses different waveforms to generate harmonics (see Figure 8.7). The Phase Modulation knob (labeled "PM") controls the amount of modulation of one waveform over a carrier sine wave. Adjusting the PM knob morphs the wave shape between a sine wave and the selected modulator wave. This is also known as phase-distortion synthesis, made popular by Casio CZ synthesizers in the mid 1980s.

Figure 8.7
© Propellerhead Software AB.

The first waveform selector includes the following:

▷ Sawtooth
▷ Square
▷ Pulse
▷ Pulse and Sine
▷ Sine and Flat
▷ Saw×Sine (combined)
▷ Sine×Sine (combined)
▷ Sine×Pulse (combined)

The second waveform selector offers the first five waveforms.

FM PAIR OSCILLATOR

The FM Pair oscillator (FM Pair Osc; see Figure 8.8) produces a unique sound through the use of frequency modulation (FM). FM is a form of synthesis that combines a sine wave oscillator called the *carrier* with another sine wave oscillator called the *modulator*. The modulator controls the frequency of the carrier, and different complex harmonics are created by varying the pitch between the carrier and modulator.

Figure 8.8
© Propellerhead Software AB.

The pitch between the carrier and modulator are always proportionally relative, and there are 32 offset values that scale the ratio between the two sine wave sources. The FM Amount knob controls the intensity of the modulator influence over the carrier. When the FM Amount knob is set to 0, there is no FM modulation; raising this control increases the frequency modulation, resulting in more complex harmonics.

MULTI OSCILLATOR

The Multi oscillator (Multi Osc; see Figure 8.9) creates huge, wide sounds by stacking several oscillators of the same waveform type. This module has all the same waveforms as the Analog oscillator, but with additional parameters:

Figure 8.9
© Propellerhead Software AB.

▷ **Amt (Amount):** This knob controls the amount of detune between the multiple oscillators.
▷ **Detune Mode:** There are eight modes or starting points, where the Amount knob will intensify the detune effect. For example, there is an Octave mode, which stacks a lower and higher note an octave apart. The Amount knob can then be used to create strange but interesting detune effects.

Noise Oscillator

Thor's Noise oscillator (Noise Osc) sounds much different from any module I've heard in a long time (see Figure 8.10). It offers several types of noise, most of which can then be manipulated by a modulating BW (Bandwidth) knob, to the right of the different noise waveforms. Noise is particularly useful when creating percussion sounds such as cymbals or snare drums.

Figure 8.10
© Propellerhead Software AB.

> ▷ **Band:** This oscillator produces a pure noise that can be changed to a pure tone by using the Bandwidth knob.
> ▷ **Sample and Hold (S&H):** This is a random type of noise, which sounds a lot like bit crushing, where a pure signal is broken down and degraded bit by bit.
> ▷ **Static:** This is an emulation of static noise that you might hear on a car radio.
> ▷ **Color:** This type of noise is associated with a color type based on its characteristics.
> ▷ **White:** This mode produces a pure white noise, which cannot be altered by the Bandwidth knob.

Additional Oscillator Parameters

In addition to the three oscillators, this section includes a couple of routing possibilities to help shape the overall sound.

> ▷ **Sync buttons:** These buttons will synchronize the wave cycle of oscillators 2 and 3 to oscillator 1. This forces the oscillators to restart when a new cycle begins on oscillator 1. A good way to demonstrate this is to create analog oscillators in the first and second slots. Set the Semi knob on the second oscillator to a non-zero value. If you audition this sound, you will hear a chord of two different notes, one from each oscillator. Now activate the Sync button, and oscillator 2 will sync to oscillator 1. The result sounds like a one note with rich harmonics.
> ▷ **BW slider:** This slider works in combination with the Sync buttons, as they adjust the sync bandwidth. This can create much more pronounced synced sound as the value increases.
> ▷ **AM slider:** This slider creates a ring-modulation effect between oscillators 1 and 2. Simply adjust the slider and then make changes to the pitch settings of either oscillator to hear the effect.

The Mixer

The Mixer is used to mix the outputs of the three oscillators (see Figure 8.11). It's fairly straightforward and easy to use. There are just a couple of key features to point out here.

> ▷ **Balance 1–2:** This knob enables you to adjust the balance between oscillators 1 and 2.
> ▷ **Sliders:** These sliders adjust the volume of all three oscillators. The first slider adjusts the combined volume of oscillators 1 and 2. The second slider adjusts just oscillator 3.

Figure 8.11
© Propellerhead Software AB.

The Filters

Need to do some sonic sculpting on those raw, savage oscillators? If so, you have a large assortment of semi-modular filters from which to choose. (See Figure 8.12.) You can have up to three filters running at once, although the third filter, filter 3, controls the final "mix" of the patch. Filters 1 and 2 are optional. However, should you choose to use them, you do have some options in the routing department. For example, oscillator 1 can be routed directly to filter 1, while in the same patch, oscillator 2 could be routed to filter 2! Another example would be routing filter 1 directly to filter 2. There are loads of possibilities. And, like I said, there are several filter types. (Ever filtered with a human throat before?)

Figure 8.12
© Propellerhead Software AB.

Before you learn about the different filters, it's a good idea to first learn about their common parameters.

▷ **Frequency/Resonance (Freq/Res):** No filter would be complete without these vital parameters. However, these parameters are a little less obvious when discussing the Formant filter, which I'll do later in this chapter.

▷ **Keyboard Tracking (Kbd):** This knob determines how the filter frequency reacts to notes played on your keyboard.

▷ **Envelope (Env):** This knob determines how the filter frequency reacts to the Filter Envelope.

▷ **Velocity (Vel):** This knob determines how the filter frequency reacts to velocity.

▷ **Invert (Inv):** This button inverts how the filter frequency reacts to the filter envelope.

▷ **Drive:** Each filter includes an input gain, which can be used to overdrive the filter effect. Note that the drive reacts differently with the Low Pass Ladder filter.

NOTE: Looking back at Figure 8.12, you'll notice the 1, 2, and 3 buttons to the immediate left of the primary filters. These buttons are used to assign three oscillators to one or both of the available filter modules. Simply click on them to activate them, load a filter, and you're good to go. Just make sure that you click on the Filter 2 to Amplifier button to route filter 2 to the Amplifier; otherwise, you won't hear it.

LOW PASS LADDER FILTER

The Low Pass Ladder filter is fashioned after classic filter modules commonly found on Moog modular synths (see Figure 8.13). There are five filter modes in addition to a built-in shaper, which reshapes the waveform with distortion.

Figure 8.13
© Propellerhead Software AB.

The Self Oscillation (Self Osc) button at the top-right corner is used to create a feedback loop of high-pitched, bell-like tones that can be further enhanced by making use of the built-in saturation shaper and the 24 dB slopes. A word of warning, though: A self-oscillating filter can get very loud and easily clip your mix, not to mention damage your hearing.

TIP: You can use the Keyboard (Kbd) knob to control the pitch to the self-oscillating filter. Just turn it up to its maximum value, and it will produce 12 semitones per octave.

There are two types of 24 dB slopes, and each processes the saturation effect differently. Type I places saturation after the filter going into the feedback loop so that only the resonant signal is shaped. Type II places the saturation at the input of the filter so that both the incoming signal and the feedback loop are shaped.

STATE VARIABLE FILTER

The State Variable filter differs greatly from the Low Pass Ladder filter because it offers filtering possibilities other than just the lower frequencies (see Figure 8.14). Instead, the State Variable filter includes Band Pass mode, High Pass mode, as well as a unique Notch/Peak mode that combines a low-pass and high-pass filter. The filter frequency is then routed to the LP/HP knob that mixes between the two filters. This description sounds a little complicated, I know, but with a little practice, you will quickly find ways to include this filter in your Thor patches.

Figure 8.14
© Propellerhead Software AB.

COMB FILTER

The Comb filter is a bit simpler than the previous two filters that you've looked at (see Figure 8.15). As you will recall from Chapter 7, "The Malström: Close-Up," a comb filter is essentially a series of delays with very short delay times assigned to each delay instance, resulting in a detuned sound. The feedback of these delays is controlled by the Resonance parameter in each filter. The difference between the Comb+ and Comb– filter is the polarity of the feedback into the delay.

Figure 8.15
© Propellerhead Software AB.

FORMANT FILTER

The Formant filter is probably one of the coolest modules I've used in Reason (see Figure 8.16). It's not your traditional filter module; its primary function is to produce vowel sounds by making use of the XY pad to emulate the vowels through filter formant. Aside from the traditional parameters in the Formant filter, the Gender knob offers the ability to alter the timbre of the filter to emulate a male voice or a female voice. Note that the Envelope (Env), Velocity (Vel), and Keyboard (Kbd) knobs affect or offset only the X slider (horizontal).

Figure 8.16
© Propellerhead Software AB.

TIP: There are quite a few "choir" patches available in Thor, but one of the best examples of the Formant filter has to be the I Am Thor patch, which is one of the default patches when an instance of Thor is created.

The Shaper

The Shaper is Thor's onboard distortion (see Figure 8.17). Its primary function is to alter the waveshape of the oscillators by adding a bit of saturation or a heavy digital distortion. It's split up into three parameters:

Figure 8.17
© Propellerhead Software AB.

> **On/Off:** This turns the Shaper on and off.
> **Modes:** There are nine modes of waveshaping, including Soft/Hard Clip, Saturate, Sine, Unipulse, Peak, Rectify, and Wrap.
> **Drive:** This adjusts the amount of waveshaping.

NOTE: Looking back at Figure 8.17, you can see two buttons below the Shaper—one pointing to the left and one to the right. These buttons determine how the Shaper is routed through Thor. Activating the button that points to the left sends the Shaper output to filter 2. Clicking on the button that points to the right sends the output of the Shaper to the Amplifier.

The Amplifier

After you have mixed, filtered, and shaped your oscillators, you're ready to move on to the Amplifier. There are three main parameters to be aware of here.

> **Gain:** This adjusts the overall volume.
> **Velocity (Vel):** This determines how much velocity affects the gain.
> **Pan:** This places the oscillators in the stereo field.

The LFO

The LFO is used to modulate the oscillators by introducing the waveform of another inaudible oscillator operating at a very low frequency. Additionally, this is a polyphonic LFO, which means that every note played will have its own LFO effect. The LFO can generate 18 waveforms from its spin controls that can be applied by making use of the following parameters:

> **Rate:** This sets the speed of the LFO in hertz (Hz). Note that if Tempo Sync is selected, the Rate knob will adjust in note values.
> **Delay:** This introduces a delay prior to the LFO effect.
> **Keyboard (Kbd) Follow:** This sets how much the rate is controlled by the notes played on the keyboard.
> **Key Sync:** This resets the LFO each time a note is played.

TIP: Thor actually includes two LFOs, the second of which is included with the global parameters.

The Envelopes

Thor includes three envelopes that all perform different tasks for your patches (see Figure 8.18). All of them include the standard ADSR parameters (Attack, Decay, Sustain, Release), but they also include a few extra bells and whistles. Let's cover each one.

THE FILTER/AMP ENVELOPES

The Filter/Amp envelopes are used to alter the character of Thor's filter and amplifier over a determined period of time. Aside from the standard parameters, they both include a Gate Trig parameter. On the surface, this parameter is meant to be used as a power button of sorts because it activates the envelopes. But the Gate Trig parameter can also be accessed by way of the modulation bus, which you'll read about later in this chapter.

Figure 8.18
© Propellerhead Software AB.

THE MOD ENVELOPE

The Mod envelope functions a bit differently from the others. For one, the Mod envelope does not have a default assignment. That has to be handled by the modulation bus. It also has a different type of envelope (Attack, Decay, Release, no Sustain), and it includes additional parameters:

▷ **Delay:** This introduces a delay before the envelope takes effect. The range is 0 ms to 10.3 seconds.

▷ **Loop:** This loops the envelope as long as a note is held on your keyboard.

▷ **Tempo Sync:** When activated, this button syncs up all the Mod envelope parameters to the tempo of the song. Each parameter is adjustable in note values.

The Global Parameters

Thor's global parameters affect the entire synth by introducing effects, filters, and a second LFO (see Figure 8.19). Let's go ahead and burn through these modules.

Figure 8.19
© Propellerhead Software AB.

THE EFFECTS

In addition to the Shaper, which you looked at earlier in this chapter, Thor includes Delay and Chorus effects to give your patches a little extra zing. You can read much more about these types of effects in Chapter 10, "Effects: Close-Up." You learned what a delay is, back in Chapter 2, "Recording," when we talked about The Echo. Thor has a very similar "Mini Echo," if you will. Chorus is a very cool effect that modulates an incoming signal slightly in and out of pitch. The result is a fattening effect that really bulks up your patches.

The Delay parameters include the following:

▷ **Time:** This adjusts the amount of time between delay repeats.
▷ **Feedback:** This determines the number of delay repeats.
▷ **Rate:** This determines the rate at which the delay time is modulated.
▷ **Amount (Amt):** This determines how intense the modulation is.
▷ **Dry/Wet:** This adjusts the amount between the unprocessed (dry) and processed (wet) signal. In this case, if the signal is completely wet, you hear only the delay repeats.

The Chorus parameters include the following:

▷ **Delay:** This is similar to the Time knob in the Delay. However, because this is a Chorus effect, the Delay parameter introduces a very short time in the effect.
▷ **Feedback:** This determines the number of delay repeats (same as with the Delay effect).
▷ **Rate:** This determines the rate at which the delay time is modulated (same as with the Delay effect).
▷ **Amount (Amt):** This determines how intense the modulation is (same as with the Delay effect).
▷ **Dry/Wet:** This adjusts the amount between the unprocessed (dry) and processed (wet) signal.

THE FILTER

The third Filter module available in Thor affects the entire synth rather than just the oscillators. Because I have already discussed the different filters available, I won't repeat myself here. The best advice I can give is to try the different filter types to see which one fits your patch. Note that this is the only filter in Thor that does not require a note to trigger it. This capability is useful when you're using the filter to process external audio or to create a sine wave using self-oscillation.

THE GLOBAL ENVELOPE

The Global envelope is a bit more complicated than the others previously discussed because it includes more parameters and must be assigned via the modulation bus. Aside from the standard ADSR parameters, the Global envelope includes the following:

▷ **Delay:** This determines the delay time before the envelope kicks in.
▷ **Loop:** Activating this causes the envelope to loop once triggered.
▷ **Hold:** This creates a hold before the Decay parameter begins.
▷ **Tempo Sync:** This sets the parameters of the envelope to the tempo of your song.
▷ **Gate Trigger:** This activates the Global envelope.

LFO 2

LFO 2 is much like the one you toured earlier in this chapter, as it has most of the same parameters (sans the Kbd Follow). However, unlike LFO 1, this LFO is not polyphonic. Also, it must be assigned to a parameter via the modulation bus, which you'll learn about next.

The Modulation Bus

Once you have crafted your Thor patch using its many oscillators, filters, and effects, you'll want to take your patches to the next level, which is handled by the modulation bus (see Figure 8.20). Here, you can add enhancements and modifications to your patch to make them ideal for live performance, or just to make them sound more creative and spontaneous in your sequences.

Figure 8.20
© Propellerhead Software AB.

Before I get in depth with the modulation bus, let's first consider its main parameters:

▷ **Source:** Sources can be pretty much anything you want them to be inside Thor. Click on the first source of any modulation bus, and you'll find that everything from audio inputs to LFOs to oscillators can be used as modulation sources.
▷ **Destination:** Once a source has been selected, you must select what that source is going to modulate, which is the destination. All destinations have an Amount slider that determines the intensity and direction of modulation for the destination.

▷ **Scale:** The Scale parameter is used to govern the modulation amount. For example, say you set up a simple modulation where the source (LFO 1) is routed to the destination (Osc1 Pitch). If you play a note, you'll hear LFO 1 modulate Osc 1, which will create a pitch-based vibrato. You'll probably not want to hear the note played that way all the time, so you can assign the modulation to an additional parameter that will control or scale the effect, such as a modulation wheel. Once you have selected this parameter, you can then use its Amount slider to determine the intensity and direction of the scale effect.

This information is a lot to take in at one time, but I have created a couple of examples for you to help make more sense out of it. Keep in mind that there are 13 modulation buses. While there is no tooltip to reference them, internally they are numbered from 1 to 13 starting from the top of the left column and going down, then from the top of the right column and going down. There are three types of modulation buses:

▷ Modulation buses 1–7 are Source→Destination→Scale buses.
▷ Modulation buses 8–11 are Source→Destination 1→Destination 2→Scale buses.
▷ Modulation buses 12–13 are Source→Destination→Scale 1→Scale 2 buses.

TIP: To the immediate right of every modulation bus is a Clear (Clr) button. Click this button to reset the bus.

Modulation Sources

At this point, it would be a good idea to list all the possible modulation sources for the Voice section (oscillators, envelopes, LFO, filter 1/2, and the Shaper), as well as the Global section (envelope, filter 3, LFO 2, and so on). Notice the small downward-pointing triangle icons on each routing slot. (This icon always indicates a pop-up menu is available.) Click on the triangle icon or anywhere to the left in the source field to access the Modulation Source pop-up menu (see Figure 8.21).

Figure 8.21
© Propellerhead Software AB.

▷ **Voice Key:** This assigns modulation according to notes and is divided into four possible parameters: Note (Full Range), Note 2 (Octave), Velocity, and Gate.
▷ **Osc 1/2/3:** This assigns any of Thor's oscillators as a modulation source.
▷ **Filter 1/2:** This assigns the audio output of filter 1 or 2 as modulation sources.

▷ **Shaper:** This assigns the audio output of the Shaper as a modulation source.

▷ **Amp:** This assigns the audio output of the Amplifier as a modulation source.

▷ **LFO 1:** This assigns LFO as a modulation source. It's perfect for creating a vibrato or tremolo effect.

▷ **Filter/Amp/Mod Env:** This assigns either of these envelopes as a modulation source.

And now, on to the global modulation parameters:

▷ **Global Env:** This assigns the global envelope as the modulation source.

▷ **Voice Mixer:** This assigns the left and right mixer inputs as modulation sources.

▷ **Last Key:** This applies modulation based on the last monophonic note played, either via the built-in step sequencer or MIDI. You can select Note, Velocity, or Gate to be your source of modulation.

▷ **MIDI Key:** This behaves similarly to Last Key, but this modulation is heard on notes globally. As with Last Key, you have a choice of Note, Velocity, or Gate.

▷ **LFO 2:** This assigns LFO 2 as a modulation source.

▷ **Performance:** This assigns performance parameters (Mod Wheel/Pitch Wheel, Breath, After Touch, and Expression) as modulation sources.

▷ **Modifiers:** This assigns the rotary knobs and buttons as modulation sources.

▷ **Sustain Pedal:** This assigns a sustain pedal to be your modulation source. If you don't have one yet, go to your local music shop and pick one up. It's worth the cost.

▷ **Polyphony:** This sets polyphony as a modulation source. You can use it to create different envelope attacks depending on how many notes you play at one time.

▷ **Step Sequencer:** This assigns one of eight parameters (Gate, Note, Curve 1/2, Gate Length, Step Duration, and Start/End Trig) as a modulation source.

▷ **CV Inputs 1–4:** This allows you to use other Reason devices (Matrix, Redrum, Dr. Octo Rex) as modulation sources via any or all of the CV inputs in Thor's rear panel.

▷ **Audio Inputs 1–4:** This allows you to use the audio outputs of other Reason devices as modulation sources.

Modulation Destinations

As you can imagine, there are also quite a few modulation destinations (see Figure 8.22).

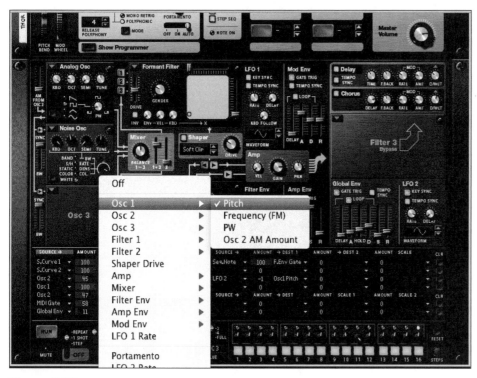

Figure 8.22
© Propellerhead Software AB.

▷ **Osc 1:** This assigns the parameters of Osc 1 (Pitch, Frequency, Pulse Width, and Osc 2 AM Amount) as modulation destinations.

▷ **Osc 2/3:** These are the same as Osc 1 without the AM option.

▷ **Filter 1/2:** This assigns the parameters of either filter 1 or filter 2 (Audio Input, Frequency, Frequency [FM], Res, Drive, Gender, LP/HP Mix) as modulation destinations.

▷ **Shaper Drive:** This assigns the Shaper drive as a modulation destination.

▷ **Amp:** This assigns the velocity, pan, and input of the Amplifier as modulation destinations.

▷ **Mixer:** This assigns the parameters of the Mix section (Osc 1+2 Level/Balance, Osc 3 Level) as modulation destinations.

▷ **Filter/Amp/Mod Env:** These assign the parameters of either envelope as modulation destinations.

▷ **LFO 1 Rate:** This assigns the LFO 1 Rate as a modulation destination.

And here are the global destinations:

▷ **Portamento:** This sets the Portamento time as a modulation destination.

▷ **LFO 2 Rate:** This sets the rate of LFO 2 as a modulation destination.

▷ **Global Envelope:** This assigns any of the Global envelope parameters as a modulation destination.

▷ **Filter 3:** This assigns several filter 3 parameters (Left/Right Inputs, Freq, Freq [FM], Resonance) as modulation destinations.

▷ **Chorus:** This assigns almost any of the Chorus parameters (Dry/Wet, Delay, ModRate, Mod Amount, Feedback) as modulation destinations.

▷ **Delay:** This assigns almost any of the Delay parameters (Dry/Wet, Time, Mod Rate, Mod Amount, and Feedback) as modulation destinations.

▷ **Step Sequencer:** This assigns any of five Step Sequencer parameters (Trig, Rate, Transpose, Velocity, and Gate Length) as modulation destinations.

▷ **CV Outputs 1–4:** These set any of the four CV outputs as destinations.

▷ **Audio Outputs 1–4:** These assign any of the four audio outputs as destinations.

Some Modulation Examples

Now that you have a good idea of how the modulation bus works, let's put that knowledge to the test by going through a few modulation exercises. Remember, adjusting modulation takes a bit of practice, so these exercises are pretty basic.

This first example illustrates a well-known effect, which is to have the modulation wheel open and close a filter. Be sure to initialize your patch before beginning by opening the Edit menu and choosing Initialize Patch.

1. In the Filter 1 slot, load the Formant filter.
2. In the modulation bus, navigate to modulation bus 1, in the upper-left corner. Click on the source field to access the pop-up menu, select Performance, and choose ModWheel as your source.
3. Assign an amount of 100.
4. Now select your destination by clicking on the destination field, selecting Filter 1, and choosing Y.

Play a note and try out the modulation wheel. The Formant filter responds by creating a vowel sound that opens and closes. You can also try assigning an amount of −100 to get the exact opposite effect.

In the next example, you create a tremolo effect and use the Rotary knob to control the effect. You can continue using the same patch from the previous example.

1. On modulation bus 2, select LFO 1 as your source.
2. Set the modulation amount to 100.
3. Open the Destination field drop-down menu, select Amp, and choose Gain as your destination.

At this point, you should now be able to clearly hear the effect. You can enhance this effect by using different waveforms in LFO 1 and changing the rate amount.

Now, let's make it a bit more of a performance effect by routing it to the Rotary 1 knob.

1. On modulation bus 2, Set the scale amount to 100.
2. Click on the modulation bus 2 Scale field to open the pop-up menu, choose Modifiers, and select Rotary 1.

Play a note and use the first rotary knob in the Thor Play parameters. This now controls the tremolo effect.

The Step Sequencer

As a synth, Thor is one commanding creation of software. And as if it couldn't get better, Thor's Step Sequencer offers a selection of powerful features and musical creativity that you can use as a source of either melodies or modulation (see Figure 8.23). Up to 16 steps in total can be sequenced with a variety of data, including note, velocity, and gate. All in all, this thing really packs a punch.

Figure 8.23

© Propellerhead Software AB.

TIP: If you've been reading this book from cover to cover, this is certainly not the first time you've seen a step sequencer. Redrum has a first-rate sequencer of its own, as does the Matrix. However, you'll find that the Thor Step Sequencer includes a few more tricks up its sleeves than either of the aforementioned sequencers, so read on carefully.

The Basics

Before you can get to sequencing Thor, you should probably take a couple of minutes to familiarize yourself with the basic layout of the Step Sequencer to better understand it.

▷ **Run:** This button is used to start and stop the Step Sequencer.
▷ **Mute:** This LED lights up whenever Thor is muted in the sequencer. However, the LED does not light up if Thor is muted from the Mixer.

Next up are the Run modes:

▷ **Off:** The sequencer does not play.
▷ **Step:** The sequence advances one step at a time each time the Run button is clicked.
▷ **One Shot:** The sequence plays through one time and then stops.
▷ **Repeat:** The sequence plays continuously until the Run button is clicked again.

After selecting a Run mode, you can select one of five sequence directions:

▷ **Forward:** The sequence simply plays from left to right and then jumps back to the left.
▷ **Reverse:** The sequence does exactly the opposite by playing from right to left and then jumping back to the right.
▷ **Pendulum 1:** This plays the sequence from left to right, repeats the last step, and then plays right to left. It then repeats the first step and starts over again.
▷ **Pendulum 2:** This plays the sequence from left to right and then right to left continuously.
▷ **Random:** This direction plays the sequence steps in random order.

Now let's move on to the right. The Rate setting controls the speed of the Step Sequencer. This can be set to either hertz or note values (if the Sync button is activated). You can change the value of this setting by clicking and dragging up or down on the knob.

As mentioned, up to 16 steps can be filled to the brim with sequencing data, and that data is determined by the Edit controls. These are just to the left of the sequencer steps. Note that as you select these controls and assign values to them in the sequence (by using the knobs of each step), the Value readout displays either the numeric or note value (either length or number) of each step.

▷ **Note:** This allows you to enter note data on a step-by-step basis. An additional switch to the right of this parameter governs the note range of the sequence. You can select two octaves, four octaves, or full range.
▷ **Velocity:** This sets the velocity of each sequenced step.
▷ **Gate Length:** This sets the length of each sequenced step.
▷ **Step Duration:** This sets the length of each step in the sequence. For example, the first step can be a 1/4 note, the next can be an 1/8 note; the possibilities are endless.
▷ **Curve 1/2:** These set the value of curve data on a step-by-step basis. As mentioned, these curves are assigned through the modulation bus.

Write a Quick Sequence

Now, it's time to put your new knowledge to the test and write in a quick first sequence.

1. Start by selecting a Thor patch that would work well for sequencing, such as a bass or lead patch.
2. Turn off a few sequencer steps to create an interesting rhythm. Try turning off steps 2, 7, 11, and 15 (see Figure 8.24).

Figure 8.24
© Propellerhead Software AB.

Click the Run button to hear the sequence. Keep in mind that you'll want to set the Play mode to Repeat. At this point, it would be a good idea to enter some notes into the sequence. Try the following notes.

  ▷ **Step 1:** C#2
  ▷ **Step 3:** C4
  ▷ **Step 4:** C3
  ▷ **Step 5:** G4
  ▷ **Step 6:** C5
  ▷ **Step 8:** C3
  ▷ **Step 9:** C3
  ▷ **Step 10:** C3
  ▷ **Step 12:** C#4
  ▷ **Step 13:** F4
  ▷ **Step 14:** D#2
  ▷ **Step 16:** D#2

> **TIP:** If you listen to your sequence and you want to start over, you can simply click the Reset button at the far right of the Step Sequencer. Just note that clicking this button resets everything (note value, gate length, curve date, and so on), so proceed with caution.

You've written out a pretty interesting melodic line, so from this point on, you should try to spice it up a bit by making use of the additional Edit parameters. For example, you could select Gate Length and write in a more interesting gate pattern that makes use of staccato note lengths versus legato. You could also try altering the velocity of different notes to create a dynamic impact. The sky's the limit really, so let your hair down and experiment.

CV/Audio Connections

Press the Tab key to flip the Rack screen around, and you'll see that Thor has many connections that can be used to sequence with the Matrix or RPG-8, modulate other devices, or be modulated by other devices (see Figure 8.25). In addition, Thor includes several audio I/Os for pushing the creative limits of soft synthesis.

> **TIP:** Take a quick look at the back of the Thor interface, and you'll notice that the programmers have provided a neat cheat sheet of sorts. It lists several modulation and routing possibilities. This can be a real helper when you are just starting down the road of modular synthesis.

Audio Outputs

The audio output connections are used to output the signal from Thor to the Reason mixer. There are a couple of options:

  ▷ **Mono/Left (1) and Right (2):** These are the main outputs of Thor. Note that if you build a mono patch with Thor, use output 1 to retain the proper effect.
  ▷ **Audio Outputs 3/4:** These are the additional audio outputs, which can be assigned from the modulation bus.

Audio Input

As you learned in the previous chapter, audio inputs on a soft synth are hot, and Thor has four of them. You can literally route just about any Reason device output to these inputs and then assign them to Thor's various modulation inputs via the modulation bus.

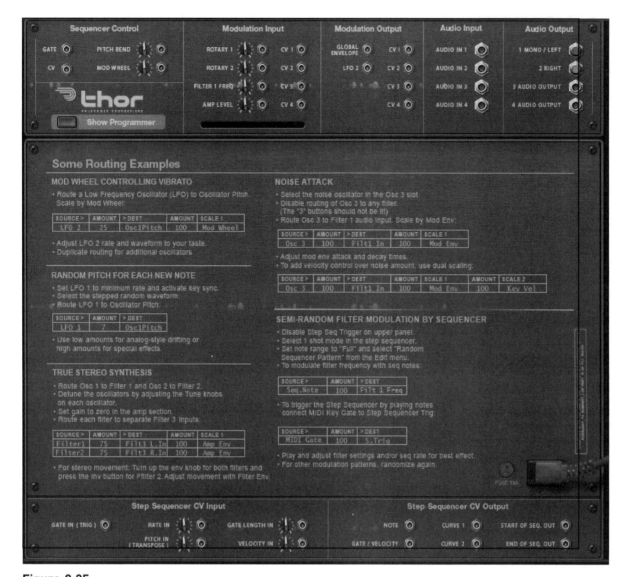

Figure 8.25
© Propellerhead Software AB.

Let's try an interesting experiment:

1. Create a new Reason song.
2. Create instances of Thor and Redrum.
3. Select the Percutron patch for Thor. This is a percussion pitch-based patch that makes use of the Step Sequencer.
4. In the Redrum sequencer, write a hi-hat pattern that has lots of dynamics.
5. Press the Tab key to flip the interface.
6. Disconnect the outputs of Redrum and connect Redrum's hi-hat output to Thor's Audio In 1 (see Figure 8.26).
7. Press the Tab key to flip the interface again.
8. Use Thor's modulation bus to route Audio In 1 as the source to oscillator 1's Pitch or FM amount (see Figure 8.27). Note that this will require you to clear a Modulation slot, as the Percutron patch uses all available slots.

At this point, you can run the step sequencers of both Reason devices, and you should now hear the hi-hat pattern modulating the pitch or FM of oscillator 1 of Thor.

Modulation Input/Output

Moving to the left, you'll see that Thor offers a lot of possible CV I/O connections for modulation (see Figure 8.28). This can lead to some serious modulating bliss if you play your cards right. For example, you could use LFO 2 to modulate in sync with the CV input of another Reason device—for example, the Damage Control CV input of Scream 4, which would cause the amount of distortion to rise and fall in time with the tempo of your song. Or, you could also use the LFO CV output of Dr. Octo Rex to modulate the filter 1 frequency 1 CV input of Thor. And the list goes on and on and on.

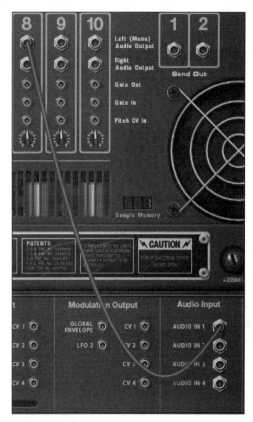

Figure 8.26
© Propellerhead Software AB.

Figure 8.27
© Propellerhead Software AB.

Figure 8.28
© Propellerhead Software AB.

Let's start with the modulation outputs:

▷ **Global Envelope:** This connection routes the output of the Thor Global envelope to any CV input.

▷ **LFO 2:** This connection routes the output of LFO 2 to any CV input.

▷ **CV 1–4:** These modulation outputs are assignable through the modulation bus and can route the CV output of just about any Thor parameter to the CV input of your choosing.

And now, the modulation inputs. Note that these have Amount knobs that intensify or decrease the effect.

▷ **Rotary 1/2:** These modulation inputs are used to route the CV outputs of any Reason device to the Rotary knobs on the front of the Thor interface. Remember that these knobs can be assigned to just about any Thor parameter.

▷ **Filter 1 Frequency:** This modulation input controls the Filter Frequency knob of filter 1.
▷ **Amp Level:** The modulation input alters the Amp envelope on the front of the Thor interface.
▷ **CV 1–4:** These inputs allow you to send modulation data to just about any Thor parameter via the modulation bus.

> **NOTE:** Keeping in line with the other Reason synths that you've already read about, Thor also includes a pair of CV inputs for the Modulation Wheel and Pitch Wheel parameters. Additionally, there are Sequencer Control inputs for the gate and CV, which are used to link up to an instance of the Matrix sequencer.

Step Sequencer CV Inputs/Outputs

Scroll down to the bottom of the Thor interface, and you'll see that the Step Sequencer also has its own set of CV inputs and outputs (see Figure 8.29). Every parameter that you alter in a Thor sequence (Note, Gate, Velocity, and so on) can be used as a CV output. Conversely, you can use the CV outputs of other Reason devices, such as the Matrix sequencer, to control most of the vital inputs of the Thor sequencer.

Figure 8.29
© Propellerhead Software AB.

▷ **Gate In (Trig):** This CV input triggers the gate input of the Step Sequencer. A good way to check this out is to route the slice gate output of Dr. Octo Rex to this input. Load up a REX file and let the fun begin.
▷ **Rate In:** This CV input controls the rate of the Step Sequencer. Try connecting the curve CV output of the Matrix sequencer to this.
▷ **Pitch In (Transpose):** This input alters the pitch of the Step Sequencer. Try connecting the LFO output of any other Reason device to this input.
▷ **Gate Length In:** This input alters the gate, or note length, of the sequencer steps.
▷ **Velocity In:** This input alters the velocity of the sequencer steps. Both this and the gate length inputs are perfect for the Matrix or perhaps Redrum.

And now, let's look at the outputs:

▷ **Note:** This outputs the note data from the Step Sequencer to any device.
▷ **Gate/Velocity:** These output gate and velocity data to any device. They might serve as an interesting way to drive the Amp envelope of another device such as Dr. Octo Rex or the Malström.
▷ **Curve 1/2:** These output data from the Curve parameters found in the modulation bus.
▷ **Start of Sequence Out:** This outputs a start message when the Step Sequencer starts.
▷ **End of Sequence Out:** This outputs an end message when the Step Sequencer stops.

Building Thor Patches

By now, you're more than ready to start programming, so let's build some Thor patches to get you going. Throughout this section, I'll help you program a bass and a pad patch. Before beginning each of these tutorials, be sure to reset Thor by selecting Initialize Patch from the Edit menu.

Programming a Bass Patch

Bass patches can be a great starting point when you are learning how to program synths because they are somewhat simple to build. And yet, with Thor and its diverse feature set, any bass patch has the chance to become something unique and creative.

Let's begin by selecting the right kind of oscillator for this patch. Because this is a bass patch, let's keep it simple and use just oscillator 1. Click on the Osc 1 pop-up menu and select Multi Oscillator. After selecting this option, press any key on your keyboard, and you'll hear a rather uninteresting "vanilla" sound play back. So without further ado, make the following changes:

▷ **Waveform:** Set to Soft Sawtooth.
▷ **Detune:** Set the Detune mode to Interval and set the Amount knob to 24.
▷ **OCT:** Set to 3 to create a really low, solid suboscillator sound.

Next, use a Low Pass Ladder filter to add presence and overdrive to the bass patch. Make the following adjustments:

▷ **Drive:** Set to 127.
▷ **Freq:** Set to 21.6 kHz.
▷ **Filter Type:** Set to 24 Type I. This is really more a matter of taste, but this filter type adds much more punch. Also, make sure the Self Osc button is turned off.
▷ **Red:** Set to 80.

Play a couple of notes now, and you'll definitely hear a difference in the low range, especially if you have a subwoofer in your studio. Let's wrap this up by adding a Comb filter in the Filter 3 slot. Once you do this, set the following values:

▷ **Freq:** 2.69 kHz
▷ **Res:** 95
▷ **Drive:** 78

Last but not least, set the Play parameters to the following values:

▷ **Polyphony/Release Polyphony:** 1
▷ **Keyboard mode:** Mono Retrig
▷ **Portamento:** On, and set the knob to 8

At the end, your bass patch should look a lot like Figure 8.30.

Figure 8.30
© Propellerhead Software AB.

Programming a Pad

With all the programming potential of Thor, it would be a crime not to program a pad sound. First things first, make sure that you initialize Thor. And away you go!

Programming the Play Parameters

To start things off, punch the following values into the Play parameters:

▷ **Pitch Bend:** 12.
▷ **Polyphony/Release Polyphony:** 8 (You can choose a greater value if you want, but just remember that you'll eat up that much more CPU.)
▷ **Portamento:** On, and set the knob to 30

Programming the Oscillators

At this point, it's time to start breathing a little more life into this patch by activating and routing the oscillators. Make the following adjustments to oscillator 1:

▷ **Oscillator Type:** Phase Mod Osc
▷ **Second:** Sine×Pulse
▷ **PM:** 74

Now move to oscillator 2, which is going to be an FM oscillator:

▷ **Oct:** 5
▷ **Mod:** 2
▷ **FM:** 91

Finish this off by activating and programming oscillator 3 and selecting the Multi oscillator:

▷ **Oct:** 5
▷ **Waveform:** Square Wave
▷ **Detune Mode:** Random 1
▷ **Amt:** 21

At this point, you should hear only oscillator 1 because you haven't routed oscillator 2 or oscillator 3 yet. Set oscillator 2 and oscillator 3 to filter 2 by clicking on their corresponding numeric buttons next to filter 2. Also note that you need to activate the Filter 2 to Amplifier button as well.

Programming the Filters and Mixer

In this patch, you'll use all three filters, but for the time being, you can start with the two primary filters. By default, Thor provides a Low Pass Ladder filter, and you can continue using that here. Make the following parameter adjustments to filter 1:

▷ **Mode:** 24 Type II, and activate Self-Oscillation
▷ **Drive:** 102, and activate Inv
▷ **Freq:** 317 Hz
▷ **Res:** 101
▷ **Vel:** 103 (This will cause the filter to open differently depending on how hard the notes are played.)

Now, set up filter 2, which is going to be a Formant filter:

▷ **Drive:** 49
▷ **Gender:** 48
▷ **X:** 43
▷ **Y:** 68
▷ **Vel:** 108

Play the patch at this point. You'll notice it has some interesting characteristics, but it's way out of balance. Let's fix that by setting the Mixer to the following values:

▷ **Balance 1–2:** 24 (This will emphasize oscillator 1 over oscillator 2.)
▷ **1+2 Level:** –5 dB.
▷ **3:** –9 dB. (This will make oscillators 1 and 2 the dominant elements in this patch.)

Finally, under the Shaper are the direction buttons. Click on the left direction button to send oscillator 1 to filter 2.

CAUTION: Make sure to save your patch frequently to ensure you don't lose any of your valuable work.

Programming the Amp, LFO, and Amp Envelope

You're almost done with the primary ingredients to this patch. Now it's time to program the Amp, LFO, and Amp envelope to start bringing it "Pad" status.

There's not much to do with the Amp, except to set the Pan to −42. This will sound a little out of balance, but it will make more sense when you look at the modulation bus.

Make the following changes to LFO 1:

▷ **Key Sync/Tempo Syn:** On
▷ **Rate:** 2/4
▷ **Kbd Follow:** 57
▷ **Waveform:** Square Wave

Finally, let's create a nice, slow attack by setting the Attack slider on the Amp envelope to 4.22s.

Programming the Global Parameters

You're getting pretty close to synthetic pad bliss, but you need to make a few adjustments to the global parameters to spice it up a bit, at which point you'll round it off by using the modulation bus. First, let's start with the effects. There's really no reason to use the Chorus, as the patch is already thick enough, so let's add some Delay. Activate this effect and set it to the following values:

▷ **Tempo Syn:** On, and set the Time knob to 6/16
▷ **Feedback:** 50
▷ **Rate:** 0.54 Hz
▷ **Amount:** 25
▷ **Dry/Wet:** 40

Next, you'll introduce a third filter to this patch. Select the Comb filter and make the following parameter adjustments:

▷ **Drive:** 60, and activate Inv
▷ **Freq:** 91.7 Hz
▷ **Res:** 61

Finally, the last of the global parameter adjustments are quick and easy:

▷ **Global Envelope:** Set Hold to 30 ms.
▷ **LFO 2:** Activate Key and Tempo Sync and set the Rate knob to 3/8.

Setting the Modulation Bus

Last but not least are the modulation bus parameters. This last section introduces some modulation to LFO 1 and 2. Make the following parameter settings to modulation bus 1:

▷ **Source:** LFO 1
▷ **Amount:** 63
▷ **Destination:** Osc 2 FM
▷ **Scale Amount:** 100
▷ **Scale:** Modulation Wheel

Play a note and use the mod wheel. At this point, you should hear the FM amount change dramatically.

Now, make the following parameter adjustments to modulation bus 2:

▷ **Source:** LFO 2
▷ **Amount:** 100
▷ **Destination:** Amplifier Pan

Play your patch now, and you will hear a pad sound that morphs over time and also offers a healthy dose of ambience.

Moving On

As you have read throughout this chapter, Thor is a synth's synth when it comes to programming, playing, and, above all, creativity. Now that you have a clear understanding of this wonder, take some time to program your own patches. The next chapter will cover one of the best software samplers I've ever used, the NN-XT.

9

NN-XT: Close-Up

T HE NN-XT IS THE SAMPLER THAT PICKS UP WHERE THE NN-19 LEAVES OFF. For people who have created Reason song files with versions of Reason prior to the addition of the NN-XT, it is a good thing that the NN-19 remains in the program for the sake of compatibility. However, after using the NN-19 as a learning tool, you will probably want to move up to the NN-XT. It's a big step toward more functionality, compatibility, and, of course, creativity (see Figure 9.1).

Figure 9.1
© Propellerhead Software AB.

What Makes the NN-XT Different?

Aside from the extreme graphic facelift, there are many other differences between the NN-XT and NN-19:

▷ **Multilayered sampling:** The NN-XT can trigger samples according to their assigned velocity.
▷ **More outputs:** The NN-XT has eight stereo outputs, or up to 16 mono outputs, with the use of the panning assignments.
▷ **More control:** The NN-XT allows individual control over each sample in a patch.

Sample format is the same for both NN-XT and NN-19 as well as Redrum and Kong. The audio file format support differs depending on which computer OS you are using. The NN-19 can read audio files in the following formats:

- ▷ **In Windows 7:** WAV, AIF, MP3, AAC, M4A, and WMA.
- ▷ **In Mac OSX 10.7:** WAV, AIFF, 3G2, 3GP, MP1, MP2, MP3, MPEG, MPA, SND, AU, SD2, AC3, AAC, ADTS, AMR, CAF, M4A M4R and MP4.
- ▷ **SoundFonts (.SF2):** SoundFonts are an open standard for wavetable synthesized audio, developed by E-mu systems and Creative Technologies.
- ▷ **REX file slices (RX2, REX, RCY):** REX files are music loops created in the ReCycle! program or when editing audio clips inline in Reason. The NN-19 lets you load REX files as patches or separate slices from REX files as individual samples.

A Guided Tour of the NN-XT

It's time to begin your guided in-depth tour of the NN-XT.

The NN-XT Main Display Panel

When you create an instance of the NN-XT, Reason does not automatically expand the device's entire interface; the reason is that it takes up a lot of room and might seem a little intimidating to the novice sampling artist (see Figure 9.2). Rather, the NN-XT main display panel is the first part of the device you will see. The main display includes all the global controls of the NN-XT.

Figure 9.2
© Propellerhead Software AB.

Loading Patches

As with all Reason devices, the Patch Browser is available to locate and load patches, scroll through them, and save them. Because you already know how to browse for patches, you're ready to consider the various formats the NN-XT can import.

- ▷ **SXT:** This is the standard NN-XT patch format extension name.
- ▷ **SMP:** This is the standard NN-19 patch format extension name.
- ▷ **SF2:** This is the common file extension name for SoundFonts. Unlike the NN-19, the NN-XT can import an entire SoundFont patch instead of just single SoundFont files.
- ▷ **RCY, REX, and RX2:** These are the commonly known file extensions for REX files. As with the NN-19, when the NN-XT imports a REX file, it chromatically maps the individual REX slices, starting from the C1 note.

Additionally, the NN-XT can sample audio just like Redrum, Kong, and the NN-19, and can be accessed from the Remote Editor, which you'll read about soon.

Just below the Patch Browser is the High Quality Interpolation button and the Note On indicator, which lights up whenever a MIDI message is received.

Global Controls

To the right of the Patch Browser are the global controls for your loaded patches:

- ▷ **Filter controls:** These knobs are used to control the Freq (Frequency) and Res (Resolution) parameters of the filter found on the NN-XT Remote Editor. Note that the filter must be turned on before you can use these knobs.
- ▷ **Amp Envelope controls:** These knobs are used to control the attack, decay, and release of the amp envelope on the Remote Editor.
- ▷ **Mod Env control:** This knob is used to control the Decay parameter of the modulation envelope in the Remote Editor.
- ▷ **Master Volume:** This knob controls the amplitude level for the NN-XT.

Pitch and Modulation

Located to the far left of the main display, the Pitch and Modulation controls are common to just about every Reason synth:

▷ **Pitch Bend wheel:** This wheel is used to bend the pitch of the sample up and down. The potential range of the pitch bend effect is determined by its corresponding controls found in the Remote Editor.

▷ **Modulation wheel:** This wheel is used to control and modify a number of parameters, such as Filter Frequency, Resonance, and Level. When used effectively, modulation is a key tool for adding expression to your sampled instruments. Note that the modulation wheel is called the wheel or simply "W."

External Control

To the right of the modulation wheel is the External Control wheel. The External Control wheel can receive three MIDI controller messages and then send that data to any of its assigned parameters in the NN-XT Remote Editor:

▷ Aftertouch
▷ Expression
▷ Breath

Additionally, the External Control wheel can be used to send these three MIDI controller messages to the Reason sequencer if your MIDI keyboard does not support these parameters.

Also note that the External Control wheel is labeled "X" in the main display, just as the modulation wheel is labeled "W." These controls will be discussed in greater detail later in this chapter.

The NN-XT Remote Editor

As stated, when an NN-XT is created in the Reason Rack screen, its main display is the only visible element. Just below the main display is the collapsed Remote Editor. Click on the arrow icon located in the lower-left corner of the NN-XT to expand the Remote Editor (see Figure 9.3).

Group parameters   Synth parameters   Sample parameters   Key Map display

Figure 9.3
© Propellerhead Software AB.

At first sight, the Remote Editor looks very complex. But as you read through the guided tour of this beauty, you will soon see that the Remote Editor is quite possibly one of the most well-thought-out and versatile devices in Reason.

There are several sections to the Remote Editor. Here's a rundown of what this section covers:

> **Synth parameters:** The parameters in this section are used to edit and manipulate your sample patches using filters, envelopes, and two LFOs.
> **Group parameters:** These parameters are used to enhance the performance or playing style of the NN-XT. They are similar to the Play parameters of the NN-19.
> **Key Map display:** This area is used to map samples across the NN-XT. Any sample information you need can be found in this section.
> **Sample parameters:** These parameters are used to set the key zones, root keys, play modes, and more for each sample loaded into the Key Map display.

These Parameters Are Not Global: While you're touring the Remote Editor, it's important to remember that, with the exception of the Group parameters, all the remaining parameters you will be using are not global. When you select a single sample from the Key Map display and make any change to the pitch, filter, or modulation, you are affecting just that single sample zone, not the rest of the sample patch. However, if you want to make global changes to the entire sample patch, you can do so in several ways. Here's one:

1. Use the Patch Browser to load a sample patch into the NN-XT. Then open the Edit menu and choose Select All Zones.
2. Click on one of the samples in the Key Map display. Then Shift-click on the additional samples.
3. Click the group of samples you want to make changes to in the Group column. This selects all the samples in that particular group. If there are additional groups, you need to hold down the Shift key and select the next groups as well.

The Synth Parameters

The NN-XT Synth parameters are used to edit and manipulate the characteristics of your samples with ease and precision. To make them easier to understand, I break these parameters into the following groups:

> Modulation
> Velocity
> Pitch
> Filter
> Envelopes
> LFOs

THE MODULATION SECTION

The Modulation section of the NN-XT is one of the most versatile of its kind (see Figure 9.4). Six parameters can be used on an individual basis or grouped together. Additionally, you can assign these parameters to either the modulation wheel (by selecting the W button under each knob) or the External Control wheel (by selecting the X button under each knob). Better yet, you can assign the parameters to both wheels simultaneously by selecting both the W and X buttons.

Figure 9.4
© Propellerhead Software AB.

Take a look at what each of these parameters does:

▷ **F. Freq:** This parameter assigns the Filter Frequency parameters to the Modulation section. When it is assigned a positive value, the filter opens as the modulation wheel's value is increased. Assigning a negative value has the opposite effect.

▷ **Mod Dec:** This parameter assigns the Decay parameter of the modulation envelope to either the modulation or External Control wheel.

▷ **LFO 1 Amt:** This parameter determines the amount of modulation of LFO 1 that is affected by the modulation wheel.

▷ **F. Res:** This parameter assigns the Filter Resonance parameter to the Modulation section.

▷ **Level:** This parameter assigns the level or amplitude of a single zone or several zones to the Modulation section.

▷ **LFO 1 Rate:** This parameter assigns the rate of LFO 1 to the Modulation section.

THE VELOCITY SECTION

The Velocity section enables you to modify a combination of five parameters according to the velocity of notes played by a MIDI keyboard (see Figure 9.5).

Figure 9.5
© Propellerhead Software AB.

▷ **Filter Frequency:** When this parameter is set to a positive value, different velocities control the Amount knob of the filter cutoff frequency. A negative value has the opposite effect.

▷ **Modulation Envelope Decay:** When this parameter is set to a positive value, different velocities control the Decay parameter of the modulation envelope. A negative value has the opposite effect.

▷ **Level:** When this parameter is set to a positive value, the velocity controls the amount of volume. A negative value has the opposite effect.

▷ **Amp Env Attack:** When this parameter is set to a positive value, the velocity controls the Attack parameter of the amplitude envelope. A negative value has the opposite effect.

▷ **Sample Start:** When this parameter is set to a positive value, the velocity modifies the starting time for the sample patch. A negative value has the opposite effect.

THE PITCH SECTION

The Pitch Bend Range setting is used to assign a bend range to the Pitch Bend wheel of the main display (see Figure 9.6). However, the Pitch Bend Range setting has a potential range of 24 semitones, or two octaves. To increase or decrease the bend value, you can click on its scroll buttons or simply click and drag on the display itself.

Figure 9.6
© Propellerhead Software AB.

Below the Pitch Bend Range setting are three parameters used to modify the pitch of individual samples in a patch. Take a look at what each of these parameters does:

▷ **Octave:** This parameter shifts the pitch of a selected sample in octave increments. The range of the Octave knob is +/−5 octaves.

▷ **Semi:** This parameter shifts the pitch of a selected sample by semitone increments. The range of the Semi knob is +/−13 semitones, or two octaves.

▷ **Fine:** This parameter is used to make minimal adjustments to selected samples by cent increments. The range of the Fine knob is +/−50 cents, or half a semitone.

The Keyboard Track knob, labeled "K. Track," is a parameter you use to control the keyboard tracking of the NN-XT pitch. It's a fairly unusual parameter that is best explained when having a patch loaded, ready to listen to the resulting effect.

Load up a bass patch from the Reason Factory Sound Bank and try the following exercise:

1. Select all the samples in the patch by opening the Edit menu and choosing Select All Zones.
2. Navigate to the Keyboard Track knob and turn it all the way down by clicking and dragging with your mouse.
3. Arm the NN-XT sequencer track so you can play your MIDI keyboard to hear the effect. All the keys should now be the same pitch.
4. Now turn the Keyboard Track knob all the way up. Play the C3 note on your MIDI keyboard, followed by C#3 and D3. You should hear the same pitch played in different octaves. Experimenting with the Keyboard Track knob (especially with more subtle settings) can result in some interesting musical scales that you may find inspiring. This can work especially well with tuned ethnic percussion and metallic sounds. It can also allow you to play some ear-grabbing passages that would be very difficult with standard tuning.

THE FILTER SECTION

As with most other Reason devices, the filter uses a combination of resonance and cutoff frequencies to shape the sound and timbre of a sample (see Figure 9.7). Take a look at the available parameters.

Figure 9.7
© Propellerhead Software AB.

To activate the filter, just click the On/Off button located at the top-right corner of the Filter section. Once it is activated, you can also use the Filter controls in the NN-XT main display.

After activating the Filter section, you can then select one of six filter modes by clicking on the Mode button or by clicking on a filter's name. Here's a brief rundown of the available filter modes and the additional parameters:

▷ **Notch:** Rejects the mid frequencies while allowing the high frequencies and low frequencies to pass.

▷ **HP 12:** Filters out the low frequencies while allowing the high frequencies to pass through with a roll-off curve of 12 dB per octave.

▷ **BP 12:** Filters out both the high and low frequencies, while allowing the mid frequencies to pass with a roll-off curve of 12 dB per octave.

▷ **LP 6:** LP 6 is a low-pass filter that filters out the high frequencies while allowing the low frequencies to pass with a gentle roll-off curve of 6 dB per octave. The LP 6's effect can be heard only when changing the value of the Frequency Filter knob because it has no resonance.

▷ **LP 12:** Filters out the high frequencies while allowing the low frequencies to pass with a roll-off curve of 12 dB per octave.

▷ **LP 24:** Filters out the high frequencies while allowing the low frequencies to pass with a steep roll-off curve of 24 dB per octave.

The Filter Frequency (labeled "Freq"), or *cutoff frequency* as it is also called, is used to specify where the filter will function in the frequency spectrum. Once the Filter section is activated, just click on the Filter Frequency knob and drag your mouse up or down to increase or decrease the cutoff effect.

The Resonance knob (labeled "Res") is used in combination with the Filter Frequency. It emphasizes the frequencies set by the Filter knob, which thins the sound out.

The Keyboard Track knob (labeled "K. Track") is used to compensate for the loss of high frequencies as you play higher notes on the keyboard. It can be used to bring the higher played notes to the forefront in a mix.

THE ENVELOPES

An envelope generator is used to modify specific synth parameters, including pitch, volume, and filter frequencies. By using an envelope creatively, you can control how these parameters are to be modified over a specific amount of time. The NN-XT includes two envelope generators. One is assigned to modulation, and the other is assigned to amplitude (see Figure 9.8). Both envelope generators have common control settings, but they serve to control different parameters of the sample zones.

Figure 9.8
© Propellerhead Software AB.

Here are the control parameters in common with both the Mod and Amp Envelopes:

▷ **Attack:** When an enveloped is triggered, the Attack parameter, labeled "A," determines how much time passes before the envelope reaches its maximum value.
▷ **Hold:** Unique to the NN-XT, this parameter is used to determine how long the envelope remains at its maximum potential.
▷ **Decay:** Once the maximum value is reached and held for a determined hold time, the Decay parameter, labeled "D," determines how much time passes before the value begins to drop.
▷ **Sustain:** After the value begins to drop, the Sustain parameter, labeled "S," determines at which level the falling value should rest.
▷ **Release:** Once the value has been set at its rested value, the Release parameter, labeled "R," determines how long it will take until the value will begin to drop to 0.
▷ **Delay:** This parameter determines the amount of delay between playing the note and hearing the effect of the envelope. The Delay knob has a range of 0–10 seconds.
▷ **Key to Decay:** This parameter creates an offset of the Decay parameter, which is determined by where you play on your MIDI keyboard. If assigned a positive value, the Decay parameter will increase. The opposite effect occurs when assigned a negative value.

The modulation envelope can be used to modify the pitch or filter parameters. Aside from the control settings that are found on both the mod and amp envelopes, the modulation envelope also has modulation amount controls that adjust the intensity of pitch and filter changes:

▷ **Pitch:** This parameter causes the envelope to control the pitch of the notes played. If assigned a positive value, the pitch bends up. The opposite effect occurs when assigned a negative value.
▷ **Filter:** This parameter causes the envelope to modulate the Filter Frequency. When it is assigned a positive value, the value of the Filter Frequency increases. The opposite effect occurs when it is assigned a negative value.

The amplitude envelope is used to alter the volume of a sample over time. Aside from the control parameters, the amplitude envelope also has a few additional knobs that control the following:

▷ **Level:** This parameter controls the volume level of a selected zone in the key zone map. It can also control the volume of an entire patch if you select all the zones.
▷ **Pan:** This parameter controls the panning of a selected zone in the key zone map. It can also control the panning assignment of an entire patch if you select all the zones.

▷ **Spread:** This parameter creates a stereo effect by placing single notes played in various places in the stereo field. The knob determines the amount of spread, whereas the type of spread is determined by the Spread modes, which are located just to the right.

▷ **Mode:** Also called Spread mode or Pan mode, this parameter has three settings: Key, Key2, and Jump. Key pans gradually from left to right across the entire range of the keyboard. Key2 pans from left to right and back again over a span of eight keys. Jump alternates the pan left or right each time a note is played.

THE LFOs

The NN-XT includes two independent low-frequency oscillators, or LFOs (see Figure 9.9). As discussed in previous chapters, LFOs do not actually produce audible sound on their own. Rather, an LFO is used to modulate the main oscillators of a synthesizer. The NN-XT's LFOs are designed to modulate the samples themselves.

Figure 9.9
© Propellerhead Software AB.

If you look at both of the LFOs, you'll notice that they share common knobs, but there are some key differences between LFO 1 and LFO 2.

▷ Although LFO 1 supports a number of waveforms, LFO 2 supports only the triangle waveform.

▷ LFO 1 can modulate the NN-XT filter, whereas LFO 2 modulates the pan.

▷ LFO 2's play mode is *always* set to Key Sync. That means the waveform of LFO 2 will always trigger whenever a note is pressed on your keyboard.

The Rate knob determines the frequency of the LFO. To increase the modulation rate, turn the knob to the right. For a slower modulation, turn the knob to the left.

It is important to note that LFO 1 has three Rate modes, as follows:

▷ **Group Rate:** When this mode is selected, the rate of LFO 1 is controlled by the LFO 1 Rate knob in the Group parameters of the Remote Editor. This ensures that all the zones in the NN-XT modulate at the same rate.

▷ **Tempo Sync:** When this mode is selected, the rate of the LFO is controlled by the tempo of the Reason sequencer. If you activate this mode and then begin to make changes to the Rate knob, a tooltip displays the different time divisions.

▷ **Free Run:** When this mode is selected, the LFO runs continuously at the rate set by the Rate knob. If Key Sync is activated, the LFO triggers every time a note is played. Also note that LFO 2 *always* runs in Free Run mode.

The Delay knob is used to set a delay between playing the note on your keyboard and hearing it. Both LFO 1 and LFO 2 Delay knobs have the same capability and range of 0–10 seconds.

LFO 1 has six waveform choices for modulation. You can select these modes by clicking on the Waveform Mode button or by just clicking on the desired waveform.

▷ **Triangle:** This creates a smooth up-and-down vibrato.

▷ **Inverted Sawtooth:** This creates a cycled ramp-up effect.

▷ **Sawtooth:** This creates a cycled ramp-down effect.

▷ **Square:** This makes abrupt changes between two values.

▷ **Random:** This creates a random stepped modulation. Also known as sample and hold.

▷ **Soft Random:** This is exactly like the previous waveform but has a smoother modulation curve.

After you select a rate, delay, and waveform mode, it's time to choose a modulation destination. Although LFO 1 and LFO 2 contain different destinations, I have placed them all in a single list to discuss them:

▷ **Pitch:** This parameter modulates the pitch of the loaded sample patch. It is commonly used for trills and vibrato, but those are just a couple of the many sound design possibilities. The Pitch knob has a range of −2,400 to 2,400 cents (up to four octaves) and is available in both LFO 1 and LFO 2.

▷ **Filter:** This parameter modulates the Filter Frequency. It is a great tool for creating a filter sweep that can open upward (when set to positive) or downward (when set to negative). Note that this parameter is available only on LFO 1.

▷ **Level:** This knob is used to modulate the output level of the NN-XT for creating a tremolo effect. Note that this is available only with LFO 1.

▷ **Pan:** This parameter is used to modulate the panning of a single or multiple zones. It is a great effect to use on orchestral percussion, such as xylophones or glockenspiels. When it is turned to the left, the panning effect moves from left to right in the stereo field. When the knob is turned to the right, the panning effect moves from right to left in the stereo field. Note that this parameter is available with LFO 2.

The Group Parameters

Located in the upper-left corner of the NN-XT interface, the Group parameters apply to all the zones in a selected group (see Figure 9.10).

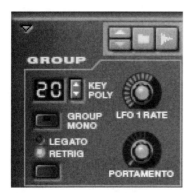

Figure 9.10
© Propellerhead Software AB.

POLYPHONY

Polyphony determines how many notes can be played simultaneously from the NN-XT. When it is set to a value of 1, the NN-XT becomes a monophonic instrument, which is perfect for playing lead synth lines or mimicking monophonic instruments, such as a flute or clarinet. When it is set to a greater polyphonic value, the NN-XT becomes the perfect device for mimicking instruments that are capable of producing many voices at one time, such as a piano, guitar, or choir. The NN-XT has a polyphony range of 1–99 voices, accessible from the Key Poly setting, so that should give you plenty of room to work with.

LEGATO AND RETRIG

Legato is the play mode of choice for monophonic sounds. While in Legato mode, play a note and hold it. Now play another note, and you will notice that the NN-XT will not retrigger the envelope but rather just change the pitch. If you combine this with a good portion of Portamento, you can create a fantastic sliding synth sound. Legato will also work with polyphonic patches. Set the Polyphony to 3 and play a three-note chord on your MIDI keyboard. Now press and hold another note, and you will hear that the new note is played legato style, but it steals one of the original notes of the chord.

Retrig is thought of as the "normal" preference for polyphonic patches. While in Retrig mode, NN-XT envelopes are triggered every time a note is played on your MIDI keyboard, which differs greatly from the legato effect. Retrig can also be used with monophonic patches. Press a note, hold it, and then play another note and release it. Notice that the NN-XT will now retrigger the sample of the first note, unlike in Legato mode.

GROUP MONO

The Group Mono setting is used in combination with notes that are grouped together in a patch. Once the notes are grouped and selected, activating the Group Mono function will bypass the Key Poly value and treat the grouped notes as monophonic. However, this function does not work with the Legato or Retrig play modes.

A real-world example of this would be the open hi-hat, closed hi-hat scenario. When you play an open hi-hat, you want the sound to be cut if you play the closed hi-hat sound. You can easily accomplish this effect with Group Mono by simply selecting both closed and open hi-hat samples, grouping them, and then activating Group Mono. Now play an open hi-hat, let it ring out, and then play a closed hi-hat sample. The open hat should immediately cut out.

LFO 1 RATE
The LFO 1 Rate knob is used to control the frequency of modulation in the LFO 1. This knob is active only when Group Rate mode is selected in the LFO section of the synth parameters.

PORTAMENTO
Portamento is used to create a sliding effect between played notes. The knob determines the amount of time it will take to slide from one note to another. It can be used with either monophonic or polyphonic patches and is a great tool for creating some interesting effects. Try loading a polyphonic patch, such as a string section or piano. Set the Portamento to 45 and play some chords. You will hear a slight sliding effect that makes the patch sound a little funny, but try adding some delay and reverb. After a while, you'll have an ambient masterpiece on your hands.

The Key Map Display
Occupying the majority of the Remote Editor, the Key Map display is where all the action happens when it comes to importing, grouping, and creating sample patches (see Figure 9.11). There are a few similarities to the NN-19 as you will see, but the NN-XT Key Map display is a much more diverse and mature interface that is intuitive and shouldn't take too long to master.

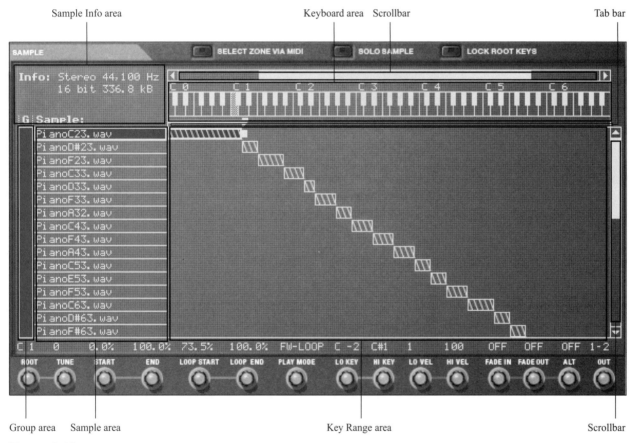

Figure 9.11
© Propellerhead Software AB.

The Key Map display is split into seven areas:

  ▷ **Sample Info:** The Info area is used to display the sample rate, bit depth, and file size of a selected sample.
  ▷ **Sample:** The Sample area is used to list the filenames of the loaded samples in a patch.
  ▷ **Group:** The Group area does not display information. Rather, it is used to select a compilation of sample zones that are assigned to a group.
  ▷ **Keyboard:** The Keyboard area is used to display key ranges, audition loaded samples, and set root keys.

▷ **Tab bar:** The Tab bar is located just below the Keyboard area and is used to display the key range of a selected sample zone. Here, you can resize a sample zone's key range.

▷ **Key Range:** The Key Range area is used to display the sample zones in a patch. Zones can be moved and resized in this area.

▷ **Scrollbars:** Vertical and horizontal scrollbars allow you to view any key range (vertical) or position on the keyboard (horizontal).

Aside from the Info area and scrollbars, which are pretty self-explanatory, let's take an in-depth look at these areas.

THE SAMPLE AREA

All the files used to create a sample patch for the NN-XT are displayed in the Sample area as a list. The Sample area can also be used as a tool to load samples into a zone. To get better acquainted with the Sample area, try this quick exercise:

1. If you have a patch loaded into the NN-XT, clear it by opening the Edit menu and choosing Initialize Patch. This gives you a clean slate to work with.
2. Next, you need to add a zone to your key map so you can load a sample. Open the Edit menu and choose Add Zone to create an empty zone into which a sample can be loaded. Notice that in the Sample area, the newly created zone is labeled "No Sample."
3. To load a sample into the zone, click on the Load Sample button in the upper-left corner of the Remote Editor or double-click on the No Sample label to open the Sample Browser. At this point, you can select a sample and load it into your new zone. Additionally, you can record a sample straight into the NN-XT by clicking on the Start Sample button.

THE GROUP AREA

After you create a number of zones and load samples into them, you can compile these zones into a group. Once you do this, a number of zones can be selected and modified at one time, making it a big time-saver. To create a group, try this quick exercise:

1. Using the previous exercise as an example, create several zones and load samples into them.
2. Once you have created a number of zones, select them all by either choosing Select All from the Edit menu or pressing Ctrl+A (Windows) or Command+A (Mac).
3. Choose Group Selected Zones from the Edit menu. This will place all the zones into one group.

THE KEYBOARD AREA

The Keyboard area is a graphical representation of the virtual keyboard in the NN-XT. It is here that key ranges can be viewed, root notes can be set, and loaded samples can be auditioned without the use of a MIDI keyboard.

Key range refers to the lowest and highest key that will trigger a loaded sample. For example, suppose you've imported a snare drum sample into a newly created zone in the key map. Because a snare drum is a sample that does not have a specific pitch, you will not need more than one or two keys on your keyboard to trigger the sample. By using a key range, you can specify that the snare sample will be heard only if the D1 or D#1 notes are pressed on a MIDI keyboard.

A root note specifies the original frequency at which a sample was recorded. If you record a piano played at middle C, C3 is its root note. It is very important to specify a sample's root note because you want to make sure that the recorded sample retains its realism and natural timbre.

> **TIP:** Later in this chapter, in the section called "The Sample Parameters," you will read about root notes in more detail. You will also get an opportunity to work with root notes again.

It is very easy to audition loaded samples in the NN-XT by using your computer keyboard and mouse. If you are on a Windows PC, just Alt-click on a key in the virtual keyboard. Notice that the mouse icon becomes a speaker icon as you press the Alt key. You also can do this on the Mac by using the Option key.

THE TAB BAR

The Tab bar is one of several ways to adjust the key range of a zone. Start by selecting a sample zone in the key map. Once it is selected, the zone's Tab bar will display the zone's key range and supply boundary handles to make adjustments. Just drag the handles to the left or right to make adjustments to the key range. The Tab bar can also be used to adjust the key range of several zones at one time and shift the positions of several zones at once. For this to work, the zones must share at least one common key range value.

KEY RANGE AREA

The Key Range area is used to adjust the key range of a selected zone and to shift the position of a zone up and down the Keyboard area. The main difference between the key range and the Tab bar is that the key range will make adjustments on an individual basis. If two zones share the same key ranges, adjustments to the key range are still made individually. Zones can also be shifted in the Key Range area on a singular or multiple basis if they are both selected.

The Sample Parameters

Located in the bottom portion of the Key Map display, the Sample parameters enable you to edit any selected zone in the key map (see Figure 9.12). Whereas the synth parameters are used to alter the timbre and tone of a selected zone, the Sample parameters are used to set up loop points, root notes, and route outputs, and to generally help you do some pretty creative things with your samples.

Figure 9.12
© Propellerhead Software AB.

ROOT NOTES AND TUNE

The Root knob is used to adjust the original pitch of a loaded sample. When a sample is loaded into the NN-XT, you need to assign a root as the original frequency of the recorded sample. For example, if you record a piano's C3 note and then import it into the NN-XT, you need to tell the NN-XT that the original pitch of the sample was C3. This is done with the Root knob.

After importing a sample into the key map, you can click and drag on the Root knob until you reach the desired root note. Another way to change the root note is to Ctrl-click (Windows) or Command-click (Mac) on the root note you want.

> **TIP:** Once you have set a root note, activate the Lock Root Keys button at the top of the Key Map display. When it is active, you can still make adjustments to the root note with the Root knob, but if you want to shift the position of the sample zone, the root note will remain in place.

The Tune knob is used to make fine adjustments to your samples. It is used to make sure that the pitch of the samples matches the tunings of your other imported samples. For example, if you import a piano sample with a root note of C3 and then import another sample with a root note of E3, you might need to make fine-tuning adjustments to ensure that the piano samples will play in tune with each other as you make the transition from C3 to E3. The Tune knob has a range of +/− half a semitone.

If you are not sure what the root note of your sample is or which way to tune it, Reason has a solution to help you out. Reason can automatically detect the root note of any imported sample with a perceivable pitch. Here's how it works:

1. Select the zone of the sample whose root note you want to detect.
2. Open the Edit menu and choose Set Root Notes from Pitch Detection. Reason will detect and assign a root note to your sample and will also make any fine-tuning adjustments.

START AND END

The Start knob is used to offset the start position of a loaded sample in the NN-XT. This function can be used for many purposes, such as the following:

> ▷ Removing unwanted noise at the beginning of a sample.
> ▷ Creating different versions of one sample. For example, if you have a sample of a person speaking the phrase "One, two, three, four," you could use the Start and End knobs to isolate each word and map it on its own key without having to perform this task in an audio-editing program.
> ▷ Creating very realistic and dynamic performances perfect for percussion and drums samples, using the Start knob along with the Sample Start Velocity Amount knob (labeled "S. Start") in the Velocity section.

The End knob is used to offset the end position of a loaded sample in the NN-XT. It is useful for removing unwanted sample portions from the end of a sample, such as noise or hiss. To make changes to the Start and End knobs, you can click and drag up or down with your mouse to move the offsets by percentages. If you want to make very fine changes to these knobs, hold down the Shift key while making adjustments to the Start and End knobs.

LOOP START AND LOOP END

In sampling terms, a loop is used to prolong the sustain of a note that is held down on your MIDI keyboard. For example, if you play a piano sample and hold down the key, notice that like a real piano, the note sustains as long as you hold it (see Figure 9.13). This is accomplished by finding a portion of the sample that can be looped continuously to sound like a sustain.

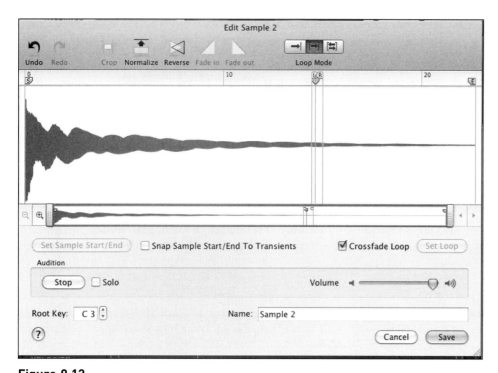

Figure 9.13
© Propellerhead Software AB.

Figure 9.13 shows a loop point that will occur toward the end of the sample. This loop point was created for this guitar sample using the NN-XT Sample Editor. The loop that has been created occurs in an area where the loop start and end differ very slightly in amplitude. When a loop is created there, the loop is not noticeable and sounds very natural when used.

All the samples in the Reason Factory Sound Bank and Orkester Sound Bank have already been assigned loop points, and you will find that this is the case for any sample collection that is commercially available. The Loop Start knob shifts the offset of the loop starting point to the right in a sample. The Loop End knob shifts the offset of the loop end point to the left in a sample.

PLAY MODE

After a pair of loop points has been established, the Play Mode knob determines how the loop will be played. The Play Mode knob offers five choices:

▷ **FW:** The sample will play through once, without looping.
▷ **FW-LOOP:** The sample will play from the sample start to the loop end, and then it will jump back to the loop start and proceed to loop continuously between the loop points until the note is released.
▷ **FW-BW:** The sample will play from the sample start to the loop end. The sample will then play backward from the loop end to the loop start and finally play from the loop start to the loop end. This process will loop continuously until the note is released.
▷ **FW-SUS:** The sample will play from the sample start to the loop end, and then it will jump back to the loop start and proceed to loop continuously between the two loop points. After the note is released, the sample will play to the absolute end of the sample that reaches beyond the loop boundaries.
▷ **BW:** The sample will play backward once, without looping.

LO KEY AND HI KEY

The Lo Key and Hi Key knobs are used to assign boundaries to the loaded samples. The low key assigns the lowest note that a sample can be played at, whereas the high key does exactly the opposite. You'll get a better idea of how this works later in the chapter when you build your own sample patch.

LOW VELOCITY AND HIGH VELOCITY

The Low Velocity and High Velocity knobs, labeled "Lo Vel" and "Hi Vel," are used to assign velocity ranges to the loaded samples. Low velocity assigns the lowest velocity at which a sample can be played, whereas high velocity does the opposite.

Understanding these knobs and how they work is essential when creating a multilayered sample patch. For example, you can create sample zones and assign them all to the same key but give them different velocities. Here's an example of how you would velocity-map four snare drum samples to the D1 note. (Note that this will include all the other sample parameters that you have read about up to this point.)

▷ **Snare 1.aif:** Root D1, Tune 0, Start 0%, End 100%, Play Mode FW, Lo Key D1, Hi Key D1, Lo Vel 1, Hi Vel 32
▷ **Snare 2.aif:** Root D1, Tune 0, Start 0%, End 100%, Play Mode FW, Lo Key D1, Hi Key D1, Lo Vel 33, Hi Vel 64
▷ **Snare 3.aif:** Root D1, Tune 0, Start 0%, End 100%, Play Mode FW, Lo Key D1, Hi Key D1, Lo Vel 65, Hi Vel 99
▷ **Snare 1.aif:** Root D1, Tune 0, Start 0%, End 100%, Play Mode FW, Lo Key D1, Hi Key D1, Lo Vel 100, Hi Vel 127

FADE IN AND FADE OUT

The Fade In and Fade Out knobs are used to assign velocity crossfades to overlapping zones. As discussed earlier in the section "The Key Map Display," it is possible to have two zones that share the same range, root note, and velocity. The Fade In and Fade Out knobs can be used to smooth the transition between these two samples, making for an interesting dynamic effect.

The Fade In knob is used to create a velocity threshold that will trigger a sample when that threshold is reached via velocity. Once the threshold is reached, the sample will fade in rather than abruptly trigger. The Fade Out knob performs the same function, except that when the threshold is reached, the sample will fade out.

Here's an example of how to use these knobs:

1. Create two zones and load a sample into each one. Set the Lo Vel setting for both zones to 1 and their Hi Vel settings to 127.
2. Set the Fade Out knob on the first zone to 40. This will tell the NN-XT to play that zone at its full level when the velocity is played under 40. Once the velocity has reached 40 and over, the sample will fade out.
3. Set the Fade In knob on the second zone to 80. This will tell the NN-XT to play that zone with a fade-in effect when the velocity equals 80. After the played velocity surpasses 80, the sample will then play at its full level.

ALTERNATE

To give your sample performance a realistic sound, you can use the Alternate knob, labeled "Alt," to semi-randomly trigger different sample zones during playback. For example, if you have a sample of a guitar chord playing with a down stroke and a sample of that same chord playing with an up stroke, you can use the Alternate knob to create a pattern where the NN-XT will determine when to alternate between the two samples. Here's how you set up the Alternate function:

1. Create two zones and load a sample into each.
2. Select both zones.
3. Set the Alt knob to the On position. The NN-XT will determine when to alternate between the two samples.

OUTPUT

The Output knob, labeled "Out," is used to assign your sample zones to one of eight stereo pairs of outputs. This capability comes in handy when you work with a sample patch that has many samples loaded in it. You can route each of these samples to any of these outputs by selecting the zone on which the sample is loaded and using the Output knob.

Moving On

Whew! That's a lot of sampling information. If you've made it through this chapter in one piece, it would be fair to say that you probably know more about sampling now than many seasoned professionals! But don't let that stop you from continuing your sampling education. Try your hand at sampling drums, pianos, basses, voices, or a few unique noises from a creaky bedroom door to see how you can twist and turn those samples into music with the NN-XT!

Effects: Close-Up

10

N O VIRTUAL STUDIO IS COMPLETE WITHOUT A HORDE OF VIRTUAL EFFECTS, and Reason 7 is no exception. There are 22 unbelievable real-time virtual effect processors here that are sure to be just what the doctor ordered when a healthy dose of audio spice is needed for your tracks. This chapter digs into 18 of these hotties and shows you how they can be used effectively and creatively. Please note that in addition to the 18 effects discussed in this chapter, Propellerhead has also included a virtual Line 6 Guitar Amp and a virtual Line 6 Bass Amp.

Effects Common Features

As you look more closely at these real-time effects, you will notice that they all share a few common parameters. Each real-time effect includes an input meter, located on the left side of each graphic interface. This meter shows the level of an incoming audio signal. Each effect also comes with a Power/Bypass switch that has three modes:

▷ **Bypass:** When this mode is selected, the input signal passes through the effect module without being processed. It is a good way to compare "clean versus processed" audio signals.
▷ **On:** When this mode is selected, the input signal passes through the effect and is processed.
▷ **Off:** When this mode is selected, the effect is turned off. No audio whatsoever will pass through this effect device.

All the real-time effects support stereo ins and outs and can be used as sends or inserts. However, some of these effects were programmed to be used as insert effects only or send effects only. To help you tell the difference, each effect has a signal flow graph that demonstrates how the effect handles mono and stereo signals. To see a device's graph, press the Tab key to flip the Rack screen around.

There are five signal flow charts used to describe the signal flow through the different effects (see Figure 10.1):

Chart A Chart B Chart C Chart D Chart E

Figure 10.1
© Propellerhead Software AB.

▷ **Chart A:** This can be used as a mono-in, mono-out device.
▷ **Chart B:** This can be used as a mono-in, stereo-out device. That means the effect will create a stereo effect, or it can also be used as a mono effect and panned.
▷ **Chart C:** Connecting both inputs and outputs in stereo makes this device a dual-mono effect because both left and right signals will be processed independently.
▷ **Chart D:** The left and right signals are summed, or combined, before being processed, which does not make it a true stereo signal. However, the effect itself is a stereo effect.
▷ **Chart E:** This is a true stereo processor because the effect uses both left and right signals to generate a new signal. This process can be found in the RV7000 Advanced Reverb, which is discussed later in this chapter.

The remainder of this chapter is a guided tour through each of Reason's real-time effects, with the exception of the Line 6 guitar and Bass Amp devices and the MClass Mastering Suite.

RV-7 Digital Reverb

Reverberation is one of the most important effects needed to create ambience and space in your Reason songs. The RV-7 Digital Reverb is the first of two real-time stand-alone (there is another reverb in Kong) reverbs available in Reason 7 (see Figure 10.2) and is sure to help you add new life to your pads and snare drums.

Figure 10.2
© Propellerhead Software AB.

The RV-7 offers several presets, including the following:

▷ **Hall:** This simulates the characteristics of a standard-sized hall.
▷ **Large Hall:** This simulates the characteristics of a large hall.
▷ **Hall 2:** This sounds very similar to Hall 1, but with a brighter attack.
▷ **Large Room:** This simulates the characteristics of a large room with hard early reflections.
▷ **Medium Room:** This simulates the characteristics of a medium-sized room with semi-hard walls.
▷ **Small Room:** This simulates the characteristics of a much smaller room. Suitable for drums.
▷ **Gated:** This provides a reverb that is fed through a gate with a quick release.
▷ **Low Density:** This makes a thin-sounding, low–CPU consumption reverb.
▷ **Stereo Echoes:** This creates an echo reverberation that pans left and right.
▷ **Pan Room:** This is similar to Stereo Echoes, but with softer attacks.

> **TIP:** Reverbs are without a doubt the most CPU-intensive of all real-time effects. With so many variables and algorithms needing to be calculated in real time, using several reverbs like the RV-7 in one Reason song can overload your computer's processor. If you plan to use several instances of the RV-7 in one Reason song, choose the Low Density preset, which was designed to use less processing power than the others.

Once you have selected the preset you want to work with, you can begin to edit the preset with these available parameters:

▷ **Size:** This knob adjusts the size of the room. Decreasing this value causes the room size to shrink. Increasing the value has the opposite result. Also note that this knob is used to adjust the delay time when using the Stereo Echoes or Pan Room presets.
▷ **Decay:** This parameter adjusts the length of the reverb's decay. Note that Decay is not used with the Gated preset.
▷ **Damp:** This parameter adjusts the equalization of the reverb effect. Increasing this value cuts the high frequencies, making for a warm and smooth effect.
▷ **Dry/Wet:** This parameter determines the balance between a processed, or *wet*, signal and an unprocessed, or *dry*, signal. When using the RV-7 as a send or aux effect, you should set this knob to its maximum. When using it as an insert effect, you should set it in the middle, or 12 o'clock position, so you can hear both wet and dry signals at once.

The Matrix Pattern sequencer can be used to control the Decay parameter of the RV-7. Just route the Curve CV output of the Matrix to the Decay input on the back of the RV-7. Switch the Matrix from Note to Curve mode, select a note value, and create a curve for your RV-7 Decay.

DDL-1

A *delay* effect is an echo of sorts, but not like that of a reverb. It is used to repeat synth phrases, thicken up pads, syncopate drum sounds, and introduce a funky tempo feeling to your songs. One of the best examples of this to be found in popular music is the guitar part for "Run Like Hell" by Pink Floyd. The whole rhythm of the song is based solely on a guitar part played through a delay in tempo with the song. Delay is simply one of those effects you cannot live without. It's an effect that can be used on any instrument, even the less conventional ones, like bass synths. The DDL-1 (see Figure 10.3) is a delay that does it all and, what's more, is incredibly easy to understand and use.

Figure 10.3
© Propellerhead Software AB.

Take a look at the available parameters:

▷ **Delay Time:** The window to the far left of the DDL-1 displays the currently selected delay time in either note-valued steps or in milliseconds. You can have a maximum of 16 steps or 2,000 milliseconds (approximately two seconds).

▷ **Unit:** This button is used to select either steps or milliseconds for the DDL-1. If you select steps, the delay effect synchronizes with the Reason sequencer. If you select milliseconds, the delay effect is in *free time,* meaning that it is not tempo related.

▷ **Step Length:** This button is used to select the note value of the DDL-1 when it is set to steps. You can select between 1/16 notes (1/16) and 1/8 note triplets (1/8T).

▷ **Feedback:** This knob sets the number of delay repeats.

▷ **Pan:** This knob pans the delay effect in the stereo field.

▷ **Dry/Wet:** This knob determines the balance between a processed, or *wet,* signal and an unprocessed, or *dry,* signal. When using the DDL-1 as a send or aux effect, you should set this knob to its maximum. When using it as an insert effect, you should set it in the middle, or 12 o'clock position, so you can hear both wet and dry signals at once.

The Matrix Pattern sequencer can be used to control the DDL-1 via CV input. Just connect the Curve CV, Note CV, or Gate CV outputs of the Matrix to one of these two parameters on the back of the DDL-1:

▷ **Pan:** Once this parameter is connected, the Matrix can pan your delay effect in Step mode. Increasing the amount of input on the back panel of the DDL-1 can intensify this effect.

▷ **Feedback:** Once this parameter is connected, the Matrix can control the amount of feedback in Step mode. Increasing the amount of input on the back panel of the DDL-1 can intensify this effect.

D-11 Foldback Distortion

The D-11 is a fantastic-sounding digital distortion effect (see Figure 10.4). It is a perfect and easy solution for adding a little more growl to your SubTractor bass lines or for going full-on industrial with Redrum. Controlled by just two parameters, the D-11 is a basic real-time effect that can be used as an insert or auxiliary send. It has two parameters:

Figure 10.4
© Propellerhead Software AB.

▷ **Amount:** This knob assigns the amount of distortion to be used.

▷ **Foldback:** This knob is used to add character to the shape of the distortion. At its minimum setting, the Foldback knob sounds dark and flat. At its maximum setting, the Foldback becomes the audio equivalent of nuclear meltdown by introducing a sharp and jarring effect into the mix.

The Matrix can control the Amount parameter of the D-11. Just route the Curve CV output of the Matrix to the Amount input on the back of the D-11, and you're set.

ECF-42 Envelope Controlled Filter

The ECF-42 is a combination filter/envelope generator that can be used to create pattern-controlled filter and envelope effects with any Reason device (see Figure 10.5). This effect should be used as an insert because it is more of a niche effect used for specific sounds rather than a universal effect such as a reverb or delay.

Figure 10.5
© Propellerhead Software AB.

Let's look at the filter parameters of the ECF-42:

▷ **Mode:** This button is used to switch between the different filter modes (BP 12, LP 12, and LP 24). Also note that you can simply click on the name of the filter mode to select it.

▷ **Freq:** This knob controls the Filter Frequency of the ECF-42. When you use the ECF-42 in its static or filter-only mode, this knob controls the overall frequency of the audio. When you use this filter in combination with the envelope generator, this knob is used as a start and end frequency for the created filter sweep effect.

▷ **Resonance:** This knob, labeled "Res," controls the resonance of the filter.

▷ **Envelope Amount:** This knob, labeled "Env Amt," is used to specify how much the filter frequency will be affected by the triggered envelope.

▷ **Velocity:** This knob, labeled "Vel," is used to specify how much the gate velocity affects the envelope.

The envelope parameters of the ECF-42 are available only when triggered by another Reason device, such as a Matrix or Dr. Octo Rex (see the upcoming sidebar for more information). Once the envelope is triggered by another Reason device, you can use any of these standard envelope parameters:

▷ Attack (A)
▷ Decay (D)
▷ Sustain (S)
▷ Release (R)

Triggering the Envelope: Unlike most of the other real-time effects in Reason, the ECF-42 does not function completely as an independent effect and requires an additional Reason device to trigger the envelope. This is done very easily by routing the gate output of any Reason device that has a gate output on the back, such as Redrum, Dr. Octo Rex, or the Matrix.

Here's how to set it up with a Dr. Octo Rex:

1. In any Reason song, create a Dr. Octo Rex and load it up with any available REX file. Click the Copy Loop to Track button to send it to the sequencer.
2. Click on the Dr. Octo Rex to select it and then select the ECF-42 Envelope Controlled Filter from the Create menu. Reason automatically sets up the ECF-42 as an insert effect for Dr. Octo Rex.
3. Press the Tab key to flip the Rack screen.
4. Route the gate output of Dr. Octo Rex to the env gate input on the back of the ECF-42.
5. Press the Tab key again and click Play.

You should now see the Gate LED on the ECF-42 light up because it is receiving gate information from Dr. Octo Rex. At this point, you can use the Envelope parameters.

The Matrix can control the Frequency, Decay, and Resonance parameters of the ECF-42. Just route any of the CV outputs of the Matrix to any of the three available ECF-42 parameters, and you're set.

CF-101 Chorus/Flanger

The CF-101 is a combination chorus/flanger effect device (see Figure 10.6). A chorus/flanger effect is commonly used to add depth and ambience to a sound by introducing a short delay to the audio signal. That delayed signal is then mixed with the original dry signal, creating a much larger sound than before. The size and broadness of the delayed signal are determined by the set delay time, feedback, and LFO modulation.

Figure 10.6
© Propellerhead Software AB.

TIP: To really understand the magic of a chorus/flanger effect, you should hear these beauties in action. Some of the best examples can be found in classic rock tunes of the 1970s and '80s. For example, the vocal track from "In The Air Tonight" by Phil Collins is drenched in chorus, whereas "Never Let Me Down Again" by Depeche Mode and "Barracuda" by Heart are examples of flanging at its best. Sure, they may be "moldy golden oldies" to some, but you can really benefit from exploring the groundbreaking work found in these tunes.

Let's look at the CF-101 parameters:

▷ **Delay:** This knob sets the delay time needed to create the chorus/flanger. For best results, use short delay times to create a flanger effect and medium-to-long delay times for chorus effects.
▷ **Feedback:** This knob controls the amount of effect being fed back into the input, which gives character to the effect.
▷ **LFO Rate:** This knob controls the modulation rate of the LFO. Increasing this parameter speeds up the frequency of oscillation.
▷ **LFO Sync:** This button synchronizes the LFO Rate setting to the tempo of the Reason sequencer. Note that when this button is activated, the LFO Rate knob displays note values rather than the standard numeric value.
▷ **LFO Modulation Amount:** This knob, labeled "Mod Amt," is used to assign a depth to the LFO modulation.
▷ **Send Mode:** This button is used to properly integrate the CF-101 with the other Reason devices. When it is activated, the CF-101 is in Send mode, which means that the device outputs only the modulated signal, making it possible to use the Aux send knob to mix in the additional dry signal. When it is not active, the CF-101 is used as an insert effect, where the device outputs a mix of the dry and wet signal.

Aside from parameters on the front of the device, the Matrix Pattern sequencer can also modify the CF-101. Press the Tab key to flip the Rack screen, and you will find two CV inputs: one for the Delay parameter and one for the LFO Rate parameter. Just route the Curve, Note, or Gate CV outputs of the Matrix to either of these parameters and experiment.

PH-90 Phaser

The PH-90 is a sweeping effect perfect for use with guitar samples, Rhodes piano patches, or pads (see Figure 10.7). At times, it can be confused with a standard chorus/flanger effect, but a phaser is a much different monster once you look under the hood.

Figure 10.7
© Propellerhead Software AB.

A phaser shifts portions of an audio signal out of phase and then sends that signal back to the original signal, causing narrow bands (called *notches*) of the frequency spectrum to be filtered out. The aforementioned sweeping effect happens when these notches are adjusted.

The PH-90 has four adjustable notches in the frequency spectrum that can be modified by way of seven parameters:

▷ **Frequency:** This knob, labeled "Freq," assigns the frequency of the first notch. Once this is set, the remaining three notches move in parallel in the frequency spectrum.
▷ **Split:** This knob changes the distance between each notch. This alters the character of the overall effect.
▷ **Width:** This knob adjusts the width of the notches. Increasing this parameter creates a very deep effect, while also making the overall sound hollow.
▷ **LFO Rate:** This knob controls the modulation rate of the LFO. Increasing this value speeds up the frequency of oscillation.
▷ **LFO Sync:** This button synchronizes the LFO Rate setting to the tempo of the Reason sequencer. Note that when this button is activated, the LFO Rate knob displays note values rather than the standard numeric value.
▷ **LFO Frequency Modulation:** This knob, labeled "F. Mod," assigns the depth of LFO modulation.
▷ **Feedback:** This knob is used to alter the tone of the phaser, in much the same way as a Resonance knob on a filter.

The Matrix Pattern sequencer can also modify the PH-90. Press the Tab key to flip the Rack screen, and you will find two CV inputs: one for the LFO Frequency and one for the LFO Rate parameters. Just route the Curve, Note, or Gate CV outputs of the Matrix to either of these parameters and experiment.

Here's an exercise to demonstrate how to use the PH-90 with Dr. Octo Rex. Be sure to create a new song and load it with a Dr. Octo Rex. Also, load a REX file and send it to its sequencer track.

1. Select the Dr. Octo Rex by clicking on it once. Then select PH-90 Phaser from the Create menu. This will automatically connect the PH-90 to the Dr. Octo Rex to be used as an insert effect.
2. Click Play, and you will hear the PH-90 in action. By default, it already sounds great, but would probably sound even better if it were synced up to the tempo of the Reason song.
3. Click the Sync button to synchronize the PH-90 effect with the song tempo. Then adjust the Rate knob until it reads 4/4, which means that the phasing effect will recycle every bar.
4. Adjust the Split knob to 0. Notice the extra sweep that has been introduced to the low end.
5. Adjust the Width knob to its maximum setting. Notice that the high and low frequencies are accented, but not the mid frequencies, which makes the overall sound hollow.
6. Experiment with setting the Feedback knob to add a singing tone to the mix.

UN-16 Unison

The UN-16 Unison module can be thought of as a simple and straightforward chorus effect (see Figure 10.8). When you use the available parameters, it produces a set number of voices that are each slightly delayed and detuned by way of low-frequency noise. This produces a very thick stereo-friendly chorus that can be used on vocal samples, guitar/drum loops, and so on.

Figure 10.8
© Propellerhead Software AB.

Let's look at the UN-16 parameters:

▷ **Voice Count:** This parameter assigns the number of voices to be produced. You can select 4, 8, or 16 individual voices.
▷ **Detune:** This knob increases or decreases the detuning of the individual voices.
▷ **Dry/Wet:** This knob determines the balance between a processed, or wet, signal and an unprocessed, or dry, signal. When using the UN-16 as a send or aux effect, you should set this knob to its maximum. When using it as an insert effect, you should set it in the middle, or 12 o'clock position, so you can hear both wet and dry signals at once.

The Matrix Pattern sequencer can control the detune parameter of the UN-16. Just connect the Curve CV output of the Matrix to the Detune input on the back of the UN-16.

PEQ-2

The PEQ-2 is a two-band parametric EQ that allows very precise control over the equalization curve of any Reason device (see Figure 10.9). There have been a few additions to the EQ department since the PEQ-2 was released that have a much wider feature set. Still, the PEQ-2 can be used when you just need simple equalization.

Figure 10.9
© Propellerhead Software AB.

The two bands of equalization, EQ A and EQ B, are controlled independently in the interface of the PEQ-2. EQ A is always active and ready to use when an instance of the PEQ-2 is created in a Reason song. To use EQ B, you must first activate it by clicking the B button, found in the lower-center portion of the interface. Once it is activated, its individual parameters are at your disposal.

The graphical display in the left portion of the PEQ-2 is used to show the frequency response curve as it is being created by the EQ parameters. This is a fantastic visual aid that helps you sculpt your EQ curve.

Let's look at the parameters of the PEQ-2:

▷ **Frequency:** This knob, labeled "Freq," assigns the center of the EQ curve. When changing this setting, you should first increase the Gain parameter to hear the effect. The range is 31 Hz to 16 Hz.

▷ **Q:** This knob determines the frequency width of the EQ curve around the set center frequency.

▷ **Gain:** This knob boosts and cuts the gain of the EQ curve.

The Matrix can control the Freq A and Freq B settings by connecting the Curve CV, Note CV, or Gate CV outputs of the Matrix to the Freq 1 or Freq 2 inputs on the back of the PEQ-2.

COMP-01 Compressor

The COMP-01 is real-time compressor that is typically used to level out audio signals that are too loud in the mix and are in danger of digitally clipping. The COMP-01 is a great solution to combat this problem and can be used as an insert effect or send effect (see Figure 10.10). Its parameters are as follows:

Figure 10.10
© Propellerhead Software AB.

▷ **Ratio:** This knob sets the gain reduction of the audio signal according to the set threshold.

▷ **Threshold:** This knob, labeled "Thresh," sets the level that dictates when the compressor effect will kick in. Any audio signal that meets this set level or goes above it is compressed, whereas signals that fall below this level are not affected.

▷ **Attack:** This knob adjusts the attack of the compression effect.

▷ **Release:** This knob adjusts the length of time needed before the audio signal is unaffected by the COMP-01, once its level has fallen under the threshold. At its lowest setting, a short release causes a pumping sound, which is good for kick drums. At its mid to high settings, the release becomes long and sustained, which is good for pads or pianos.

▷ **Gain:** This meter displays the amount of gain reduction and increase in decibels.

To use the COMP-01 as an insert effect (which is its intended use), refer to the "PEQ-2" section earlier in this chapter.

The BV512 Vocoder/Equalizer

One of the coolest effects in Reason 7 is the BV512 vocoder (see Figure 10.11). This effect is commonly used to create robotic voices in dance and performance music. Another popular use of a vocoder is to create a "choir of synthetic voices" as heard in songs by Moby and New Order. Possibly the single most famous use of a vocoder in popular music is the opening of the 1980s hit "Mr. Roboto" by Styx. A beautiful and very artistic use of vocoder can be found in another 1980s track, "O Superman," by Laurie Anderson.

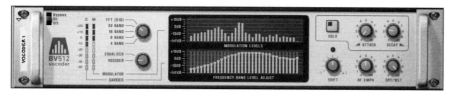

Figure 10.11
© Propellerhead Software AB.

What Is a Vocoder?

A vocoder is an effect that uses two separate sources of input to create a new audio signal by applying the frequency bands of one signal to the other. These two separate audio sources are as follows:

▷ **The carrier.** The carrier is ideally an audio source that is constantly generating sound. A good example of this is a string pad playing from the SubTractor in a sequence that is looped continuously.

▷ **The modulator.** The modulator is typically an audio source such as a spoken voice or vocal track. Another typically used modulator is a drum loop for creating rhythmically enhanced sounds.

Once you have these two elements, they are then routed to their appropriate vocoder inputs. The modulator is divided into a set number of bands (4, 8, 16, 32, or 512) by using band-pass filters. These separate bands are then sent to an envelope follower, which is a device that continuously monitors and analyzes the signal levels. Meanwhile, the carrier is processed with the same number of bands as the modulator. The same frequency ranges used in the modulator's band-pass filters are also applied to the carrier. This way, the carrier will have the same frequency characteristics as the modulator. That means if the modulator gets louder or more dynamic in shape, the carrier will emulate this.

> **TIP:** If you want to hear good audio examples of vocoding, listen to just about any CD by Laurie Anderson ("O Superman"), Daft Punk ("Around the World"), Air ("Remember"), or Zapp and Roger ("More Bounce to the Ounce").

Let's look at the basic parameters of the BV512:

▷ **Level meters:** These meters display the signal level of the carrier and the modulator.

▷ **Band switch:** This switches between the number of filter bands (4, 8, 16, 32, or 512).

▷ **Equalizer/Vocoder switch:** This switches the BV512 between Vocoder mode and Equalizer mode. Note that when the BV512 is in Equalizer mode, the modulator input is not used.

▷ **Modulation Levels display:** This displays the overall spectrum of the modulation signal.

▷ **Frequency Band Level Adjust:** This displays the levels of the individual filter bands. When this section is used in Vocoder mode, each band adjusts the sound and shape of the vocoder. When this section is used in Equalizer mode, each band adjusts the amplitude of the individual frequencies in the EQ curve. After making adjustments to the individual bands, you can use the Reset Band Levels option from the Edit menu.

▷ **Hold:** When activated, this button freezes the current filter settings. The modulator signal no longer affects the carrier in this mode. Clicking it again releases the filter settings.

▷ **Attack:** This affects the overall attack of the frequency bands. Increasing the Attack setting can create some very cool pad sounds. Note that when the BV512 is in Equalizer mode, this parameter is not available.

▷ **Decay:** This parameter affects the overall decay of the frequency bands. As with the Attack, this parameter is not available when the BV512 is used as an equalizer.

▷ **Shift:** This shifts the carrier signal filters up and down, creating a sweeping effect.

▷ **High Frequency Emphasis:** This knob, labeled "HF Emph," increases the high frequencies in the carrier signal.

▷ **Dry/Wet:** This knob mixes between the unprocessed (dry) signal and the processed (wet) signal.

The BV512 as an Equalizer

The BV512 can also be used as a graphic equalizer. Capable of supporting up to 512 bands of equalization, the BV512 is perfect for enhancing individual devices in a Reason song or can even be used as a mastering equalizer.

Follow these steps to learn how to use the BV512 as a mastering equalizer:

1. Near the top of the Rack screen, click the Show Insert FX button on the Master Section Device.
2. Right-click on the Master Section Device and select Clear Insert FX from the menu.
3. Locate the BV512 Vocoder device in the Device Palette screen of the Tool Window and drag the BV512 Vocoder into the Insert slot of the Master Section.
4. If the Bypass button on the Master Section is lit blue, click on it so that the Master Section insert effects will not be bypassed.
5. On the BV512 Vocoder, set the Equalizer/Vocoder switch to Equalizer. Also, set the Band switch to 512 for the best-quality equalization. (Read the upcoming note for details.)

At this point, you can now load some Reason devices, sequence them, and play them through the BV512 as a mastering EQ. Feel free to add an MClass Maximizer below the BV512 Vocoder if you so desire!

NOTE: As you know, the BV512 supports up to 512 bands of EQ, but what does this really mean? If you use the Band switch to change between 32 bands and 512 bands of EQ, there is no visual difference in the interface of the BV512, but there is a noticeable auditory difference, thanks to Fast Fourier Transform (FFT). FFT is a very detailed and precise form of analysis and processing in which waveforms are represented as a sum of sines and cosines. (Math geeks rejoice!) That means using the BV512 as a vocoder or as an EQ in 512FFT mode produces very precise and detailed control over the shaping of the effect. One point to keep in mind is that when you are making adjustments to the BV512 in 512FFT mode, a majority of the available bands in the interface will control the high frequencies rather than the low frequencies.

Basic Vocoding Tutorial

Let's apply what you have just learned about vocoding by going through a basic vocoding tutorial. In this section, you open a Reason song that I have prepared; it consists of an NN-19 (the modulator) playing a single sample, a SubTractor (the carrier) playing chords, and the BV512 Vocoder. Through this step-by-step method, you learn how to route the carrier and modulator to the BV512, adjust the frequency band, and create a unique signal that you can edit further by using the synth parameters of the SubTractor.

NOTE: Before you start this tutorial, take a minute to visit the Cengage Learning website (www.cengageptr.com), where you will find a Reason song called "Vocoder Tutorial." This song file is a published song, which means that all the elements specifically created for this tutorial are self-contained in the song file.

1. Open the "Vocoder Tutorial" song. You will see the DDL-1 delay, a SubTractor, the NN-19, and the BV512 at the bottom. The NN-19 has a loaded sample of my voice, and the SubTractor has the Bowy patch loaded. Also notice that there is a sequence written for both the SubTractor and the NN-19, but if you click Play, you won't hear anything because the audio has not yet been routed.
2. Press the Tab key to flip the Rack screen. This gives you a perfect starting point to begin routing your carrier and modulator.
3. Route the output of the SubTractor to the carrier input left of the BV512 (see Figure 10.12).

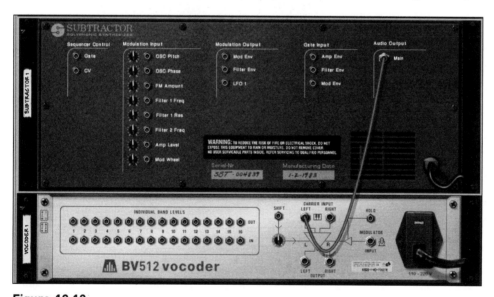

Figure 10.12
© Propellerhead Software AB.

4. Route the left output of the NN-19 to the modulator input on the BV512 (see Figure 10.13).
5. Route just the left output of the BV512 to the channel 1 left input of the Mix Channel of the NN-XT. This is a mono signal.
6. Click Play on the Transport panel. You should now hear the BV512 in action. It should be a strong signal that is very bass-heavy and slightly distorted. That means some adjustments will need to be made to the frequency band level section of the BV512.
7. Because this is your first time using the BV512, use the Band switch to switch to the 16-band display, and make some adjustments to the lower frequency bands (see Figure 10.14).

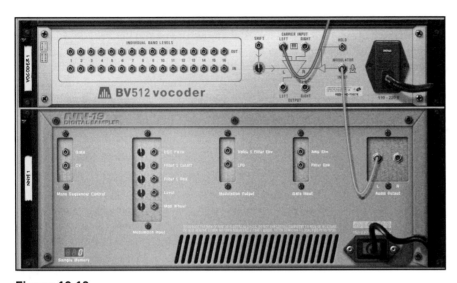

Figure 10.13
© Propellerhead Software AB.

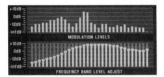

Figure 10.14
© Propellerhead Software AB.

This should give you a pretty good idea of how the BV512 works. You can experiment further by changing the band range of the BV512, making additional adjustments to the synth parameters of the SubTractor, or replacing the SubTractor with the Malström for a whole new sound.

Using Dr. Octo Rex as the Modulator: Another interesting application for the BV512 is to use a drum loop as the source of modulation. This creates a very interesting rhythmically driven audio signal. Try the following exercise:

1. Create an instance of Dr. Octo Rex and load a 1/16-note patterned REX file. Something from the Abstract Hip-Hop folder in the Reason Factory Sound Bank should work well.
2. Click the To Track button on the Dr. Octo Rex interface to load the REX file into the Reason sequencer.
3. Press the Tab key to flip the Rack screen. Disconnect the NN-19 from the BV512.
4. Disconnect Dr. Octo Rex from its Mix Channel. Connect the left output of Dr. Octo Rex to the modulator input of the BV512.
5. Click Play to hear the rhythmic bliss of vocoding in action. Try to add some delay to the signal, or use some of the synth parameters of either Dr. Octo Rex or the SubTractor for a whole new sound.

Automation

All the parameters in the BV512 can be automated in the same way as any Reason device. If you would rather draw in your automation data than record it in real time, the only hoop you have to jump through to begin automating is to create a sequencer track. You can see how by working through the following exercise. Before you begin, start a new Reason song and create an NN-19 and a BV512.

1. Right-click on the BV512 and select Create Track for Vocoder 1. This creates a sequencer track that is automatically routed to the BV512.
2. Right-click on the vocoder track and select Parameter Automation.
3. A window pops up giving you a list of parameters to select. Select the ones you want and click OK.
4. The Reason sequencer now displays these parameters as lanes on the vocoder sequencer track. Switch to the Edit mode and draw your automation moves.

For more on automation, check out Chapter 12, "Automation."

CV Connections

As if it couldn't get any better, the BV512 offers many individual inputs and outputs on the back of the device that allow for some interesting routing possibilities (see Figure 10.15).

Figure 10.15
© Propellerhead Software AB.

▷ **Frequency band outputs:** These CV outputs use the amplitude of an individual frequency band to control the parameter inputs of other Reason devices. For example, you could route the output of band 8 to the FM Amount input of the SubTractor.

▷ **Frequency band inputs:** These CV inputs can be controlled by the Matrix to alter the amplitude of each frequency band in the BV512. Note that once you make a connection from the Matrix to a specific frequency band, the Matrix exclusively controls that band's amplitude.

▷ **Shift:** This input controls the Shift parameter on the front of the device and can be used to create fantastic sweeping effects.

▷ **Hold:** This input is to operate the Hold parameter and can be used to create a step-driven vocoder effect. It's perfect for creating percussive vocoder stabs on vocals and pads. Note that you must use the Gate CV output of the Matrix to make this input work.

Scream 4 Sound Destruction Unit

Aside from the comical Wes Craven-esque name (programmers always have a good sense of humor), the appropriately titled Scream 4 is a digital distortion effect that takes vocals, drums, and synth patches to a whole new level (see Figure 10.16). Divided into three sections (Damage, Cut, and Body), Scream 4 can shape, mold, and destroy any audio signal it comes into contact with. Another welcome addition to Scream 4 and the upcoming RV7000 (discussed later in this chapter) is the ability to load, edit, and save customized presets. Scream 4 already comes with a lot of great sounding presets, but it never hurts to make your own. If you were looking for a distortion box with more to offer than the D-11, this is it!

Figure 10.16
© Propellerhead Software AB.

The Damage Section

Let's look at the various parameters of Scream 4. This section looks at the parameters and presets for the Damage section (see Figure 10.17).

Figure 10.17
© Propellerhead Software AB.

▷ **Damage:** This button turns the Damage section on and off.

▷ **Damage Control:** This knob is used to assign an amount of input gain to Scream 4. The higher the value, the more distortion there is.

▷ **Damage Type:** This knob lets you select the type of distortion.

▷ **P1/P2:** These knobs work differently with each Damage type. These types are covered next.

There are 10 Damage types available with Scream 4:

▷ **Overdrive:** This standard analog-type distortion responds well to variable dynamics. When it is selected, the P1 knob is used as a tone control. The P2 knob controls the presence, which increases the mid to high frequencies before it's passed through the distortion effect.

▷ **Distortion:** This preset is similar to the Overdrive preset, but it is capable of creating a much thicker distortion effect. Note that the P1 and P2 knobs work the same here as they do with the Overdrive preset.

▷ **Fuzz:** This preset is a heavy distortion that is strong even at low Damage Control settings. Note that the P1 and P2 knobs work the same as they do with the Overdrive preset.

▷ **Tube:** This preset simulates a classic tube distortion (*à la* Led Zeppelin or Jimi Hendrix). When you use this preset, the P1 knob acts as a contour or high-pass filter. The P2 knob controls the bias, or balance, of the tube distortion. When the P2 knob is set to a 12 o'clock position, the bias is very balanced in shape. When the P2 knob is set to its maximum resolution, it creates an uneven balance to the distortion, which sounds very close to a tube-driven amplifier.

▷ **Tape:** This preset is a simulation of tape saturation, which can add compression and punch to the distortion. The P1 knob acts as a tape speed, which helps to preserve the higher frequencies when set to high speeds. The P2 knob controls the compression ratio.

▷ **Feedback:** This preset is a combination of heavy distortion and looped feedback. Feedback is created when a sound source is fed back to itself. A good example is an electric guitar or microphone that is placed too close to its amplifier or speaker. The Damage Control knob assigns the amount of gain to the feedback loop, and the P1 and P2 knobs control the size and "howl," or frequency, of the feedback, respectively.

▷ **Modulate:** This preset creates a distortion that resonates by combining two copies of itself before it is fed through a distortion. The P1 knob controls the resonance ring, and the P2 knob controls the filter frequency.

▷ **Warp:** This preset creates a strong, stinging distortion by multiplying its incoming signal with itself. The P1 knob controls the sharpness of the distortion, and the P2 knob controls the bias, or balance, of the distortion.

▷ **Digital:** This preset is meant to be used as a low-fidelity, gritty distortion. The P1 knob is used to alter the bit depth from the highest resolution possible to a down-and-dirty single bit of resolution. The P2 knob alters the sample rate of the distortion and ranges from clean and pristine to crunchy and static.

▷ **Scream:** This preset is similar to the Fuzz preset, but includes a band-pass filter including high resonance and gain before distorting. The P1 knob controls the tone of the distortion, and the P2 knob controls the filter frequency.

The Cut Section

The Cut section of Scream 4 acts as EQ controls, allowing for many creative possibilities in carving and shaping an interesting EQ curve for your distortion (see Figure 10.18). Click on the Cut button to activate the EQ. At this point, you can adjust the low, mid, and high bands of equalization to your liking. At any time, you can reset any of the three bands by Ctrl-clicking (Windows) or Command-clicking (Mac) on the band slider to reset it to its default position.

Figure 10.18
© Propellerhead Software AB.

The Body Section

The Body section of Scream 4 is used to create different effects, such as speaker cabinet simulations and auto-wahs (for us guitarists), by placing the signal in different simulated enclosures (see Figure 10.19). Five body types can be selected and then edited by resonance and scale parameters.

Figure 10.19
© Propellerhead Software AB.

▷ **Body:** This button switches the Body section on and off.
▷ **Resonance:** This knob, labeled "Reso," creates a resonance effect for the selected body type.
▷ **Scale:** This knob controls the size of the selected body. Note that this knob is inverted; turning the knob clockwise creates a smaller size, whereas turning it counterclockwise increases the size.
▷ **Auto:** This knob controls the amount of the envelope follower (see the upcoming sidebar).
▷ **Type:** This knob switches between one of five available body types.

The Envelope Follower: The envelope follower is used to change the body scale according to the incoming dynamic level. The louder the incoming sound, the more the scale parameter is increased. This creates what is commonly known as an "auto-wah" effect, which is set by the Auto knob.

To demonstrate the versatility of this effect, try the following exercise. Before you begin, start a new Reason song.

1. Create a Dr. Octo Rex and load a REX file from either the Abstract Hip-Hop folder or the Techno folder in the Reason Factory Sound Bank. Click the To Track button to load the Dr. Octo Rex pattern into the Reason sequencer.
2. Create a Scream 4 and route it to be used as an insert effect.
3. Activate the Body section, select body type B, and turn the Auto knob clockwise.
4. Adjust the Resolution knob.
5. Click Play. Notice how the body scale opens up with the various dynamics of the REX loop.

The CV Connections

Using CV outputs can enable the Matrix to control any of four Scream 4 parameters.

▷ **Damage Control:** This changes the amount of distortion.
▷ **P1:** This increases or decreases the P1 parameter. Note that the damage type determines what this parameter affects.
▷ **P2:** This increases or decreases the P2 parameter. Note that the damage type determines what this parameter affects.
▷ **Scale:** This increases or decreases the size of the selected body.

Additionally, Scream 4 includes an Auto CV output, which can be routed to the CV input of another Reason device. For example, Scream 4 could be routed to a modulation parameter of the SubTractor or Malström.

RV7000 Advanced Reverb

The RV7000 is a true stereo professional reverb effect that sounds too good to be true (see Figure 10.20). It has nine reverb and echo algorithms that can be used along with an EQ and gate for molding and shaping your reverb in ways that just can't be done by most hardware and software reverbs.

Figure 10.20
© Propellerhead Software AB.

The Main Panel

The RV7000 is a two-part effect unit, much the same way that the NN-XT is a two-part sampler. When you first load the RV7000, the part of the device you see is the main panel, which controls the global parameters of the device (see Figure 10.21).

Figure 10.21
© Propellerhead Software AB.

Notice that the RV7000 has a Patch Browser in the left corner of the main panel. This makes it possible to load, edit, and save customized patches for the device.

Take a look at the global parameters:

> ▷ **EQ Enable:** This button switches the EQ section off and on.
> ▷ **Gate Enable:** This button switches the Gate section off and on.
> ▷ **Decay:** This knob controls the rate of decay in a reverb or the amount of feedback in an echo algorithm.
> ▷ **High Frequency Damp:** This knob, labeled "HF Damp," assigns an amount of decay time for the high frequencies in the reverb. Increasing this value makes the reverb sound warm and dull.
> ▷ **High EQ:** This knob, labeled "Hi EQ," controls the high shelving EQ. Increase the value of this parameter to boost the high frequencies in the reverb.
> ▷ **Dry/Wet:** This knob mixes between the unprocessed (dry) signal and the processed (wet) signal.

The Remote Programmer

The Remote Programmer is where all the individual edits of the RV7000 are completed (see Figure 10.22). To activate the Remote Programmer, click on the arrow button next to the virtual cable slot. The RV7000 then performs a little animation and loads up right below the main panel.

Figure 10.22
© Propellerhead Software AB.

Once the Remote Programmer is open, you can select one of nine algorithms. To see each of these algorithms, scroll through them using the knob located on the top left of the Remote Programmer. Each of the algorithms emulates a specific type of reverb or echo and offers a number of editable parameters.

> ▷ **Small Space:** This emulates a small room.
> ▷ **Room:** This emulates a standard-sized room with adjustable shape and wall composition.
> ▷ **Hall:** This emulates a standard hall.
> ▷ **Arena:** This emulates the characteristics of a large arena.
> ▷ **Plate:** This creates a classic plate reverb.
> ▷ **Spring:** This emulates a spring-driven reverb, which can be found on the back of most old Fender guitar amps.
> ▷ **Echo:** This creates a tempo-synced echo.
> ▷ **Multi Tap:** This creates a tempo-synced multi-tapped delay.
> ▷ **Reverse:** This creates a well-known backward effect in which the dry signal comes after the reverb.

As you will see, each one of these algorithms has its own set of attributes and parameters that you can alter. That said, let's run down the list of each one, starting with Small Space:

> ▷ **Size:** This assigns a size to the space.
> ▷ **Modulated Rate:** This sets the rate of modulation of the space, which helps even out the character of the reverb. It works alongside the Mod Amount parameter.

▷ **Room Shape:** This selects one of four room shapes.
▷ **Low Frequency Damp:** This controls the rate of decay for the low frequencies.
▷ **Wall Irregularities:** This adjusts the positioning of the walls in a small space.
▷ **Predelay:** This adjusts the amount of predelay, which is the delay between the source signal and the starting point of the reverb.
▷ **Modulation Amount:** This assigns the amount of modulation to the reverb.

The next algorithm is the Room algorithm. Note that the Hall algorithm has the same parameters, but much larger size settings.

▷ **Size:** This assigns a size to the space.
▷ **Diffusion:** This clarifies the *bounce*, or reflection, of the reverb.
▷ **Room Shape:** This selects one of four room shapes.
▷ **ER->Late:** This sets the time between the early reflections and tail end of the reverb.
▷ **ER Level:** This adjusts the level of the early reflections.
▷ **Predelay:** This adjusts the amount of predelay.
▷ **Modulation Amount:** This assigns the amount of modulation to the reverb.

The Arena algorithm is used to emulate the reverberations of a full-sized area. This algorithm is unique in that it controls the left, right, and center reflections that are present in an arena setting.

▷ **Size:** This assigns a size to the space.
▷ **Diffusion:** This clarifies the bounce of the reverb.
▷ **Left Delay:** This sets the predelay time for the left side of the reverb.
▷ **Right Delay:** This sets the predelay time for the right side of the reverb.
▷ **Stereo Level:** This adjusts the level of both the left and right channels of the reverb.
▷ **Mono Delay:** This sets the predelay time for the center of the reverb.
▷ **Mono Level:** This adjusts the level of the center of the reverb.

There are only two adjustable parameters for the Plate algorithm:

▷ **LF Damp:** This controls the rate of decay for the low frequencies.
▷ **Predelay:** This adjusts the amount of predelay.

The Spring reverb algorithm emulates the behaviors of the actual spring found on the back of old guitar amps.

▷ **Length:** This sets the length of the spring.
▷ **Diffusion:** This clarifies the bounce of the reverb.
▷ **Dispersion Freq:** This controls the amount of dispersion of the different frequencies created by the initial reflection. This parameter works in combination with the Dispersion Amount.
▷ **Low Frequency Damp:** This controls the rate of decay for the low frequencies.
▷ **Stereo On/Off:** This determines whether the reverb is mono or stereo.
▷ **Predelay:** This adjusts the amount of predelay.
▷ **Dispersion Amount:** This controls the amount of the dispersion effect.

The Echo algorithm is an echo or delay-like effect, which can be tempo-synced.

▷ **Echo Time:** This adjusts the time between each echo. Note that when Tempo Sync is not active, this parameter has a range of 10–2,000 milliseconds (up to two seconds). When Tempo Sync is active, this parameter is set in note values, such as 1/8 or 1/16.
▷ **Diffusion:** This clarifies the bounce and number of reflections of the echo. This parameter works in combination with the Spread parameter.
▷ **Tempo Sync:** This turns the tempo sync off and on.
▷ **LF Damp:** This controls the rate of decay for the low frequencies.
▷ **Spread:** This adjusts the space of the additional reflections set by the Diffusion parameter.
▷ **Predelay:** This introduces an additional delay before the first echo.

The Multi Tap algorithm produces four separate delays, each with its own adjustable parameters. The settings of this algorithm differ greatly from the others, as each tap is assigned its own set of parameters. The four individual Tap settings can be selected with the Edit Select knob in the upper-right corner of the Remote Programmer. There are a few common parameters used in taps 1–4, including the following:

▷ **Tempo Sync:** This turns the tempo sync off and on.
▷ **Diffusion:** This clarifies the bounce and number of reflections of the echoes.

▷ **LF Damp:** This controls the rate of decay for the low frequencies in the echoes.
▷ **Tap Delay:** This adjusts the delay time of each tap. Note that when Tempo Sync is not active, this parameter has a range of 10–2,000 milliseconds (about two seconds). When Tempo Sync is active, this parameter is set in note values, such as 1/8 and 1/16.
▷ **Tap Level:** This adjusts the amplitude of each tap.
▷ **Tap Pan:** This adjusts the panning assignment for each tap.
▷ **Repeat Tap.** This is a master feedback control parameter that adjusts the repeat time of the entire set of delays. This can be accessed by scrolling through each of the Tap Delays until you reach Repeat Tap.

One of the grooviest algorithms in the RV7000, the Reverse, mimics the backward effect that you hear so often in ambient electronic music. Its parameters are as follows:

▷ **Length:** This adjusts the time between when the source signal is processed and played back. Note that when Tempo Sync is not active, this parameter has a range of 10–4,000 milliseconds (about four seconds). When Tempo Sync is active, this parameter is set in note values, such as 1/8 and 1/16.
▷ **Density:** This controls the thickness of the reverse effect.
▷ **Rev Dry/Wet:** This mixes between the dry (unprocessed) signal and the wet (processed) signal.
▷ **Tempo Sync:** This turns the tempo sync off and on.

The CV Connections

You can connect the Matrix CV outputs to one of three CV inputs on the back of the RV7000 to control the three parameters in step time:

▷ **Decay:** This parameter controls reverb decay or echo/delay feedback.
▷ **HF Damp:** This parameter controls the HF Damp parameter on the RV7000 main display.
▷ **Gate Trig:** This CV input is used to trigger the Gate section of the RV7000.

The Spider Audio Merger & Splitter

First introduced in Reason 2.5, the Spider Audio Merger & Splitter is not an actual real-time effect (see Figure 10.23). It is a utility that serves two basic functions:

▷ It merges up to four separate audio inputs into a single output.
▷ It splits one audio input into four separate outputs.

Figure 10.23
© Propellerhead Software AB.

Press the Tab key to flip the Rack screen around. You will see that the Spider is split into two sections (see Figure 10.24). On the left is the Merge section, and the Splitter is on the right. Next, you will learn how to use the merging and splitting capabilities of the Spider.

Figure 10.24
© Propellerhead Software AB.

Using the Spider to Merge Audio

Merging audio with the Spider may not seem like such a hot idea the first time you think about it. But as this tutorial progresses, you might find yourself coming up with some interesting routing ideas that you may not have thought possible.

First, the basic idea: You can route the outputs of any Reason device to any of the four stereo inputs on the Spider. For example, you could route the outputs of the Malström, the stereo outputs of Redrum, the outputs of Dr. Octo Rex, and the outputs of two SubTractor synths to the Spider inputs (see Figure 10.25). These signals are then merged internally and routed to the stereo outputs of the Spider, which can be sent off to the inputs of a Mix Channel device, a stereo compressor, and so on.

Figure 10.25
© Propellerhead Software AB.

The Merge section of the Spider has a couple of rules when it comes to using mono signals from Reason devices such as the SubTractor or individual outputs from Redrum or the NN-XT.

▷ When you route the mono output of a Reason device to the left mono input of the Spider and don't connect anything to its corresponding right input, the Spider will output the signal to its left and right outputs.
▷ When you route the mono output of a Reason device to the right mono input of the Spider and don't connect anything to its corresponding left input, the Spider will output the signal to its right channel only.

Let's look at an example of how to use the Merge section effectively by routing Dr. Octo Rex and Redrum to the Spider to send them all to a single insert effect.

1. Create a new Reason song and load it with Redrum and Dr. Octo Rex. Additionally, write a pattern for Redrum and load a REX file into Dr. Octo Rex. Send it to its sequencer track.
2. Create a Spider Audio Merger & Splitter at the bottom of the Rack screen.
3. Create a COMP-01 next to the Spider. Press the Tab key to flip the Rack screen around. Notice that the output of the Dr. Octo Rex device has automatically routed itself to the COMP-01 to use it as an insert effect.
4. Disconnect Redrum from its Mix Channel Device and Dr. Octo Rex from the COMP-01. At this point, if you click Play, you won't hear any signal.
5. Route the left output of Redrum to any of the left inputs of the Spider's Merge section. The right output of Redrum should automatically route itself to the Spider's right input as well.
6. Route the left output of Dr. Octo Rex to any of the left inputs of the Spider's Merge section. The right output of Dr. Octo Rex should automatically route itself to the Spider's right input as well (see Figure 10.26).
7. Route the left output of the Spider's Merge section to the left input of the COMP-01.
8. Press the Tab key again and then click Play. You should now see and hear the COMP-01 processing both Redrum and Dr. Octo Rex (see Figure 10.27).

The Echo

You'll notice that I'm mentioning a delay type of device again after we already covered delay/echo devices earlier in this chapter. That's because The Echo (see Figure 10.28) is more than just an echo device, as you will soon discover.

With The Echo, it's all about modes. If you create an instance of The Echo and start using it as is, it will behave very much like the DDL-1 Digital Delay or the RV7000 discussed earlier. Unlike these other delays, though, The Echo is designed with live performance in mind. In fact, with its Roll slider and Trig buttons, you can use it similarly to a DJ effect. We're going to explore this later in this section.

Let's start off by talking about the basics. The Echo is divided into six main sections with subsections:

▷ Delay
▷ Feedback/Diffusion
▷ Color/Filter
▷ Modulation/LFO
▷ Output
▷ Mode

The Delay Section

This section lets you control the speed, panning, and right channel timing offset. It also provides a way to ping-pong your delay, such that the echo goes back and forth in your speakers via stereo. Out of this whole device, you'll spend the most time with the Time knob. By changing the time, you change the speed with which the echoes play back, which affords you new grooves, new rhythms, and a new feel. The result depends entirely on what you put through it. Moving the Time knob up slows down the echoes and also makes them longer. In the highest levels, you actually get a partial loop! In lower levels, you can create really cool glitch/stutter effects. You should give the Sync and Keep Pitch buttons much further attention than you normally would with similar features on other delays. When disabling Sync, you get an echo device that has a very large array of timings. Lower the Time knob, and you will get seriously nasty glitches and sound effects

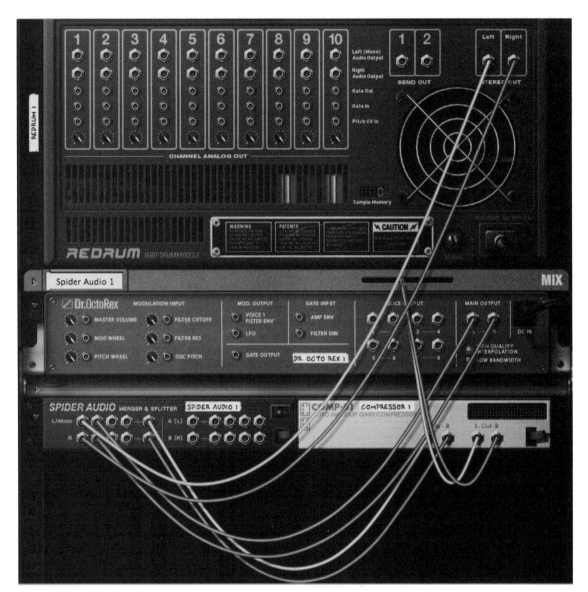

Figure 10.26
© Propellerhead Software AB.

Figure 10.27
© Propellerhead Software AB.

Figure 10.28
© Propellerhead Software AB.

that can introduce an interesting flavor to your music, especially if automated. Scrolling Time in out of sync also gives you some crazy effects, especially if Keep Pitch is disabled. When this setting is enabled, it disables the pitching that occurs when you scroll the Time knob. As you do this, you'll get a record-scratching effect, which can be very useful in hip hop, dubstep, and breakbeat. This effect can be enabled and disabled on a whim with the Keep Pitch button. When it is enabled, you can more easily create the illusion of timing changes in rhythms and melodies with simple shifts of the Time knob.

The Feedback/Diffusion Section

Feedback allows you to control how long it takes for echoes to die out once they are triggered. At the same time, the Feedback knob increases the number of echoes heard. The higher you raise the knob, the more echoes you get. You can also use the Offset knob to modify where the feedback appears in your mix. Cranking the Offset setting causes the feedback stream to wander over to the right channel. Decreasing it causes the feedback coming from the echo to slowly move to the left. This capability can be very helpful for building soundscapes of echo feedback that travels the stereo spectrum. Diffusion is used for "smearing" your echoes. This, in a sense, makes the echoes seem much less intense, with the diffusion rounding off the attack and decay of each echo. The overall result is an echo that does not seem so manufactured; it's more authentic.

The Color/Filter Section

A delay doesn't always have to be a carbon copy or reproduction of the signal that runs through the delay/echo unit. Using the Color section of The Echo, you can introduce character and aggression to your echoes. The Color setting actually has four modes:

▷ **Limiter:** Limiter ("Lim") mode pushes up the volume of even the lowest echo but does not cause the echo to peak, which would cause distortion. Use this mode to maintain a relatively clean signal with highly defined echoes, emulating the limiting that happens with tape saturation.
▷ **Overdrive:** The rest of the modes are all about introducing distortion, including Overdrive ("Ovdr") mode. This creates a distortion that affects largely boosts and distorts the higher frequencies.
▷ **Distortion:** The Distortion ("Dist") mode distorts and boosts the mid range and low end.
▷ **Tube:** This resembles the classic tube-based amplifiers. Use this mode for a more "vintage" sound.

The Filter section is highly useful. One of the problems with echoing low-end and mid-range frequencies is that when you double the low end, you create "mud" in your mix. This eliminates the low-end dynamics and gives you a nasty wall of sound. Use the Filter settings to eliminate low frequencies in your echoes and maintain clarity in your mix.

The Modulation/LFO Section

The Modulation and LFO section can cause slight to serious pitching to your incoming signal. But why would you want that from a delay/echo device? In the case of the Envelope knob, labeled "Env," you can create from subtle to drastic pitch bends in real time on your incoming signal. The Envelope knob bends the first note play, or first signal in, only once. As an example, the first note of a piano input will be bent once, and then the note will continue to play out bent, but no further bending will occur. It can be quite beautiful to have a touch of the Envelope setting engaged on guitar, as a matter of fact. This gives you a small chorus-style effect, which greatly fattens your guitar. The Wobble knob introduces a subtle pitch shift to your echoes that is meant to resemble the vintage tape echoes of the past. For the most part, this effect gives your echoes a distinct vintage or psychedelic feel. The Rate knob in the LFO subsection causes a linear bending of your signal similar to the Envelope modulation, except this is continuous bending, not just the initial signal. That means you will continue to hear pitch bending going up and down until the echo finally dies out. To hear the effect, you need to raise the Amount knob. The LFO, with minimal Amount and Rate values, is very subtle and introduces an all-encompassing chorus effect. Alternatively, you can use drastic rate levels to create everything from alien- to distortion-type effects.

The Output Section

The Output section contains only two knobs: Dry/Wet and Ducking. The Dry/Wet knob, as with all other effects in this chapter, allows you to increase the wetness of the delayed/echoing signal. But you'll discover that The Echo has many more uses than all the other effects. In fact, with Roll mode (see the following exercise), you actually need to turn the Dry/Wet knob all the way up. This is a setting you won't normally find recommended with a delay/echo device! To sum it up: For regular usage, keep the Dry/Wet knob in the middle; turn it to 10 o'clock for standard echo/delay; and turn it all the way up for roll- and DJ-style effects. Ducking causes The Echo to lower the echo effect every time it receives an incoming signal from the source device. For example, if I strum my guitar, The Echo immediately lowers the delayed signal. One problem with echo/delay effects is that you can lose your original source signal in the myriad echoes being produced. By using the Ducking knob, you can retain definition of your incoming signal while getting some really great delayed ambience in the background.

The Mode Section

Use the Mode section to change the overall functionality of The Echo. In Normal mode, The Echo functions for the most part like every other delay device in Reason. (Because the rest of this chapter explains in depth how echo/delay devices work, I won't go into any depth on it here.) The Triggered and Roll settings defy how any echo/delay devices work in this chapter, so I'll spend the rest of this section addressing these modes.

Triggered mode causes The Echo to stop producing its echo effect unless you click the Trig button. The longer you hold down the Trig button, the longer it will create echoes for your incoming signal. This capability is useful when you want to echo only one word from a verse or chorus or you want to echo only the snare drum during a loop. You can get very creative with this feature! What's interesting is that clicking the Trig button does not kill the decay of the echo effect. It still decays gradually, according to the level of your Feedback knob.

Roll mode is my absolute favorite feature of The Echo. When you're in Roll mode, you cannot hear any delay unless you raise the Roll slider. I encourage you to turn the Dry/Wet knob in the Output section all the way up when doing this. Raising the Roll slider creates incredible shifts in timing, which utterly depend on the level of the Time and Feedback settings. Because I feel this is something you experience better than read about, let's do a quick exercise.

Using Roll Mode with The Echo

Let's use Roll mode with The Echo:

1. Create a Dr. Octo Rex and then create an instance of The Echo (see Figure 10.29).

Figure 10.29
© Propellerhead Software AB.

2. Load any drum loop you want into the Dr. Octo Rex. I used the 2+4 Nailed loop. To find it, launch the Reason Factory Sound Bank, open the Dr. Octo Rex Patches folder, and then open the Acoustic Drums folder (see Figure 10.30).
3. If The Echo unit does not say Init Patch, right-click on the unit and select Initialize Patch (see Figure 10.31). This puts the unit in a zeroed, blank state with no real settings.
4. Put your The Echo unit into Roll mode (see Figure 10.32).
5. Click the Run button to start your Dr. Octo Rex. As you do, you'll notice that the loop seemingly has no effect on it from The Echo. This is as it should be. While this is taking place, move the Roll slider to the right (see Figure 10.33). You'll notice a significant stutter. Try this several times while adjusting the Time knob.

After you run through this exercise, I'm sure you can see the implications for the power of this feature. With lower Time settings, you can introduce stutters. With higher Time settings, you can introduce very natural change-ups to your drum loops, making them something other than a repeat of the same thing over and over again!

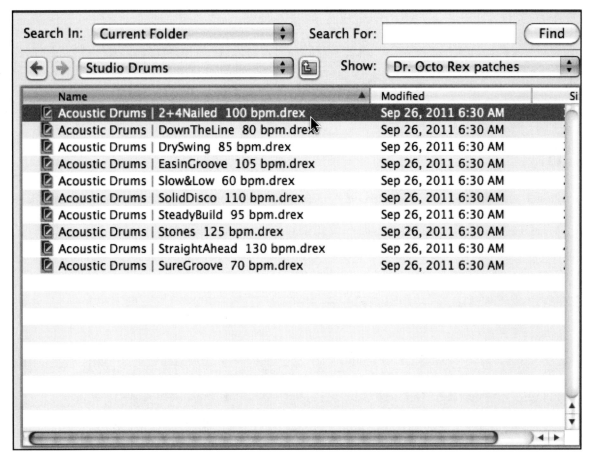

Figure 10.30
© Propellerhead Software AB.

Figure 10.31
© Propellerhead Software AB.

Figure 10.32
© Propellerhead Software AB.

Figure 10.33

© Propellerhead Software AB.

The Alligator

Of every Reason effect, the Alligator offers the most instant gratification. Propellerhead's name for the Alligator, Triple Filtered Gate, does not really give you the best description of what it does. Really, though, there's no other title I can think of that comes close other than "Chews up everything that you put into it and spits out something else." Well, that's what an alligator would do, right?

The Alligator depends on three gates that you can trigger (shown in Figure 10.34). They make up the core of its magic. Sound is fed into all three gates simultaneously, but no sound passes through the gates until they open.

Figure 10.34

© Propellerhead Software AB.

How do you open the gates? Well, there are many ways. The easiest is the pattern generator, shown in Figure 10.35. Each pattern number is a different order and set of timings from the last. The greater the number, the more interesting and weird some of the patterns get.

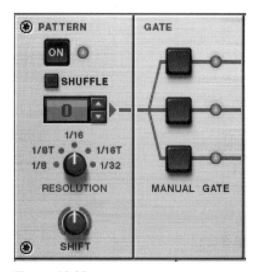

Figure 10.35

© Propellerhead Software AB.

You can use the Resolution knob (see Figure 10.36) to slow down or increase the speed of your pattern in the allotted note values in relation to your host tempo. Even though your actual song tempo may be quite high, it's sometimes good to have patterns playing in slower resolutions, like 1/8 notes. This creates a greater dimension in your song.

Figure 10.36
© Propellerhead Software AB.

The Shift knob (see Figure 10.37) works in increments of 1/16 notes. Each shift forward or backward takes you forward or back one step in timing. Use this knob to offset your pattern timing to give each pattern a new feel. Because shifting forward or backward moves the place where the Alligator pattern starts, shifting can almost make it sound as though you have a new pattern altogether. If you combine Shift and Resolution movements, there are tons of possible patterns.

Figure 10.37
© Propellerhead Software AB.

If you're doing a style of rhythm in your song that has a more relaxed beat, like house or hip hop, you may want to use the Shuffle button (see Figure 10.38). When Shuffle is enabled, it's tied to the Global Shuffle found in the ReGroove Mixer.

Figure 10.38
© Propellerhead Software AB.

> **NOTE:** On an initialized SubTractor that is running through the Alligator, sequence some half, whole, and quarter notes. After you play with this for a minute, try adjusting the Pattern number, the Shift knob, and the Resolution setting. You'll be amazed at what the Alligator can do with even its most basic settings!

Alligator Envelopes

Now that you know how to trigger the gates of the Alligator using the built-in pattern generator, let's talk about controlling how the gates open and close. Currently, when you run the Alligator with the Pattern settings, the sound allowed through is longer and more open. What if you could cause the sound to pass through in smaller increments, making your incoming signal sound more choppy and tight? There are a couple of ways of doing this:

▷ The Amplitude Envelope settings
▷ The Filter Envelope settings

The Amplitude Envelope Settings

The Amplitude Envelope settings, labeled "Amp Env" (see Figure 10.39), consist of three knobs: A (Attack), D (Decay), and R (Release). Adjusting these knobs affects how the gates open and close when they are triggered.

Figure 10.39
© Propellerhead Software AB.

If you adjust the Attack (A) knob, the amp envelope will cause the gates to open a little more slowly, cutting off the beginning part of the signal. This makes outgoing bursts from the gates seem a little more hushed and less harsh.

When adjusting the Decay (D) knob, you can clamp down on how long the gates stay open. For example, sustained notes going through will sound much choppier if you lower the decay time. If the decay time is up all the way, the sounds coming through the gates will play out much longer and fluidly. Use lower decay settings to create choppier drum loop effects or tight melodic patterns.

The Release (R) knob in low amounts causes the Alligator gates to stay open just a little bit after they've been triggered. In higher amounts, the gates will lazily close, making it sound as though a sound is slowly fading out like a bell has been struck. This effect is useful for sustained synth notes because it causes your sustained notes to sound more like piano or bell parts that gradually fade out over time. Higher sustain can also be good for allowing sections of drums to fade out without cutting off abruptly. Lower the release time to simulate abrupt, choppy rhythms and grooves.

The Filter Envelope Settings

The Filter Envelope settings, labeled "Filter Env" (see Figure 10.40), sculpt how sounds pass through the gates, but very differently. Whereas the amp envelope controls how the gates actually open and close through volume, the filter envelope controls how the filters open and close.

Figure 10.40
© Propellerhead Software AB.

By default, the filter envelope does nothing if you manipulate the A, D, and R knobs. You need to enable the filter envelope knobs on one or each of the gates for this to work (see Figure 10.41).

Figure 10.41
© Propellerhead Software AB.

Adjusting the filter envelope knob on a gate causes the filter envelope to have a lesser or greater effect in how the filter opens and closes in relation to the filter envelope settings. For example, if the Attack (A) knob is raised, the filter will appear to sweep at the beginning of the note. The faster the sweep depends on the amount of attack you've assigned.

You can turn the filter envelope amount in the opposite direction as well, toward the negative polarity. When you do this, the filter envelope settings work in reverse. For example, if Attack (A) is raised and the filter is reversed on the low pass–enabled gate, the filter will seem to close up when the gate is opening instead of fading in. Reversing polarity can be very helpful when you are using the high-pass or band-pass filters because the higher frequencies almost need to be reversed to actually hear the signals in higher frequency registers.

Alligator Filters and Channel Options

We've talked about the filter envelope, but strangely, we haven't talked about the filters themselves! Let's amend this. The filters on each gate are what ultimately give character and differentiation between each gate triggered by coloring each gate with shades of frequencies (see Figure 10.42).

Figure 10.42
© Propellerhead Software AB.

Because of the dedicated filters for each gate, you can almost consider each gate an instrument in its own right. For example, the high-pass gate can be considered a module that outputs tinnier, upper frequency–style sounds. If you run a drum loop through the Alligator and all gates are running together in pattern, the patterns distributed from the high-pass filter (see Figure 10.43) will greatly resemble a hi-hat. This depends on the Frequency (labeled "Freq") and Resonance (labeled "Res") settings, of course. To make this gate more audible when using the filter envelope, try reversing the polarity.

Figure 10.43
© Propellerhead Software AB.

The band-pass filter (shown in Figure 10.44) outputs mid range–style patterns. Think of this filter as outputting instruments along the lines of toms and snares. However, increasing the frequency on this gate can make it behave like the high pass, and lowering the frequency will make it behave like the low pass.

Figure 10.44
© Propellerhead Software AB.

You can think of the low-pass filter on gate 3 for bass and kick drum–type patterns. Personally, I use this one more than any other. And, yes, through the Volume knobs, you can disable or lower the volume of each filter (see Figure 10.45).

Because the low-pass-filtered gate is designed to enhance or boost low signals, especially with use of the filter envelope, I suggest keeping it center panned as opposed to panning left or right. You can pan each filter through use of the Pan knobs located on each gate (see Figure 10.46).

Through use of the Pan knobs, individual gate volumes, and filters, one single-source input going through the Alligator literally gets spit out as three different parts. This makes it much easier to populate a sparse arrangement, making something that is very simple into something much more complex.

Figure 10.45
© Propellerhead Software AB.

Figure 10.46
© Propellerhead Software AB.

> **TIP:** Did you know you can disable the filters on each of the gates? Using the small On buttons (see Figure 10.47) at the beginning of each gate channel strip, you can turn filter activity off completely. Use this On/Off function when you don't need filtering but want standard gates.

Figure 10.47
© Propellerhead Software AB.

Alligator Effects

Besides being an effect that essentially turns one signal into several instruments, the Alligator is also a multi-effects processor. You get a Phaser effect and a Delay effect that can be routed to each gate in varying amounts through the Gate Mix section (see Figure 10.48).

Figure 10.48
© Propellerhead Software AB.

These individual knobs afford you the ability to have, for example, some delay on the high-pass gate, while at the same time giving no delay to the low-pass channel. The behaviors of each of the effects can be modified below in their labeled locations. Let's talk about the controls of each device.

The Delay is a simple device that produces echoes on its own, similar to The Echo, discussed previously in this chapter. Keep in mind that this is a much simpler version of The Echo, RV7000, and resembles mostly the DDL-1 Digital Delay in Reason. What's helpful about having the Delay built into the Alligator is that it's just that much less patching you have to do, and as I mentioned earlier, you're much closer to instant gratification. The Delay falls short of having many of the additional features the previously listed effects devices have, but it can be synced to the Reason host tempo and can be panned, which is encouraged when using all the Alligator's gates because this frees up space in your mix.

The Phaser allows you to add a thickness to your gates when the rate is turned up higher. When it's lower, you can get very subtle sweeping psychedelic effects, which can be made much more severe using the Feedback knob.

Another brilliant effect feature added to the Alligator is the LFO, shown in Figure 10.49. LFO modulation can be introduced on each of the filters, where they can add subtle to extreme filter modulation. Like the Delay, the LFO can be synced through use of the Sync button. And, as with the filter envelope, subtle to extreme amounts can be added in positive to negative polarities using the LFO Amount knobs on each gate channel in the Filter section (see Figure 10.50).

Figure 10.49
© Propellerhead Software AB.

Figure 10.50
© Propellerhead Software AB.

Believe it or not, the Alligator also has distortion features available. Although there's no real control over the type of distortion, the Drive knobs available on all gate channels can be used to add some grit and aggression to each of your gates (see Figure 10.51). When they are used in conjunction with the filter envelope with massive filter sweeps, you can easily emulate old synths like the TB-303.

Figure 10.51
© Propellerhead Software AB.

The Dry Section

You may want to pay a small bit of attention to the Dry section. The Volume knob in this section allows you to introduce the original source signal unaltered into your Alligator mix (see Figure 10.52). This can be handy when you want to double the drums via the Alligator while keeping the original drum mix (or loop) or you want to use the sustained signal (like a pad) along with the Alligator's gated parts. The latter is an excellent strategy when used with automation because you can bring in the sustained notes in certain parts of the song and then keep the gated parts going the rest of the time. It's like having a lead with three other synth parts, all generated from one synth or sampler! And because you can pan the dry signal, you can even keep your incoming signal in certain sections of your stereo field as opposed to always being in the center.

Figure 10.52
© Propellerhead Software AB.

Pulveriser

The Pulveriser (see Figure 10.53) introduces some of the most severe compression I've ever heard in any software package mixed with modulation, distortion, and a filter. It's even capable of using the incoming signal to modulate selectable parts of the Pulveriser device internally. In short, the Pulveriser is another seemingly simple device with a few far-from-obvious tricks up its sleeve. Let's start with the basics.

Figure 10.53
© Propellerhead Software AB.

The Pulveriser as a Compressor

Setting up the Pulveriser as a compressor is easy. It's simply a matter of creating the device and raising the Squash knob until you get the desired effect. Unlike most compressor knobs, the Pulveriser's Squash knob controls not only the compression ratio, but also the threshold and make-up gain all in one shot (see Figure 10.54).

Figure 10.54
© Propellerhead Software AB.

It's easy to mistake the Follower section of the Pulveriser, with its Threshold knob, as what you would use to set your compression threshold and adjust your attack and release. This section actually does something entirely different, though! In fact, the Release knob is the only knob you will find on a conventional compressor that is separate from the Squash knob. This knob controls how fast the compressor opens up after it has been closed down. Setting the Release low with a high Squash setting causes you to get that pumping sound that is so desirable for drum loops, basses, kicks, and so on.

The Pulveriser for Distortion

Once you've added compression via the Squash knob and set your release, you might consider adding some dirt using the Dirt knob (see Figure 10.55). When you raise the Dirt value, you raise the Pulveriser's built-in distortion. You cannot modify the type of distortion given here, but it's really good distortion, and it can get very severe as you raise it higher and higher.

Figure 10.55
© Propellerhead Software AB.

When you add the Routing switch into the mix (see Figure 10.56), you get even greater possibilities. By default, the compressed signal (Squash) goes through the distortion (Dirt) and then the filter. When you adjust the Routing switch, though, you can have the filter go through the compressor (Squash) and then the distortion (Dirt). This is really helpful, because in the first mode, you have the ability to filter a compressed signal, and in the second mode, you are ultimately compressing and distorting a filtered signal.

Figure 10.56
© Propellerhead Software AB.

> **NOTE:** Try running a drum loop through a Pulveriser. On the Pulveriser, add significant amounts of Squash with a very low release. Lower the Filter Frequency setting to midway and raise the Peak knob. Next, adjust the Routing switch at the bottom of the Pulveriser and listen to the difference! While the drums are playing, adjust the Filter and Peak knobs for extra fun.

The Tone knob begins our descent into the filtering aspect of the Pulveriser. The Tone knob is a dedicated low-pass filter that clips off more and more of the high end the more you lower it. If the Tone knob is all the way up (5 o'clock), no filtering is taking place. As we get into the next section, realize that you actually get two filters on this crazy device!

Pulveriser Filter Modulation

The Pulveriser supplies a Filter section (see Figure 10.57) that is similar to many other devices in Reason. You get the familiar notch, low pass, band pass, high pass, and comb filters found in devices like Thor, Malström, and Kong.

Figure 10.57
© Propellerhead Software AB.

Of course, this wouldn't be a Propellerhead device if it didn't have a way to modulate the filter. This is where the device becomes unique: with the Follower section. Remember when I mentioned that the Threshold knob in the Follower section of the Pulveriser has nothing to do with the compression settings? Well, let's talk about what it does! On its own, with no additional settings, the Follower (see Figure 10.58) is just a red light that reacts more and more intensely the lower you take the knob. As with all threshold functions, the lower you bring down the threshold, the more reactive the result is. The attack and release determine how quickly or slowly the Follower opens, closes, and shuts down.

Figure 10.58
© Propellerhead Software AB.

The Follower becomes much more powerful when it's assigned to modulate specific parameters of the other functions on the device, like the filter, using the small modulation knobs all over the Pulveriser. Say you have a synth bass coming in playing 1/8 notes. You can set the Pulveriser's Follower Threshold setting to sit at a point where the light blinks steadily with each hit of bass synth. Then you can route the Follower to Frequency knob (see Figure 10.59) to send modulation to the filter. Each time the bass synth plays, the filter will open!

Figure 10.59
© Propellerhead Software AB.

There are several modulation paths from the Follower to other sections of the Pulveriser. This is also true for the Tremor device in the Pulveriser.

Tremor

Tremor (shown in Figure 10.60) is a syncable LFO unit capable of controlling the filter cutoff frequency and output level of the Pulveriser. This makes the Pulveriser a kind of cousin to the Alligator because you also can use the Pulveriser for gating effects. The main difference is that the Pulveriser relies on a single LFO to modulate each effect's output or filter.

Figure 10.60
© Propellerhead Software AB.

Tremor also features a very cool Spread function that modulates the phase and panning of the incoming signal. This is cool for opening up a drum loop or another instrument that is taking up a lot of space in your mix!

Using the modulation knobs on either side of Tremor (see Figure 10.61), you can decide whether you want to modulate the output of the Pulveriser or the frequency of the Pulveriser's filters. Doing this can cause the signals to rhythmically blend with other thick signals by cutting the frequency when other parts are introduced. You can even use higher frequency rates to get severe distortion.

Figure 10.61
© Propellerhead Software AB.

Neptune

Not all of us have perfect pitch...myself included. Although I'm not a bad singer, when you go back and listen to recordings of my performance, you'll hear certain sections when I get out of tune. Because Reason allows for audio recording, it's of great importance that I tell you how to get yourself back in tune—with Neptune.

It's important to start off by saying that Neptune (see Figure 10.62) can sound as natural or as synthetic as you want it to sound. In the past 15 years, there has been no end to misuse of pitch-correction devices and software to create voice effects that sound almost human. If this is your goal, Neptune will meet you there, too.

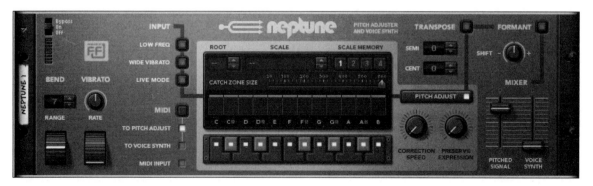

Figure 10.62
© Propellerhead Software AB.

What's even more astounding about Neptune is that it also goes beyond regular pitch correction and provides a powerful harmonization unit that can be used in multiple ways. Need backup harmonies? Neptune has you covered. Need a small barbershop quartet? Neptune's still got your back.

Neptune for Pitch Correction

Pitch correction actually sounds much more daunting than it really is. For the most part, you just choose a scale and go. It's in this middle section of Neptune, the Pitch Adjust section, that most of your work will actually take place (see Figure 10.63).

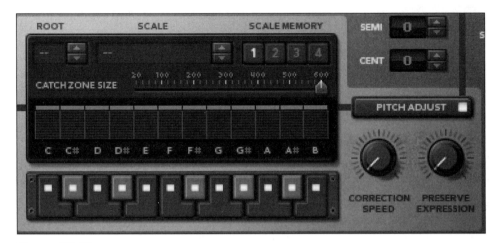

Figure 10.63
© Propellerhead Software AB.

If you know what scale you're singing in, just click the Scale drop-down menu (see Figure 10.64) and choose the appropriate scale. Next, set the root key you're singing in (see Figure 10.65).

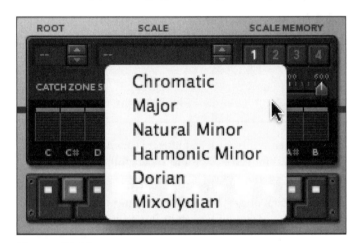

Figure 10.64
© Propellerhead Software AB.

At this point, it's safe to listen and see how your pitch-correction settings are working. If you discover a certain key being hit that you don't like, simply select the key in the Pitch Adjust section (see Figure 10.66). Clicking the key disables it as a possible note, leaving only the enabled notes as possibilities as your recording signal goes through the unit.

Now you'll need to decide how natural you want your pitch correction to be. With the Correction Speed knob set to the lowest possible setting (see Figure 10.67), Neptune slowly moves your pitch to the key's right pitch. Pitch correction is almost unnoticeable in this mode. If you move the Correction Speed knob to 12 o'clock, pitch correction is noticeable but very natural. If you boost it all the way up, you get robot voice.

If you have vibrato in your vocal recordings that you want to keep, you can use the Preserve Expression knob. The more you turn this knob up, the more original vibrato you will hear from the recording.

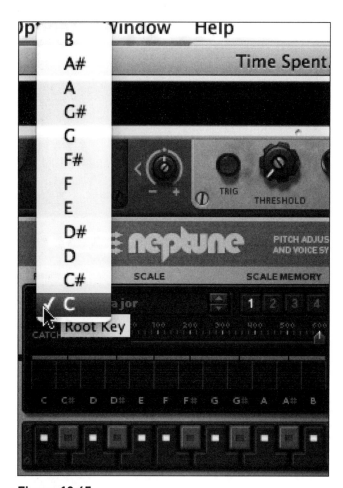

Figure 10.65
© Propellerhead Software AB.

Figure 10.66
© Propellerhead Software AB.

Figure 10.67
© Propellerhead Software AB.

Controlling Neptune Through MIDI

One of the coolest things about Neptune is the ability to control your vocal's pitch with your MIDI keyboard! To set this ability, right-click on your Neptune unit and select Create Track for Neptune, as shown in Figure 10.68.

After creating this track, you will notice that there is a keyboard present under the Neptune icon in the sequencer (see Figure 10.69). That means you have MIDI keyboard control over this device.

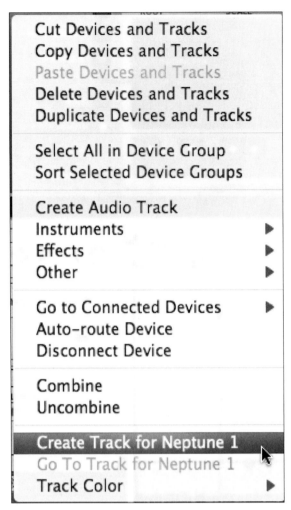

Figure 10.68
© Propellerhead Software AB.

Figure 10.69
© Propellerhead Software AB.

Run your recorded audio by starting the sequencer and playing your MIDI keyboard. Your keyboard now controls the pitch of your voice. If you'd like to keep your original voice recording as the main part but add in some harmonies that you control by keyboard, switch to Voice Synth Mode, as shown in Figure 10.70.

Figure 10.70
© Propellerhead Software AB.

Neptune is a powerful device for vocals, but it can also be used for monophonic instruments such as violin and bass. Experiment!

Audiomatic

Another effects device that you may want to familiarize yourself with is the Audiomatic Retro Transformer. (That's a mouthful, huh?) This device is included along with the purchase of Reason 7, and is a lot like Instagram for audio. How could this be? Read on!

If you pull up an Audiomatic, the first thing you'll notice will be the 16 orange buttons that adorn the front panel. These buttons trigger audio effects that can transform the overall "feel" of your sound greatly or subtly. Every effect works slightly differently. Some effects squash your audio, some add some high end, some widen the sound, and so on. It just depends on which effect you choose!

Audiomatic is intended to be used along with another extremely cool feature that has been added in Reason 7 known as parallel mixer channels. Parallel mixer channels, also known as parallel compression, have become a favorite trick for many producers as they afford you the ability to quickly and easily get a bigger sound for drums, basses, voice, etc., by doubling a source signal through several channels. Each of these copied channels can be used to add slightly different characteristics to your source signal. For example, suppose your SubTractor part is dry (or lacking any form of effect). Your second parallel channel, which is the exact same signal as your original SubTractor part, may have some distortion on it, with the EQ doing a HP filter just to add body to the upper parts of the bass while killing the lower frequencies. A third parallel channel might go through an LP filter with a 250 Hz boost to give a little body. When all these channels play back at once, you get a much bigger sound, because the original source, the SubTractor, is being doubled three times. But, each version has different tonal qualities.

Let's try seeing this in action with Audiomatic!

1. Create a Dr. Octo Rex. Then click the Browse Patch button and go to the Dr. Octo Rex Patches folder in the Reason Factory Sound Bank. In this directory, choose the Guitar Loops folder, the Electric Rhythm Guitar folder, and the Kirk Riffs Key Of A file (see Figure 10.71). This set of loops will be great because electric guitar is a perfect instrument for doubling and distorting.

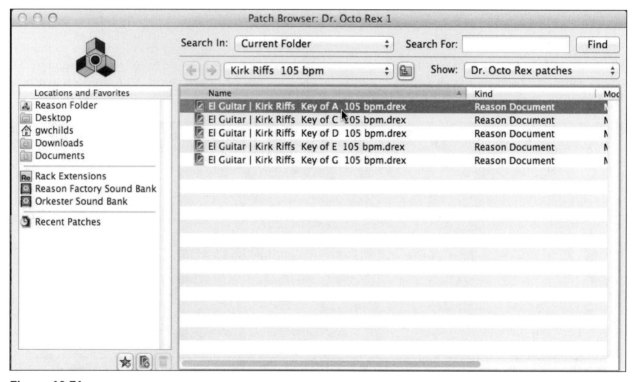

Figure 10.71
© Propellerhead Software AB.

2. Now that you have a fully loaded Dr. Octo Rex, add in a parallel channel. To do this, right-click on the Mix device in your rack that is labeled for your recently created Dr. Octo Rex and choose Create Parallel Channel (see Figure 10.72). When you do, a second Mix device will appear. This device will be labeled starting off with a "P1" in its title, which, of course, stands for "parallel channel 1."

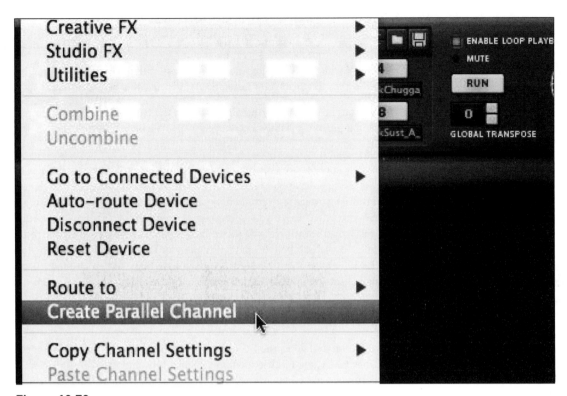

Figure 10.72
© Propellerhead Software AB.

3. The new parallel mix channel looks like it's been set up as a regular old mix channel. But, if you were to open up this device, turn it around, and look at the routing from the original mix channel to the new parallel channel, you'd notice something different. The original mix channel device is sending signal to the P1 mix channel through the parallel output. No new devices have been created. It's still just the good old Dr. Octo Rex. (See Figure 10.73.)

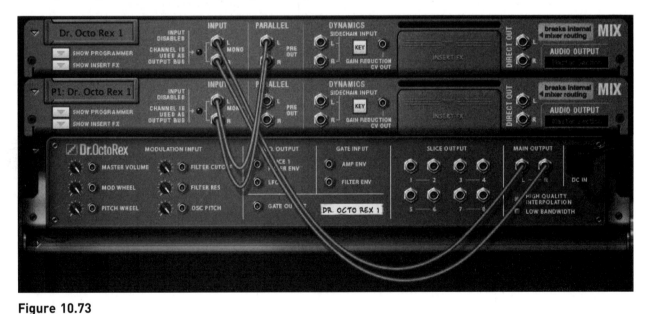

Figure 10.73
© Propellerhead Software AB.

4. Because these channels are exactly the same, sonically speaking, now would be a good time to start making them sound a little different so they aren't exact copies. Also, as mentioned, changing the parallel channel's sonic qualities makes the instrument sound bigger. On the parallel channel, create an Audiomatic device. To do so, right-click the P1 channel, choose Creative FX, and select Audiomatic Retro Transformer (see Figure 10.74).

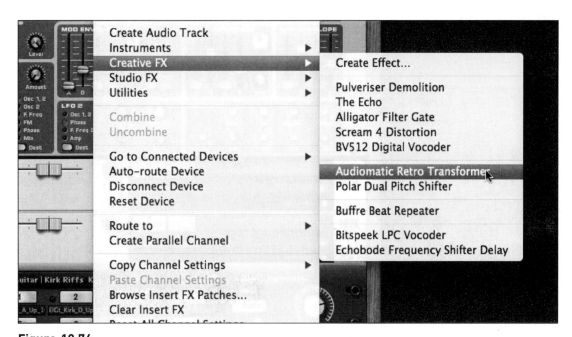

Figure 10.74
© Propellerhead Software AB.

5. If you play the Dr. Octo Rex device now, you'll notice that there is already a difference between the original mix channel, and the parallel channel. The Audiomatic Retro Transformer is already in effect. You can hear the difference by clicking the Solo buttons on the mix channels. To hear a big difference, click the Cracked button on the Audiomatic device (see Figure 10.75). This adds a nice layer of distortion to the parallel channel and instantly makes the guitar rock. You can also raise the Gain knob on the Audiomatic device to overdrive the signal a little. And, you can use the Transform knob to modify the effect in new and strange ways. You'll notice that if you turn the Transform knob up when in the Cracked mode, the signal gets thinner. Because you're doubling your signal, it might be nice to keep the signal a little thinner so that both tracks can work together nicely.

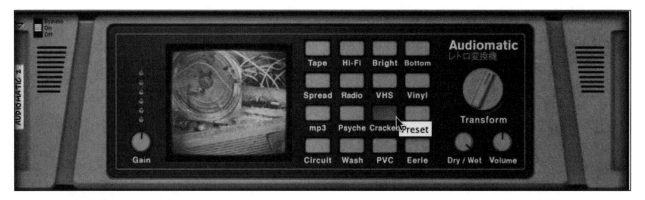

Figure 10.75
© Propellerhead Software AB.

6. Because you have the higher registers taken care of with your first parallel channel, it might be nice to add some body in the mid frequencies. Right-click on the parallel mix device and choose Create Parallel Channel (see Figure 10.76). (You always create an additional parallel channel from the last parallel device added in the chain. If you try to add another parallel channel from the original mix device, it will be grayed out!)

7. On the second parallel channel, change it up a bit. For this channel, add a Scream device. To do so, right-click on the P2: Dr. Octo Rex, choose Creative FX, and select Scream. To ensure more mid-range qualities for this channel, enable the Cut function on the Scream device. Then increase the Mid slider while lowering the Low and Hi sliders (see Figure 10.77).

8. Now that the mid range has been boosted, choose a distortion type that will blend well with what's already going through Audiomatic. In Scream, select the Distortion damage type selection. Then try dialing in your sound with the P1 and P2 knobs. Also, try using the mixer levels and Pan knobs for each channel to create a good mix between all the different channels running this one guitar loop.

Figure 10.76
© Propellerhead Software AB.

Figure 10.77
© Propellerhead Software AB.

That's really all there is to parallel channels. And, as you can see, it is easy to use the Audiomatic Retro Transformer. But, don't think to stop there with Audiomatic and parallel channels. With regard to Audiomatic on its own, try using it as a mastering effect on your master out. It gives an amazing feel to a final mix. For parallel channels, try doubling vocals and doubling synths (or tripling, or quadrupling). When you have seven channels of the same thing, try sending them all to an output bus, the way you did in Chapter 3, "Recording and Effects." This is a great way to group all of your channels and keep the mix intact under one final fader.

Moving On

Judging by the length of this chapter, the number of possibilities with the effects in Reason should keep you happy and occupied for a long, long time to come. In the next chapter, you'll start working with an amazing device that is designed to combine other devices—get ready for the Combinator!

The Combinator: Close-Up

I F THERE WERE A SINGLE RACK DEVICE CREATED FOR REASON THAT ADDS MORE POWER TO THE APPLICATION THAN ANY OTHER, the Combinator would have to be it! In short, the Combinator (see Figure 11.1) allows you to combine multiple devices (all controllable by a single sequencer track), route them any way you like, and save the entire setup as a single patch. As you read this chapter, you will discover how this seemingly simple concept offers limitless possibilities.

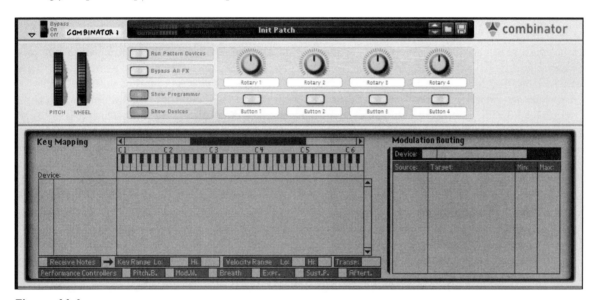

Figure 11.1
© Propellerhead Software AB.

Keep 'Em Combinated

Reason includes numerous Combinator presets, which appear as Combi (.cmb) patches in the Factory Sound Bank. Becoming familiar with these presets can help you determine which ones will be useful to you as you work on your projects, and should also provide inspiration and direction in creating your own Combi patches.

Combi patches can be divided into two basic types:

> **Effect Combis:** As you might guess, effect Combis are used to process sound rather than to generate sound as an instrument would. The MClass Mastering Suite Combi is an effect Combi.

> **Instrument Combis:** These Combis include sound-generating instrument devices, such as SubTractor, Thor, NN-XT, or Redrum, and can also contain effect devices. The only upper limits to the fatness of layered sounds that can be created in this way would be what your computer and your brain can handle!

By the way, remember that the Mix Channel and Audio Track devices in Reason are similar to the Combinator and have much of the same functionality, including the ability to load effect Combis (but not instrument Combis)!

A Guided Tour of the Combinator

Open a new document and create a Combinator. Take a look at the topmost panel of the Combinator (the part that still shows when the Combinator is folded) and note that, in addition to the usual Select/Browse/Save patch buttons, there is also a Bypass/On/Off switch like that found on Reason effect devices. Also included are input/output level meters, a MIDI note-on indicator, and an External Routing indicator, which lights up if you route audio or modulation output from any Combinator device to another device outside the Combinator. The External Routing indicator (see Figure 11.2) can be considered a warning indicator because it alerts you to the presence of external connections, which will not be saved with the Combi patch.

Figure 11.2
© Propellerhead Software AB.

The Controller Panel

The Combinator's Controller Panel consists of the following elements:

▷ **Pitch wheel:** This sends pitch bend info to all instrument devices contained in a Combi. The bend range is set individually in each instrument device's Range field.

▷ **Mod wheel:** This sends modulation data to all instrument devices contained in a Combi. The effect of this modulation data is determined by the individual mod wheel assignments made in each instrument device. The Combinator mod wheel can also be custom routed to control other knobs, sliders, and so on, in addition to the instrument modulation wheels to which it is automatically routed.

▷ **Run Pattern Devices:** This starts or stops all pattern devices in a Combi, such as a Matrix sequence or a Dr. Octo Rex pattern. This button is automatically activated when you click Play on the Transport panel.

▷ **Bypass All FX:** This bypasses all effect devices included in a Combi, switching all insert effects to Bypass mode and switching off all effects connected as send effects to a mixer device. This button does not affect effects already bypassed or turned off.

▷ **Show Programmer:** This shows or hides the Programmer panel.

▷ **Show Devices:** This shows or hides all devices included in a Combi.

▷ **Rotary knobs:** These can be assigned to control parameters in any devices included in a Combi. Rotary knob control assignments are made in the Modulation Routing section of the Programmer panel. You can customize Rotary knob labels by clicking on the label and typing in a name.

▷ **Button controls:** These can be assigned to control any button-controlled parameters in devices included in a Combi. Note that the Button controls switch between only two values, so if the device parameter you are controlling has more than two possible values (like an On/Off/Bypass switch or an LFO Waveform button), a Combinator Button control will toggle between only two of those values. As with the Rotary knobs, you can assign useful names to your Button controls by clicking on the labels and typing away.

The Programmer

Now let's click the Show Programmer button and dive into the pretty blue screen, which is really the nerve center of your Combinator. The Programmer may look slightly daunting at first, but it is actually rather straightforward and not at all difficult to master (see Figure 11.3). It controls the following five areas of functionality:

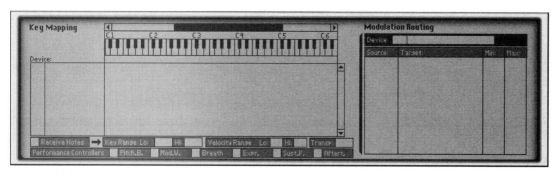

Figure 11.3
© Propellerhead Software AB.

▷ **Key Range:** This controls the lowest and highest note that will trigger any selected instrument device in the Combinator. This parameter cannot be adjusted unless Receive Notes is active for the selected instrument device.

▷ **Velocity Range:** This controls the lowest and highest velocity that will trigger any selected instrument device in the Combinator. As with the Key Range, the Velocity Range cannot be adjusted unless Receive Notes is active for the selected instrument device.

▷ **Transpose:** This controls the pitch of a selected device in a Combi patch. The range is +/−3 octaves.

▷ **Performance Controllers:** This indicates which controller messages (pitch bend, modulation, and so on) received by the Combinator are passed along to the combined devices. For example, if you have a SubTractor in your Combi patch and the Pitch and Modulation controllers are selected, whenever you use those controllers via the Combinator, the same messages will be sent along to the combined device. In other words, everything is linked up and will work in combination with each other.

▷ **Modulation Routing:** This assigns any parameters of the selected device in the Combinator to any of the virtual Rotary or Button controls on the Combinator's Controller panel. Unlike the Key Range and Velocity Range sections of the Programmer, the Modulation Routing section can control non-instrument devices (such as effects) as well as instrument devices like the NN-XT or the SubTractor.

Combinator Routing

Make sure that Show Devices is enabled. Then press the Tab key to flip your Rack screen around and take a look at the back of the Combinator (see Figure 11.4).

Figure 11.4
© Propellerhead Software AB.

Audio Connections

The audio connections on the back of the Combinator are used to send audio to the Mix Channels as well as to receive it! This is also the place where devices within the Combinator connect so that they can be heard externally.

▷ **Combi Input L/R:** These are the inputs for the Combinator, used for effect Combis. In a mastering Combi, you would likely have the outputs of your main reMix plugged into these inputs.

▷ **Combi Output L/R:** These connect with any device outside the Combinator, usually a mixer or (in the case of a mastering Combi) the Reason hardware interface.

▷ **To Devices L/R:** These connect to the input of any device in the Combi. To Devices L/R is internally routed to Combi Input L/R.

▷ **From Devices L/R:** These connect to the output of a device (the last in a chain of devices or a mixer) in a Combi. From Devices L/R is internally routed to Combi Output L/R.

CV Connections

Control voltages within Reason are an amazing way to make the virtual devices go above and beyond. The Combinator is no exception!

▷ **Gate In:** This allows the Combinator to receive Note On, Note Off, and Velocity information from the Gate CV output of another device, typically a Matrix, a Redrum, or an RPG-8 Monophonic Arpeggiator.

▷ **CV In:** This allows the Combinator to receive Note Pitch information from another device, typically from the Note CV output of a Matrix or RPG-8.

▷ **Modulation Inputs:** This allows the mod wheel, pitch wheel, or any of the four Combinator Rotary controls to be modulated by CV.

▷ **Programmer CV Inputs:** These inputs are used to route the CV output of any Reason device to a specific parameter of a device loaded in a Combi patch via the Programmer. For example, you can have the filter section of an instance of the SubTractor loaded in a Combi patch modulated via an instance of the Matrix.

Before you jump headlong into designing your first Combi patch, let's take a moment to look at another Reason device designed for use with the Combinator: the microMIX 6:2 line mixer.

microMIX

Want to mix and route some devices in your Combinator, but you don't need all the bells and whistles of reMix? Propellerhead has you covered. Although reMix can be used in Combinator patches, the microMIX line mixer was created specifically for mixing device outputs in a Combi in cases where the more advanced capabilities of reMix may not be required. Although microMIX is tailor-made for use with the Combinator, it can, of course, be used for other applications anywhere in your Reason song, such as submixing large drum kits or for adding a few extra channels when your main reMix is filling up. It should be noted that in the Rack screen, this device is labeled "microMIX," but in the Create menu, it is referred to simply as "Line Mixer 6:2." Go ahead and create an instance of this bad boy so you can follow along.

Each of the six channels in a microMIX (see Figure 11.5) includes an output Level control, a Pan knob (which can be controlled externally via CV), a Mute button, a Solo button, one Auxiliary Send Level knob (labeled "Aux"), a customizable channel label, as well as a three-segment output level meter. Rounding out the front panel is the Master knob, which controls the summed output level of all the channels in the microMIX. Finally, you have the Auxiliary Return Level knob, labeled "Aux Return," which controls the level of the signal coming back from whatever effect device has been connected to the Auxiliary Send output of the microMIX.

Figure 11.5
© Propellerhead Software AB.

Now flip your rack around to see the back of the microMIX (see Figure 11.6). The rear connections and controls on the microMIX are as follows:

▷ **Audio In L/R:** This connects the audio outputs of any audio device to the microMIX. When connecting the output of a mono device, you should use the left input.

▷ **Pan CV In:** This allows voltage control of the channel pan by other Reason devices.

▷ **Auxiliary Send:** This connects to the input of an effect device. When connecting to a mono-input device, use the left Auxiliary Send output.

▷ **Auxiliary Return:** This connects to the output of an effect device.

▷ **Auxiliary Pre/Post:** This allows you to choose whether the Auxiliary Send signal coming from each channel is sent to the effect device before it goes to the channel fader (Pre) or after the channel fader (Post). Using the Auxiliary Send in the pre-fader position allows you to send a signal to the effect device even if the individual channel output level controls are at zero. This might be especially effective when using a reverse reverb effect, for instance, where it would not be desirable to hear the original input (dry) signal.

▷ **Master Out L/R:** This is self-explanatory and is usually connected to the From Devices inputs in a Combi. Outside a Combi, the Master Out will auto-route to its own channel on the Reason mixer.

Figure 11.6

© Propellerhead Software AB.

Creating Your First Combi

Now that you have become acquainted with the theory and function of the Combinator, let's create a Combi patch. Start with an empty song file and then create a Combinator. The following performance-oriented tutorial should help you get comfortable using the various features of the Combinator.

1. Click in the black space at the bottom of the Combinator, called the Holder, and notice the red insertion line (see Figure 11.7). This is where new devices will be added to the Combinator. Note that the Holder is visible only when the Show Devices button is lit on the Combinator Control Panel. Create a microMIX in the Combinator.

Figure 11.7

© Propellerhead Software AB.

2. Press Tab to flip the Rack screen around and note that the Combi Output L/R has been auto-routed to the Mix Channel inputs and that the Master Out L/R of the microMIX has been auto-routed to the Combinator's From Devices L/R inputs. Click in the Holder space under the microMIX to show the insertion line; then create an RV7000 Advanced Reverb. Note that the Auxiliary Send of the microMIX is routed to the Audio Input L/R of the RV7000 and that the Audio Output L/R of the RV7000 is routed to the Auxiliary Return of the microMIX (see Figure 11.8).

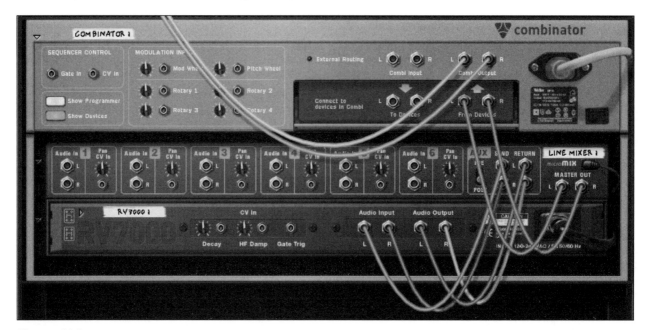

Figure 11.8

© Propellerhead Software AB.

3. Click in the Holder under the RV7000 and create a Malström. It should auto-route to Audio In 1 of the microMIX.
4. Under the Malström, create a Matrix while holding down the Shift key on your computer keyboard. This prevents any auto-routing. Then connect the Curve CV output of the Matrix to the Wheel Modulation Input of the Malström (see Figure 11.9).
5. Under the Matrix, create a SubTractor followed by another Malström.

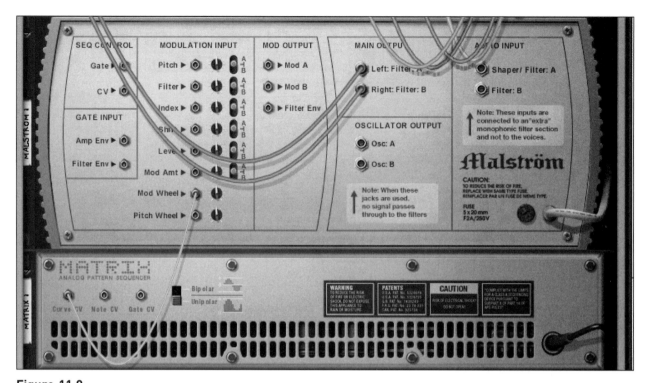

Figure 11.9
© Propellerhead Software AB.

Now that your ingredients are in place, press Tab to flip the rack around so you can see the front of your devices (see Figure 11.10). Now choose some patches for your synths.

Figure 11.10
© Propellerhead Software AB.

1. Open the Patch Browser of the first Malström and choose Redeath Bass from the Bass folder in the Malström Patches folder in the Reason Factory Sound Bank.
2. Open the SubTractor's Patch Browser and select Singing Synth from the MonoSynths folder in the SubTractor Patches folder in the Reason Factory Sound Bank.
3. Open the Patch Browser of the second Malström and choose Verbless from the PolySynths folder in the Malström Patches folder in the Reason Factory Sound Bank.

Setting the Key Ranges

On the Combinator, click the Show Programmer button, and look at the Programmer's Key Mapping section. On the far left, you will see a list of the devices in the Combi. As mentioned, the Key Range setting pertains mainly to instrument devices and some creative FX devices. Also, it can be adjusted only when the Receive Notes setting is active for the instrument device.

The Key Range setting can be adjusted in a few different ways. Try clicking on Malström 1 in the Combi Programmer Device List to select it. You can then click and hold on the Key Range Lo or Hi fields and move your mouse up or down to adjust the lowest and highest notes that will trigger the Malström 1. Alternatively, you can click and drag the markers at either end of the Key Range bar to the right of Malström 1. You may have to use the scroll arrows above the keyboard display to see the end markers. Finally, you can drag the entire horizontal bar to the left or right, moving the whole key zone at one time.

For this tutorial, you are going to split your keyboard so that the lowest notes trigger your Redeath Bass patch (Malström 1) and the upper keys trigger a layered lead sound. The keyboard I happen to be using is an Axiom 61, which has 61 keys, so I have plenty of room for both bass and lead sounds. If you are using a controller with fewer keys, you should adjust your split in a way that is comfortable for you. The main thing is to make sure Malström 1's key zone covers the lowest notes on your keyboard and comes right up to, but does not overlap, the key zone of your lead sound.

1. With Malström 1 selected in the Programmer Device List, click the right scroll arrow above the keyboard display and hold it until you see the right end marker of Malström 1's Key Range. By default, the Key Range is set to cover the entire keyboard. Click on the end marker at the far right of Malström 1's horizontal bar and drag it to the left until it reaches G1. You have now set the Hi Key of Malström 1's key zone to G1 (see Figure 11.11).

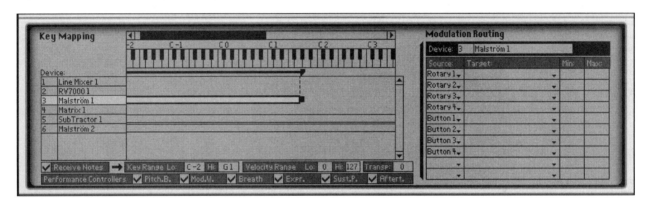

Figure 11.11
© Propellerhead Software AB.

2. Select SubTractor 1 in the Programmer Device List. If necessary, click the left scroll arrow above the keyboard display and hold it until you can see the left end marker of SubTractor 1's Key Range. Click and drag SubTractor 1's Key Range Lo marker until it reaches G#1.
3. Select Malström 2 in the Programmer Device List. Click and hold in the Key Range Lo value field and drag your mouse up until the value reads G#1. This is the same adjustment you made to SubTractor 1, done with an alternative technique. Now you have a perfectly split keyboard (see Figure 11.12).

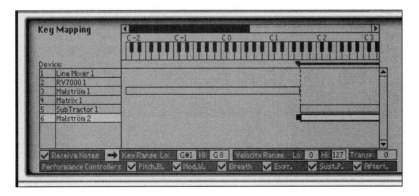

Figure 11.12
© Propellerhead Software AB.

Before you continue with the next part of this tutorial, in which you will set the Velocity Range, some minor tweaks are in order. If you have been playing this patch at high velocities, you may have already noticed that some of your signal levels are a bit out of hand. To fix this, follow these steps:

1. On the microMIX, turn the Channel 2 SubTractor down to a value of 92 and turn the microMIX Master level down to 80. You could also rein in the SubTractor's level by inserting a compressor, but for the sake of simplicity, just turn the channel down a bit for now.
2. Add a bit of reverb. Turn up the Channel 2 SubTractor Aux Send to a value of 48 or so.
3. Give the Malström on Channel 3 a larger dose of reverb by turning up the Channel 3 Aux Send to a value of 86.

Setting the Velocity Range

Okay, now you're ready to set the velocity range. Follow these steps:

1. Select Malström 2 in the Programmer Device List.
2. Click in the Lo Vel field of the Velocity Range setting and drag your mouse up until you've set a value of 85.

Notice the diagonal stripes that have appeared on the horizontal Key Range bar of Malström 2, which will be present any time there is a velocity range of less than 127. In this case, Malström 2 will not be triggered at velocities below a value of 85. You may wish to vary this number a bit depending on the feel of your controller keyboard. You want to hear the SubTractor alone when playing soft-to-medium velocities and to hear the additional layer of Malström 2's Verbless patch when striking the keys vigorously. This is a simple example, but I hope it will stimulate your imagination to consider the many far-out possibilities for multilayered sounds offered by the Combinator.

Run Pattern Devices

By now, you may be asking, "What did he stick that Matrix in there for, anyway?" Why, just for a little added fun! Follow these steps:

1. Set the Matrix to Curve Edit mode and draw in any old curve pattern that strikes your fancy. It's okay to leave the Steps and Resolution controls on the Matrix at their default settings (16 and 1/16, respectively).
2. On the Combinator Control Panel, click the Run Pattern Devices button.
3. Play some low bass notes (below G#1) on your controller keyboard and check out the modulation action on your Malström Redeath Bass sound.

Once again, it's worth noting that Run Pattern Devices is also activated automatically when you click Play on the Transport panel, and it is deactivated when you click Stop. Also, you will notice when browsing Combinator patches that Combis containing pattern devices (such as Matrix or Thor) will contain [Run] at the end of their patch name.

Modulation Routing

In the Modulation Routing section of the Programmer, you can decide what the Rotary knobs and Button controls on the Combinator Control Panel will be doing. From a performance standpoint, this is most useful when you can control those Rotary knobs and Button controls with an external MIDI controller. I discuss how to do this (Reason makes it *super* easy) in detail in Chapter 12, "Automation." For now, let's concentrate on assigning the functions of the Rotary knobs and Button controls in the Combinator Programmer.

To assign a function to a Rotary knob or Button control, first select the device in the Programmer's Device List that contains the parameter you would like to control. Then, in the Modulation Routing section, select a parameter from the Target menu located to the right of the Rotary knob or Button control (Source) you are assigning. In this way, Rotary Knob 1, for instance, can control several different parameters for each device in the Device List simultaneously. Let's apply some of these controls to the Combi.

1. Select Malström 1 in the Device List. Note that it is now displayed in the Device field in the Modulation Routing section.
2. Assign Rotary Knob 1 to control the Oscillator B Shift of Malström 1 by selecting Oscillator B Shift from the Target menu to the right of Rotary 1 (see Figure 11.13).
3. Set the minimum value to −30 by clicking in the Min field and dragging your mouse down until the desired value has been selected (see Figure 11.14).
4. Find Button 1 in the Source column of the Modulation Routing section. Click in the Target field to the right of Button 1 and select Shaper Mode from the menu. The Malström has five Shaper modes, but because the Button controls can only toggle between two values, set the minimum value to 0 and the maximum value to 1. This will toggle between the Sine and Saturate Shaper modes (Saturate being the default for the Redeath Bass patch).
5. Select Line Mixer 1 in the Device List. In the Target field to the right of Rotary 2, select Channel 2 Aux Send from the menu. Set the maximum value to 99 by clicking in the Max value field and dragging the mouse down until you've selected the desired value. Now the amount of reverb on your SubTractor sound can be controlled with Rotary Knob 2.

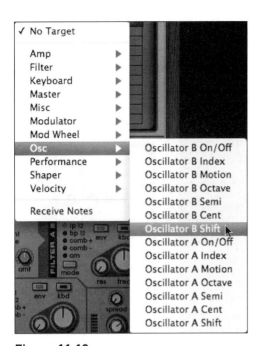

Figure 11.13
© Propellerhead Software AB.

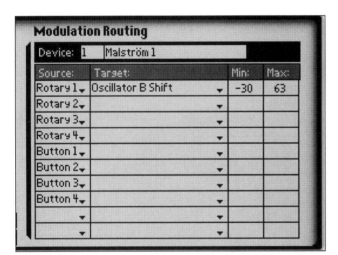

Figure 11.14
© Propellerhead Software AB.

If you've made it through the relatively simple Combi patch we've just created together, you should have a good grasp of the basic building blocks you can use to make much more complex and imaginative Combis. The sky's the limit!

Uncombine/Combine

Before you leave your first Combi behind, if you think you might like to play with it later, be sure to save it by clicking on the Save Patch button (located to the right of Patch Browser button). Then try the following:

1. Make sure the Combinator is selected (highlighted with a light blue border) by clicking on it once. Then select Uncombine from the Edit menu. Alternatively, right-click (Windows) or Control-click (Mac) on the Combinator and select Uncombine from the pop-up menu. Now the Combinator is gone, but the devices it contained still remain and the routing is intact except that the Master outputs of microMIX are now routed to the Mix Channel, as you might expect. Of course, you no longer have any Key Range or Velocity Range information.

2. Shift-click on microMIX, RV7000, and the Malström so that all three devices are selected, highlighted with a light blue border. Then, from the Edit menu, choose Combine. Now you have a new three-device Combi.

3. Click on the right or left edge of the Matrix located just below the Combinator and drag it into the Holder until the red insertion line appears (see Figure 11.15), and drop it there. The Matrix is now part of the Combi.

Figure 11.15
© Propellerhead Software AB.

4. Shift-click on the remaining SubTractor and Malström so that they are both selected. Then select Combine from the Edit menu or right-click (Windows) or Control-click (Mac) on either of the two selected devices and select Combine from the pop-up menu. Now you've got a second Combinator.

5. Click on the right or left edge of the bottom Combinator and drag it into the Holder until you see the red insertion line; then let it go. The bottom Combinator has ceased to be, and its devices have been added to the first Combinator.

As you can see, the Combinator is a dynamic part of constructing your Reason songs.

Select Backdrop: More Than One Way to Skin a Combi

The last stop on our Combinator tour is not really musical, but you may find it to be a fun feature. Like Kong, the Combinator allows you to design and load your own skins. You may use any JPEG image you desire, but whatever JPEG you use should have a resolution of 754×138 pixels. In your Reason song, you can click on your Combinator and then choose Select Backdrop from the Edit menu. You are then able to select a Combi backdrop from among the JPEGs stored on your computer. In Figure 11.16, you can see what I did with Photoshop and perhaps a little too much time on my hands.

Figure 11.16
© Propellerhead Software AB.

> **NOTE:** By the way, there used to be a Template Documents folder in the Reason program folder (or application folder) that included some Combi backdrop templates, but as of Reason version 6.0.1, that folder seems to have disappeared, even though it is mentioned in the Reason Operation Manual.

With that, we have come to the end of the introductory tour of the Combinator.

Moving On

As we end this chapter on the Combinator, I feel I should offer a few parting words. First, do not underestimate the Combinator. It is one of the most powerful devices in Reason. With it, you can mix multiple instruments to create new instruments, and create custom effects by merging other effects devices. By creating, mixing, and matching like this, you can end up really customizing you own sound and creating your own environment. Make sure and open up the Combinators that come with the factory sound bank when you run across them. In each one, you can get new ideas for your own Combinator patches!

Automation

O NE OF THE GREAT ADVANTAGES OF TODAY'S RECORDING TECHNOLOGY FOR ANY STUDIO, virtual or hardware, is the capability to automate your mix. Automation refers to the capability to automatically control equipment by recording its movements. A good example of automation is a hardware mixer with motorized faders that are programmed to move automatically with the mix (also known as *flying faders*). Reason's automation can record the movements of nearly any device parameter, and those movements recur as you play back the song. In this chapter, you learn to automate Reason's parameters. It's easy and fun!

Simply put, Reason is one of the easiest programs to automate. Nearly any parameter in the Rack screen can be automated just by creating a device and making sure that it is armed to automate. You can then choose one of two ways to create your automation data:

▷ **Live automation.** Live automation involves using an external MIDI controller that is capable of sending out controller data that's read by the Reason sequencer and recorded as automation data, or using your mouse to move the controls on the Reason devices in real time. In either case, you are recording the same data in real time.

▷ **Drawn automation.** This method involves using the Pencil tool to draw automation information directly into clips in the sequencer. You might recall that you did this back in Chapter 4, "The Reason Sequencer: Close-Up." However, in this chapter, you look at automation with the Pattern lane.

Let's look at both of these methods in detail.

Live Automation

Live automation is generally the first choice of most Reason users because it gives you a real-time, hands-on approach to channeling your creativity. There are two ways to automate live in Reason:

▷ Using your mouse
▷ Using an external MIDI controller

Using the Mouse to Automate

If you do not have an external controller, you can use your mouse as a means of automating your Reason parameters. In this tutorial, you automate a couple of the Reason mixer's faders and knobs. Before beginning, start with an empty rack and create a couple of audio tracks. Ready? Follow these steps:

1. Click the Record button on the Transport panel to start recording.
2. As soon as the sequencer begins to record, select a mixer channel fader to automate and make volume changes to it by clicking and dragging up and down with your mouse (see Figure 12.1). Notice that the Automation Override indicator lights up to show that automation has been recorded and that a new part is being created on the audio track.
3. Press the space bar to stop recording and click the Stop button to return the song position pointer to bar 1. Notice the new data that has been written into the sequencer track and that a neon green framed box has been drawn around the mixer channel (see Figure 12.2).

At this point, you can begin to automate any additional mixer parameters.

Reason 7 Power!: The Comprehensive Guide

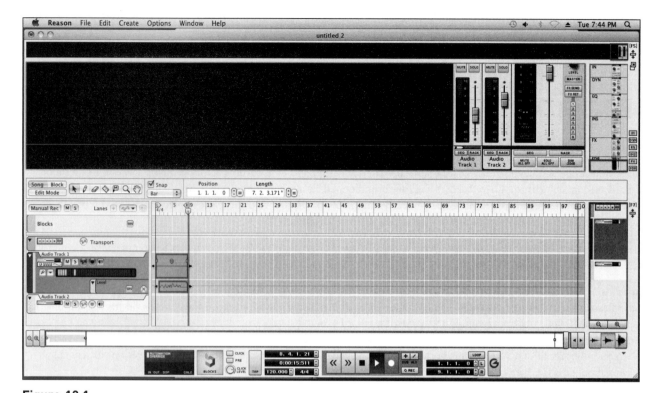

Figure 12.1
© Propellerhead Software AB.

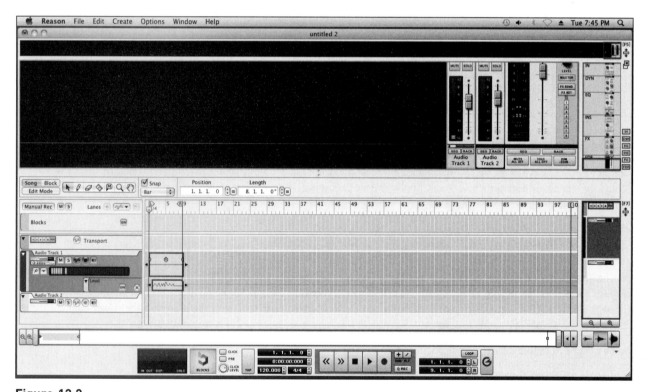

Figure 12.2
© Propellerhead Software AB.

> **TIP:** At some point, you might decide that you want to clear the automation from a particular parameter and start over. You can do this by right-clicking (Windows) or Control-clicking (Mac) on any automated parameter and choosing Clear Automation from the pop-up menu (see Figure 12.3). When you select this option, the neon green box disappears, the newly created automation part on the sequencer track is gone, and you can now record new automation data.

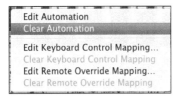

Figure 12.3
© Propellerhead Software AB.

Using an External Controller to Automate

The use of an external controller is a great solution if you find using a mouse to automate Reason parameters a bit cumbersome. An external controller can send MIDI controller data to any of the Reason devices, making it perfect for creating volume changes or synth parameter changes as well as for operating the transport controls.

Reason includes control-surface templates for most of the popular controllers on the market today, so chances are if your controller has MIDI-assignable knobs and/or faders, they will already be pre-assigned to control some of the most common device parameters in Reason.

This tutorial shows you how to automate a mixer channel using the Novation Impulse 49, which has several knobs, sliders, and pads that send out MIDI controller information (see Figure 12.4). No need to start a new song; just keep using the same one from the previous example.

Figure 12.4
© Propellerhead Software AB.

Additionally, make sure you have set up your external controller as a MIDI input device by choosing it from the Control Surfaces screen in the Preferences window (see Figure 12.5). Note that you may need to consult your manufacturer's manual to figure out how to properly map the knobs and slider to the Reason mixer or other devices.

1. Click the Record button on the Main Transport. This makes the sequencer start recording.
2. As soon as the sequencer starts to record, make volume changes to channel 1 by using the external controller's slider. This controls the level of Audio Track 1. (See Figure 12.6.)
3. Press the space bar to stop recording. The automation data is written on the Audio Track "Level" automation lane, and a neon green framed box appears around the channel 1 fader (see Figure 12.7).

It's pretty nifty how Reason already has presets that work great with several of the most popular controllers. But what if your controller has no corresponding preset in Reason? Or what if Reason does have preset controller assignments for your controller, but you want to make different assignments to suit your individual needs? Good news—Reason makes this custom assignment easy!

Once again, make sure you have set up your external controller as a MIDI input device by choosing it from the Control Surfaces screen in the Preferences window. Then do the following:

1. Start a new song with an empty rack and create an instance of Malström. The Malström sequencer track should be armed to receive MIDI input.
2. Right-click (Windows) or Control-click (Mac) on the Filter Env A fader and choose Edit Remote Override Mapping from the pop-up menu.

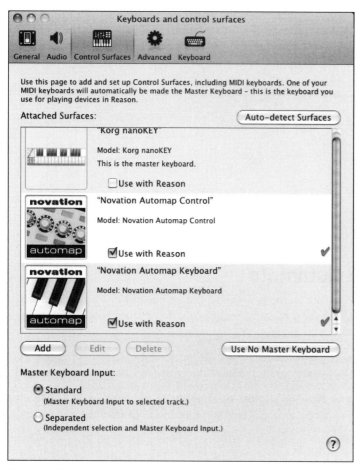

Figure 12.5
© Propellerhead Software AB.

Figure 12.6
© Propellerhead Software AB.

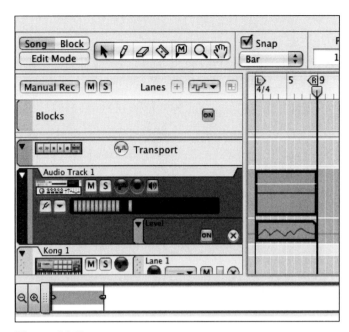

Figure 12.7
© Propellerhead Software AB.

3. In the Edit Remote Override Mapping window, select the Learn From Control Surface Input check box. Move the fader or knob on your control surface with which you would like to control Filter Env A, and you should see the Control Surface Activity display flash. Now click OK.

4. Move that same knob or fader on your control surface, and you will see that the Filter Env A fader also moves. How easy was that?!

Surface Locking

Surface locking allows you to specify that a MIDI control surface will always control parameters of a Reason device, even if that device is not set to receive MIDI input in the Track List. When a MIDI control surface is locked to a device, it can control the parameters of the device, but it cannot be used to *play* the device. Therefore, the master keyboard cannot be locked to a device because it would no longer be able to play any devices. If you want to lock your master keyboard to a device, you must first choose Use No Master Keyboard from the Control Surfaces screen in the Reason Preferences window.

Locking a MIDI control surface to a device is quite easy. Simply right-click (Windows) or Control-click (Mac) on the device you want to control and select Lock To [Your Control Surface Name] from the pop-up menu. If you do not see this option, either you have no MIDI control surfaces connected to Reason or you have only one control surface connected and it has been designated as the master keyboard. Note that you can lock several control surfaces to a single device if you want.

To unlock a device, right-click (Windows) or Control-click (Mac) on the device and deselect the Lock To item by selecting it in the pop-up menu.

> **NOTE:** After reading this tutorial, you might find yourself wanting to get an external controller for your studio. You'll be happy to know that there are many affordable solutions at your local music-instrument shop. To select the right controller, you should first decide whether you want to purchase a controller with knobs, faders, or both. They can all be used to automate Reason's device parameters, but you might find controlling the mixer faders with controller knobs a little confusing. My advice is to purchase an external controller that has both knobs and faders. There are, of course, many external controllers to choose from, but it comes down to how much money you are willing to part with. Visit your local music-instrument shop for more information, or try some online resources such as Harmony Central (www.harmony-central.com). I would also like to mention that not all controllers are created equal. Companies like Livid Instruments (lividinstruments.com) and Nektar (nektartech.com) put in an exceptional amount of time to ensure the compatibility of their products with Reason, and have really excellent support. The main thing: Do your homework!

Automation Override

Once you have written in your live automation data, you might want to add more automation data to the same parameter or redo it entirely. There are two ideal ways to do this. One way is to switch to Edit mode and use the editing tools in the Sequencer screen's toolbar to redraw and erase automated parameters. This method is covered later in this chapter. The other way is to use the Automation Override function, located in the Sequencer screen's Transport panel (see Figure 12.8).

Figure 12.8
© Propellerhead Software AB.

The Automation Override function makes it possible to replace an entire automation movement or simply add to an existing one. You can see for yourself how to use the Automation Override function by performing the following exercise. Get ready by starting a new Reason song and creating an instance of SubTractor.

1. Record a quick automation of the SubTractor's modulation wheel with either your mouse or a MIDI controller. Use the previous tutorials as examples if you are unsure how to do this.
2. When the automation data has been recorded, click Stop twice, and you should see the automation data in the SubTractor sequencer track (see Figure 12.9). Click Play to view the automation data play back.

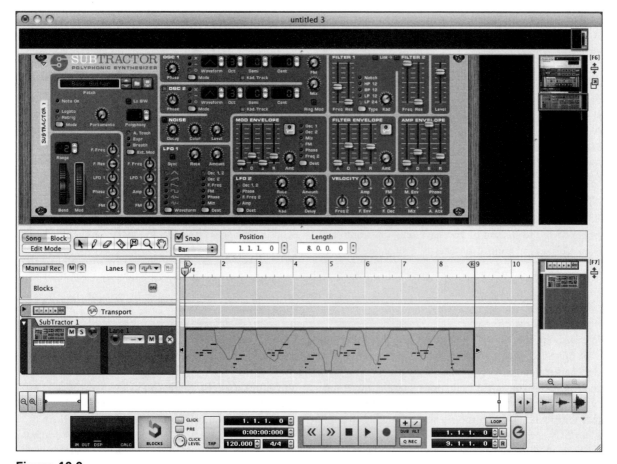

Figure 12.9
© Propellerhead Software AB.

3. Click Stop twice to go back to the beginning of your sequence. Click Record to begin recording a new automation.
4. Record a new automation performance of the modulation wheel. Notice that the Automation Override indicator is lit up, which means that new automation data is being recorded and is replacing the previously recorded automation.

5. About halfway through the automated sequence, click the Automation Override button. Notice that new automation data is no longer being recorded and that the previously recorded automation has become active again and is controlling the modulation wheel.

6. Click Stop. You should see your new and old automation data displayed in the sequencer track. Click Play to verify.

That pretty much covers live automation. The next section looks at drawn automation.

Drawn Automation

Another way of automating Reason's parameters is by manually drawing the automation into the Reason sequencer. This process can appear to be a little tedious at first, but it is very helpful for correcting or modifying any previously written automation data. You may even find it to be easier for some automation functions.

Drawing Automation in the Controller Lane

In this tutorial, you automate the individual parameters of the SubTractor by drawing in automation via the Reason sequencer. Before you begin, start a new Reason song and then create an instance of the SubTractor. It's also a good idea to quickly write in a sequence so you can hear the changes as they are being written.

1. Press Ctrl+E (Windows) or Command+E (Mac) to enter the Sequencer screen.

2. Click the Maximize Sequencer Window button. You can stretch and shrink the Note and Velocity lanes to your liking.

3. Click on the Track Parameter Automation button. This displays a pop-up menu of almost every controller that can be displayed and automated (see Figure 12.10).

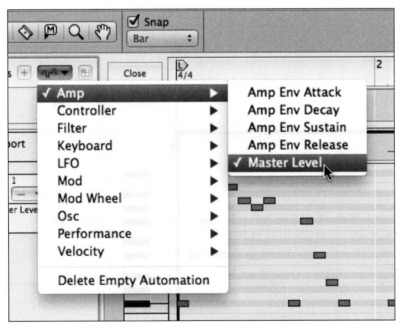

Figure 12.10
© Propellerhead Software AB.

4. Choose Master Level. The sequencer displays the Master Level controller (see Figure 12.11).

Figure 12.11
© Propellerhead Software AB.

5. Select the Pencil tool and draw in a part by clicking and dragging as long as you want the automation to occur. Then draw in some automation data (see Figure 12.12).

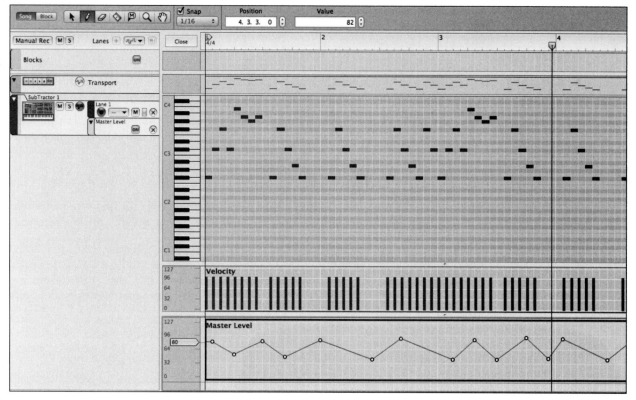

Figure 12.12
© Propellerhead Software AB.

6. Press the F6 and F7 button simultaneously to display the Sequencer and Rack screen at the same time.
7. The SubTractor Master Level slider has a neon green framed box around it. Click Play on your sequencer, and you will see the slider move up and down to match the movements of the automation you drew in. You'll also see a new lane on the SubTractor sequencer track.

TIP: After your automation is recorded or drawn in, you may find it looks a little messy from all the automation points. This is where the Automation Cleanup function found in the Sequencer Tools tab of the Tool Window can come in handy. Simply select the automation data you want to tidy up and then select the Automation Cleanup function. Set your desired amount of cleanup, click on the Apply button, and that's that.

Automating the Pattern Lane

The Pattern lane is used to write in automation data for the Pattern section of the Matrix and Redrum, which are pattern-driven devices (see Figure 12.13). It is also used for automating loop selection for Dr. Octo Rex.

Figure 12.13
© Propellerhead Software AB.

This tutorial shows you how to draw in pattern data to automate the Pattern section of Redrum. This can be done from either Song view or Edit mode, so I'll keep it in the Song view for this example. Before beginning, take a minute to start a new Reason song and create an instance of Redrum. Although it's not necessary, you might also want to load up a Redrum kit and create a few patterns.

1. Right-click on the Redrum sequencer track and select Create Pattern/Loop Lane from the pop-up menu. This creates a separate lane just below the note lane.
2. Set the Snap menu to Bar. This will allow you to write in automation that is one bar in length at a time.
3. Select the Pencil tool. Notice that the Pattern/Loop menu appears near the Inspector to the right of the Sequencer screen's toolbar. Also notice that Pattern A1 appears by default. Draw in a pattern in the pattern lane at bar 1 (see Figure 12.14).

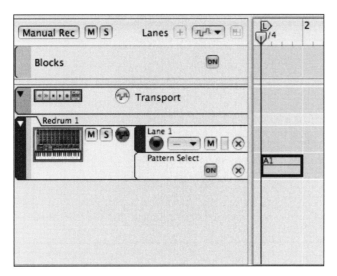

Figure 12.14
© Propellerhead Software AB.

4. Click on the Pattern/Loop menu located in the Inspector to the right of the Sequencer screen's toolbar and choose A2 (see Figure 12.15).

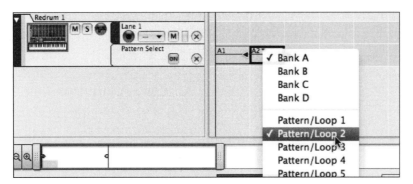

Figure 12.15
© Propellerhead Software AB.

5. Navigate to bar 2 in the Pattern lane and click to write in a bar of pattern A2 (see Figure 12.16).

Automating Live Pattern Changes

As you know, nearly any parameter in any Reason device can be automated live, and this definitely includes the Pattern section of the Matrix and Redrum. Try the following exercise:

1. Using setup from the the previous tutorial, clear the automation from the Pattern section of Redrum. To do this, simply delete the A2 clip.
2. Select the Selection tool and click the Record button to start recording pattern changes. Pattern A1 should already be playing.
3. While recording, click on Redrum's Pattern A2 button on the downbeat of bar 2. As Pattern A2 begins to play at bar 2, the sequencer track should now reflect that it has recorded a pattern change.
4. Stop the sequencer.

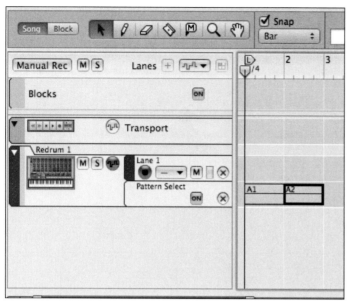

Figure 12.16
© Propellerhead Software AB.

Once the pattern changes are recorded, you can keep them as is. You can also redo them by drawing them into the pattern lane.

> **TIP:** Select a pattern in the pattern lane of the sequencer, and you'll see a little pull-down menu next to the name of the pattern. Click on this menu to switch the selected pattern to another one (see Figure 12.17).

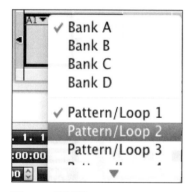

Figure 12.17
© Propellerhead Software AB.

Conclusion

In this chapter, you learned just about all there is to know about automation in Reason. If you are a seasoned DAW user, you'll probably agree that automating in Reason is much easier than it is with almost any other program out there.

This brings us to the end of our journey together through the amazing, virtual studio that is Reason. I hope that you found the exercises and information in this book helpful and that it has helped you create the music that you've always dreamed of making. I would encourage you to check out the Propellerhead website (www.propellerheads.se), as it has several of its own tutorials. Also, make sure that you sign up with the Reason community. This is a great place to ask questions of other users, as well as share things that you've been working on and more.

Also, don't forget that there are more Reason Rack Extensions being added every day. Keep an eye on the Propellerhead store (www.propellerheads.se/shop/). The synthesizer or effect of your dreams may be just around the corner!

Index

Index

Index

Index

Index

Index